# Designing a Microsoft
# Windows 2000
# Networking Services Infrastructure

# Designing a Microsoft Windows 2000 Networking Services Infrastructure

iUniverse.com, Inc.

San Jose   New York   Lincoln   Shanghai

Designing a Microsoft Windows 2000
Networking Services Infrastructure

Published by iUniverse.com, Inc.

For information address:
iUniverse.com, Inc.
5220 S 16th, Ste. 200
Lincoln, NE 68512
www.iuniverse.com

Cover Creation by Shay Jones

Graphic Production by Matt Bromley, Associate Consultant
Domhnall CGN Adams, Corporation Sole—http://www.dcgna.com
5721-10405 Jasper Avenue
Edmonton, Alberta, Canada T5J 3S2
(780) 416-2967—dcgna@yahoo.com

CD-ROM Duplication by Paragon Media, Seattle, Washington

ISBN: 0-595-14813-1

Printed in the United States of America

# Acknowledgments

We are pleased to acknowledge the following professionals for their important contributions in the creation of this study guide.

**Technical Writer**—Caleb Thompson, MSC, MCT, MCSE, MCP+I, Network+, A+

**Editor**—Grace Clark

**Indexer**—Loral Pritchett

**Cover Creation, Text Conversion, and Proofreader**—Shay Jones, AA, MCSE, MCP

**Technical Review**—Steve Patrick and Jay Graham

**Graphic Designer**—Matt Bromley

**V.P., Publishing and Courseware Development**—Candace Sinclair

# Course Prerequisites

The Designing a Microsoft Windows 2000 Networking Services Infrastructure study guide targets individuals who have the following skills:

- Proficiency of Windows 2000 technologies

- General knowledge for designing a Directory Services infrastructure for Microsoft Windows 2000

- Hands-on experience implementing and administering

- Windows 2000 Directory Services

The Designing a Microsoft Windows 2000 Networking Services Infrastructure exam tests an individual's knowledge for creating a networking services infrastructure design that supports the required network applications of an organization. Skills are enhanced when the student can provide a networking solution to an organization's needs and probable scenarios.

In addition, we recommend that you have a working knowledge of the English language, so that you are able to understand the technical words and concepts this study guide presents.

To feel confident about using this study guide, you should have the following knowledge or ability:

- The desire and drive to become an MCSE certified technician through our instructions, terminology, activities, quizzes, and study guide content

- Basic computer skills, which include using a mouse, keyboard, and viewing a monitor

- Basic networking knowledge including the fundamentals of working with Internet browsers, e-mail functionality, and search engines

- IP, remote connectivity and security

# Hardware and Software Requirements

To apply the knowledge presented in this study guide, you will need the following minimum hardware:

- For Windows 2000 Professional, we recommend 64 megabytes of RAM (32 megabytes as a minimum) and a 1-gigabyte (GB) hard disk space.

- For Windows 2000 Server, we recommend a Pentium II or better processor, 128 megabytes of RAM (64 megabytes minimum), and a 2-GB hard drive. If you want to install Remote Installation Server with Windows 2000 Server, you should have at least two additional gigabytes of hard disk space available.

- CD-ROM drive

- Mouse

- VGA monitor and graphics card

- Internet connectivity

To apply the knowledge presented in this study guide, you will need the following minimum software installed on your computer:

- Microsoft Windows 2000

- Microsoft Internet Explorer or Netscape Communicator

# Symbols Used in This Study Guide

To call your attention to various facts within our study guide content, we've included the following three symbols to help you prepare for the Designing a Microsoft Windows 2000 Networking Services Infrastructure exam.

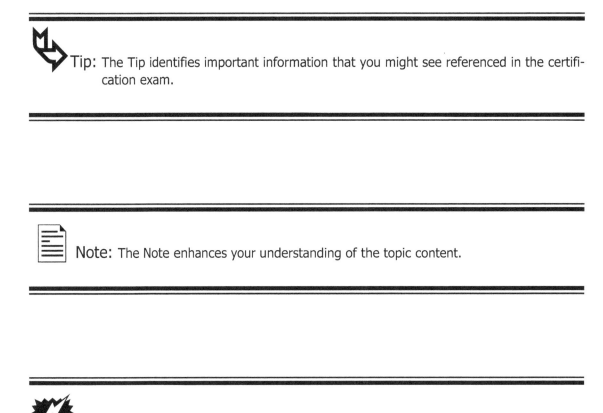

**Tip:** The Tip identifies important information that you might see referenced in the certification exam.

**Note:** The Note enhances your understanding of the topic content.

**Warning:** The Warning describes circumstances that could be harmful to you and your computer system or network.

# How to Use This Study Guide

Although you will develop and implement your own personal style of studying and preparing for the MCSE exam, we've taken the strategy of presenting the exam information in an easy-to-follow, ten-lesson format. Each lesson conforms to Microsoft's model for exam content preparation.

At the beginning of each lesson, we summarize the information that will be covered. At the end of each lesson we round out your studying experience by providing the following four ways to test and challenge what you've learned.

**Vocabulary**—Helps you review all the important terms discussed in the lesson.

**In Brief**—Reinforces your knowledge by presenting you with a problem and a possible solution.

**Activities**—Further tests what you have learned in the lesson by presenting ten activities that often require you to do more reading or research to understand the activity. In addition, we have provided the answers to each activity.

**Lesson Quiz**—To round out the knowledge you will gain after completing each lesson in this study guide, we have included ten sample exam questions and answers. This allows you to test your knowledge, and it gives you the reasons why the answers were either correct or incorrect. This, in itself, enhances your power to pass the exam.

You can also refer to the Glossary at the back of the book to review terminology. Furthermore, you can view the Index to find more content for individual terms and concepts.

# Introduction to MCSE Certification

The Microsoft Certified Systems Engineer (MCSE) credential is the highest-ranked certification for professionals who analyze business requirements for system architecture, design solutions, deployment, installation, and configuration of architecture components, as well as troubleshooting system problems.

When you receive your MCSE certification, it proves your competence by having earned a nationally recognized credential as an information technology professional who works in a typically complex computing environment of medium to large organizations. It is recommended that a Windows 2000 MCSE candidate should have at least one year of experience implementing and administering a network operating system environment.

To help you bridge the gap between needing the knowledge and knowing the facts, this study guide presents guidelines, strategies and a plan for implementing a Microsoft Windows 2000 Networking Services Infrastructure.

The MCSE exams cover a vast range of vendor-independent hardware and software technologies, as well as basic Internet and Windows 2000 design knowledge, technical skills and best practice scenarios.

---

 Note: This study guide presents technical content that should enable you to pass the Designing a Microsoft Windows 2000 Networking Services Infrastructure certification exam on the first try.

---

# Designing a Microsoft Windows 2000 Networking Services Infrastructure Study Guide Objectives

Successful completion of this study guide is realized when you can competently design a networking services infrastructure that supports the needs of an organization. In addition, you will want to create solutions for a single technology, such as DHCP, to provide Internet Protocol (IP) address configuration support. Furthermore, you will also want to understand several technology options such as Open Shortest Path First (OSPF), Routing Information Protocol (RIP), and Internet Group Management Protocol (IGMP) to design an IP routing scheme.

You must fully comprehend each of the following objectives and their related tasks to prepare for this certification exam:

- Describe the attributes of a Windows 2000 networking services infrastructure design

- Define the design requirements for a Transmission Control Protocol/Internet Protocol (TCP/IP) solution

- Design a DHCP solution for automating IP configuration

- Design a DNS service for name resolution

- Evaluate WINS as a solution for name resolution

- Evaluate and create an Internet connectivity design using Network Address Translation (NAT)

- Evaluate and create an Internet connectivity design using Microsoft Proxy Server 3.0

- Evaluate and create private network connectivity designs using Routing and Remote Access

- Evaluate and create a design to connect a remote user to a private network using Routing and Remote Access

- Evaluate and create a design to connect a remote user to a private network using Remote Authentication Dial-In User Service (RADIUS)

- Develop a management strategy for networking services

- Evaluate strategies to address interaction issues for the placement of services within an infrastructure

- Evaluate and create designs based upon the applications in use by an organization

# Figures

# List of Tables

# Table of Contents

## Lesson 1

# Designing a Windows 2000 Network

As a network engineer, you will be responsible for designing, implementing, and managing networks of all sizes. Windows 2000-based networks can range from the simplest 10-computer Local Area Network (LAN) to a multi-national enterprise, with tens of thousands of users. No matter the size of the network, you will need to be very familiar with the services provided by Windows 2000.

By now, you should be familiar with Active Directory, the directory database that provides the underlying structure of all Windows 2000 networks. You should also be familiar with many of the Windows 2000 services discussed in this book—the Domain Name System (DNS), Dynamic Host Configuration Protocol (DHCP), and Routing and Remote Access Service (RRAS), to name a few.

Throughout this book, you will learn how to make use of these services in a Windows 2000 network, how to plan and implement the services, and how to meet the business needs of an organization. The focus of this book is not on the detailed installation and configuration processes, but rather the design and implementation considerations. Each lesson discusses four common business needs—Security, Performance, Availability, and Functionality—and how the Windows 2000 services relate to these business needs. You will be presented with business scenarios to help you apply the theories.

After completing this lesson, you should have a better understanding of the following topics:

* Introduction to Windows 2000 Services

* Windows 2000 Network Design

# Introduction to Windows 2000 Services

Before you learn how to design Windows 2000-based networks and implement the services included with Windows 2000 Server, a review of the common protocols and services available in Windows 2000 is in order.

A protocol is a language—a set of rules defining how the computers on a network communicate. All computers on the same network must share a common protocol, just as all participants in a conference call must speak the same language.

Although Windows 2000 supports numerous networking protocols, this book deals almost exclusively with the Transmission Control Protocol/Internet Protocol (TCP/IP). TCP/IP is the protocol of the Internet, and is also the default protocol used in Windows 2000 networks. There are few occasions when you will need to use a different protocol (except when supporting non-Microsoft clients), and many of the services supported by Windows 2000 servers only work with TCP/IP.

A service is a program that runs on a network server and provides functionality to the network. For example, the Active Directory service, which runs on domain controllers, allows users to log on to the network and locate resources.

## Supporting IP Addressing

TCP/IP uses numeric addresses to identify each host (object) on the network. These numeric addresses are called IP addresses, and are 32 bits long. IP addresses are written as four octets separated by decimal points (for example, 192.168.2.45), with each octet representing 8 bits.

**Note:** The current version of IP—version 4 or IPv4—supports 32-bit addresses. The next release, IP version 6 or IPv6, will support 128-bit addresses. IPv6 will allow TCP/IP to support many more hosts, but the fundamentals of the TCP/IP protocol will not change when the newer version of IP is implemented.

## Dynamic Host Configuration Protocol (DHCP)

Every host on a network must have a unique IP address. No two computers on the Internet, for example, can use the same IP address. IP addresses are assigned to hosts manually or dynamically. If you choose to assign IP addresses manually, you must implement a number scheme to ensure that you do not assign the same address twice. On a small network, this may not be a problem; but as the network grows, maintaining a list of IP address assignments can become cumbersome. Dynamic IP addressing allows you to configure one or more servers to issue addresses.

DHCP is a service that issues IP addresses to requesting hosts. By default, all Windows 2000 clients are configured to receive their IP address (and other TCP/IP information) from a DHCP server. When a Windows 2000 client connects to a network, it sends a request for an IP address. A DHCP server responds to the request, issuing the necessary TCP/IP information. The client uses this information to participate as a host on the network.

**Tip:** DHCP provides hosts with an IP address and subnet mask. You can also configure DHCP to provide a default gateway address, and addresses for DNS and Windows Internet Naming Service (WINS) servers.

## Domain Name System (DNS)

IP addressing provides a very functional method for transferring information among computers, but is not the most user-friendly system. If we have to remember the IP address of each server, network printer, and client computer on our network—or worse yet, the Internet—network productivity will stop. The Domain Name System (DNS) provides a more friendly way for people to identify hosts on a network.

Each TCP/IP host has not only a unique IP address, but also a hostname. The hostname provides a friendly name by which people can identify computers. Within a domain (a logical collection of computers), each computer must have a unique hostname. For example, in the lightpointlearning.net domain, there can only be one computer named fred. The hostname is fred, and the Fully Qualified Domain Name (FQDN) is fred.lightpointlearning.net. By ensuring the hostname is unique within a domain, you are also ensuring that the FQDN is unique. FQDNs, then, are globally unique. No two computers attached to the Internet have the same FQDN.

DNS is a service that provides hostname resolution—it converts an FQDN to the host's IP address. When you enter an FQDN in a Web browser (like www.lightpointlearning.net. for example) your Web browser queries a DNS server for the IP address. DNS resolves www.lightpointlearning.net to an IP address. Using this address, your Web browser communicates directly with www.lightpointlearning.net.

### Windows Internet Naming Service (WINS)

For many years, Microsoft networks used the Network Basic Input/Output System (NetBIOS) protocol. NetBIOS is very easy to implement—each computer is assigned nothing more than a unique NetBIOS name—but was originally designed to only work with the NetBIOS Enhanced User Interface (NetBEUI) protocol. NetBEUI is not routable, and so is only useful on the smallest networks.

NetBIOS was redesigned to work with the TCP/IP protocol suite, allowing NetBIOS names to be used on segmented networks. In order for NetBIOS to work with TCP/IP, NetBIOS names must be resolved to IP addresses. Just as DNS resolves hostnames to IP addresses, WINS resolves NetBIOS names to IP addresses.

---

 **Note:** All Microsoft Windows clients support NetBIOS. In a Windows 2000-based network, you should only use NetBIOS if you need to support clients or older applications that were designed to work specifically with NetBIOS names.

---

## Routing Information

One of the strengths of the TCP/IP protocol is its ability to route information from one network segment to another. Networks are segmented to reduce traffic and data congestion. In order to get information from one segment to another, the network protocol must be routable (Figure 1.1).

# Figure 1.1 Segmented Network

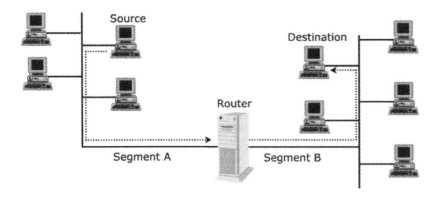

## *IP Routing*

Windows 2000 supports two dynamic IP routing protocols. Routers use these protocols to update the essential tables used in the forwarding of IP datagrams (packets of information) between network segments. The two routing protocols supported by Windows 2000 are the Routing Information Protocol (RIP) and Open Shortest Path First (OSPF).

 Note: Both RIP and OSPF are dynamic protocols—each automatically updates the routing information tables so that the information always remains up-to-date.

## *Demand-Dial Routing*

When linking two network segments by way of a dial-up connection, Windows 2000 servers can act as demand-dial routers. When a router needs to forward information from its Local Area Network (LAN) to a remote LAN, it automatically establishes a connection, and disconnects when the data transmission finishes.

Demand-dial routing can be used to connect a remote office to a corporate LAN without the expense of a dedicated leased-line (full time) connection. It can also be used as an emergency backup system to a leased-line connection.

## Providing Remote Networking

More and more users are connecting to corporate LANs from remote locations: telecommuters need to fully participate in network activities from their home offices, traveling sales representatives may need to access a customer database, and off-site network technicians may need to access servers. Windows 2000 provides three services that aid in connecting remote users to the company LAN.

### Dial-up Access

The Routing and Remote Access Service (RRAS) supports user authentication through dial-up connections. A user connects to the RRAS server using a standard analog modem and telephone line. Once connected, the RRAS server relies upon the Active Directory to authenticate users, so the logon process is very similar to when the user accesses the network locally.

In addition to user authentication, RRAS supports numerous security features, including Caller Identification, phone number callback features, and data encryption.

### Remote Authentication Dial-In User Service (RADIUS)

RADIUS is a standard protocol used to centralize dial-up access. RADIUS servers provide a single central locale for logon information, while permitting numerous remote dial-up servers. Many of the larger Internet Service Providers (ISPs) use RADIUS servers—they contain a central location of user accounts and passwords, but provide local servers for establishing the dial-in connection.

By using RADIUS, a company can have the benefits of a centrally stored user database (easier administration and simplified backup and recovery) while providing local access phone numbers to users over a large geographic area.

Tip: Internet Authentication Service (IAS) is Microsoft's implementation of RADIUS.

### Connection Manager

The Connection Manager service, which works with the Phone Book Service, automates dial-up and Virtual Private Network (VPN) connections. Using Connection Manager, you can configure a client computer to automatically connect to a LAN and also receive updates to phone books.

## Providing Secure Networking

With the increase in the demand for remote access to a network, has come the need to increase network security. Within a LAN, many security measures can be taken to ensure access to resources is restricted to authorized users. However, once data begins to be carried over public lines (whether they are telephone lines or the Internet), extra care must be taken to protect the data from unwelcome people.

### Internet Protocol Security (IPSec)

Windows 2000 supports IPSec, a protocol that authenticates sending and receiving computers and also encrypts data. Using IPSec, the sending user can be certain that the data is being sent to the proper computer, and that it is unreadable by all but the intended user. Likewise, the receiving computer can be certain of the data's origin.

 **Note:** Use of IPSec is not limited to remote access connections. You can implement IPSec on a LAN or intranet to further increase security.

### Virtual Private Networks (VPNs)

VPNs make use of the Internet—a very public system for data transfer—to transmit data securely from one computer to another. As the name implies, a VPN is virtually private. The data actually travels over public lines, but it is encrypted and sent through a logical tunnel, keeping the data private.

VPNs use a tunneling protocol to create the private path on which data will travel, and also use one or more protocols for data encryption and computer identification and verification. Windows

2000 supports two tunneling protocols, the Point to Point Tunneling Protocol (PPTP) and Layer 2 Tunneling Protocol (L2TP).

## Controlling Internet Access

Almost every company has a connection to the Internet. For many companies, this connection is two-way: employees can access Web pages and check e-mail, while the public can access the company's own Web pages. Furthermore, remote users who have established a VPN may access the company's intranet through the Internet. Controlling the intranet-Internet connection is of utmost importance for a network manager. Windows 2000 provides two methods for controlling access to and from the Internet: Microsoft Proxy Server and the Connection Sharing service. Both of these methods use Network Address Translators (NAT).

### Proxy Server

Microsoft Proxy Server is an add-on product for Windows NT 4.0 Server and Windows 2000 Server. It is not included with either product. Proxy Server acts as both an Internet proxy (which allows many people to share a single Internet connection) and a firewall (which keeps unwanted users out of the corporate intranet). You can configure Proxy Server to filter Internet traffic, regulating and monitoring the Web sites users visit.

### Connection Sharing

Connection Sharing is a service included with Windows 2000 that acts very much like Proxy Server. Internet Connection Sharing (ICS) acts as an Internet proxy, allowing multiple users to share a single Internet connection. These computers must be on the same subnet, since ICS issues its own private IP addresses. It does not support many of the advanced features of Proxy Server, but it does also serve as a simplified firewall.

# Windows 2000 Network Design

Network design and implementation is an ever-evolving process. Understanding this process is fundamental to success as a network engineer, and is the primary purpose of this book and the Microsoft exam.

With older Microsoft certifications, you needed to have a thorough understanding of networking and the Microsoft products. Now, you must also have a solid understanding of network creation. More specifically, you must be able to identify key business needs and expectations, and then plan and implement a network that meets these demands. In general, you can create a network by applying the following three principles:

**Design**—Network design includes evaluating the needs of the customer, selecting the technologies and services needed to meet customer expectations, evaluating costs, and (usually) considering the current network infrastructure.

**Implementation**—The actual implementation of the network typically involves installing and configuring hardware and services. Ideally, time and money will allow you to first configure a test network, and migrate new services and features into the existing network structure without interruption.

**Management**—Network management never ends. Even the most carefully designed and implemented networks need constant attention. When not troubleshooting problems, management includes predicting future network demands and needs and monitoring and analyzing current network use.

Of course, the processes of network design, implementation, and management are ever changing. Business needs change with time, and you need to be able to change the network to keep up with the new demands. During the management stage, you may discover the need for a new service. You then redesign the network for this service and implement the changes.

## Understanding Business Needs and Design Factors

The primary factor in designing a network is an understanding of what the customer needs and expects from the network. These needs can usually be placed into one of four design factors, and as you consider a network design (or the implementation of a particular service), you should consider the design with respect to these factors. The four factors are as follows:

**Functionality**—Analyze how a particular service meets the needs of the business. For example, if your customer wants to create a secure method for transferring data across the Internet, you must come up with a functional way to do this. Installing a DHCP server to handle secure data transmissions is not a functional design plan; building a Virtual Private Network is.

 **Note:** If a design is not functional, each of the other design factors is irrelevant.

**Security**—This is a top concern for most clients, and you must ensure that your network design meets or exceeds the security demands of the client. While you want to provide the highest possible level of security, you must also consider cost, compatibility, and performance issues. The most secure methods of transferring data may not work with all of the clients on the network, are certain to cost more, and typically decrease network performance.

**Availability**—Availability is a measure of how often the service is available when needed. If you are asked to implement a method for resolving hostnames to IP addresses on a network of 10,000 computers, you will install one or more DNS servers. One DNS server will be functional, but not highly available, whereas 25 DNS servers will provide much higher availability.

**Performance**—Performance is often a subjective measurement. Oftentimes, users complain about the speed of a network service, but the costs to increase performance are prohibitive. You should always try to meet or exceed performance expectations.

 **Note:** Performance and availability requirements are often inseparable.

## Implementing the Network

After you analyze the business needs for the network, you develop a plan for implementing the network. Your network implementation depends on the business needs, first and foremost. They not only define the network requirements, but may also hinder network implementation. Typically, you must find a balance between the perfect implementation and a financially reasonable approach.

 **Tip:** You must always find a network design that meets the needs of the customer. Exceeding their expectations is good business, but failing to meet their requirements is not an option.

## Supporting and Managing the Network

Network management can be approached in two ways. You can perform the day-to-day tasks, and then deal with the major issues as they arise. Or, you can monitor the network, collect service-specific data, and analyze the data. Of these two approaches, the latter is clearly better. It is always beneficial to detect and correct potential failures before they cause a network failure.

 **Note:** As the manager of a network, nothing is worse than a loss in company productivity because of network failure.

Just as thorough planning of the network design is important before implementing the network, developing a management methodology is important before you begin network management. When developing a strategy, consider the following:

**Data Collection**—Identify the data that is most important to collect, consider how often the data needs to be collected to get a reasonable picture of network status, and then identify the tools you need to collect the data.

**Data Analysis**—Once data is collected, identify the tools you will use to analyze the data, how often this analysis will occur, and what trends or problems you will look for in the data.

**Fault Tolerance**—Although your network may be running smoothly, you need to verify that your network can withstand certain failures. These tests often occur when you least expect (or want) them. To avoid unintentional tests of fault tolerant systems, you should plan to perform failure analysis tests that gauge network performance when one or more services or servers fail. Carefully plan the timing and duration of these tests to reflect common network usage without jeopardizing real network usage.

**Meeting the Business Goals**—Ongoing analysis of the network should include a summary of how the technology is meeting the four business goals outlined above—functionality, security, availability, and performance.

# Vocabulary

Review the following terms in preparation for the certification exam.

| Term | Description |
|---|---|
| Connection Manager | A service in Windows 2000 that provides connectivity and phone book services to clients. |
| Connection Sharing | A Windows 2000 service that acts as a basic proxy server and firewall. |
| datagram | A single piece of network data on a TCP/IP network. |
| DHCP | The Dynamic Host Configuration Protocol automatically assigns IP addresses and other TCP/IP configuration information to requesting clients. |
| dial-up access | Connecting to a network using a modem and standard telephone lines. Dial-up access also includes using an Integrated Services Digital Network (ISDN) line or Asymmetric Digital Subscriber Line (ADSL). |
| DNS | The Domain Name System resolves hostnames to IP addresses. |
| domain | A logical collection of computers all sharing the same DNS information. |
| dynamic routing protocols | Windows 2000 supports two dynamic routing protocols—RIP and OSPF. Routers using these protocols automatically update their routing information. |
| firewall | A hardware or software device that filters traffic from the Internet to the intranet, preventing unauthorized access to the network. |
| FQDN | The Fully Qualified Domain Name includes the hostname and the full domain name for a host. |

| Term | Description |
| --- | --- |
| host | Any object attached to a TCP/IP-based network. |
| hostname | A name assigned to each host on a network that simplifies network use. |
| IP address | The 32-bit number assigned to each host on a TCP/IP network. For each host on a network, the TCP/IP number must be unique. |
| IPSec | The Internet Protocol Security provides data encryption and computer authentication for network security. |
| L2TP | Layer 2 Tunneling Protocol is one of two tunneling protocols supported by Windows 2000. |
| LAN | A Local Area Network consists of computers within a single area, connected by a cable. |
| name resolution | The process of converting a hostname or NetBIOS name to an IP address. |
| NetBEUI | NetBIOS Enhanced User Interface is an older, non-routable protocol designed to work with NetBIOS. |
| NetBIOS | The Network Basic Input/Output System is an older Windows proprietary protocol. |
| NetBIOS name | The name used on NetBIOS networks to identify each computer. |
| OSPF | Open Shortest Path First is one of two dynamic (automatic) routing protocols supported by Windows 2000. |
| PPTP | Point to Point Tunneling Protocol is one of two tunneling protocols supported by Windows 2000. |

| Term | Description |
| --- | --- |
| protocol | A protocol defines the rules of communication on a network. |
| protocol suite | A collection of several protocols designed to work together, TCP/IP is an example of a protocol suite. |
| Proxy Server | A Microsoft product that uses a single Internet connection to many client computers. |
| query | A query is a request to a DNS or WINS server to provide name resolution. |
| RADIUS | Remote Authentication Dial-In User Service provides centralized management of remote access connections. |
| RIP | Routing Information Protocol is one of two dynamic (automatic) routing protocols supported by Windows 2000. |
| routable | A protocol that can be used on networks with more than one segment. |
| route | The path an IP packet travels from one computer to another. |
| routers | Software or hardware devices that connects network segments, and passes and filter the network traffic that passes through them. |
| RRAS | Routing and Remote Access Service in Windows 2000 provides network routing services and dial-up and VPN connectivity. |
| segment | One portion of a TCP/IP network, a segment is connected to other segments with routers. |
| service | A program that runs on a server and provides functionality to the network. |
| subnet mask | Part of the TCP/IP configuration information, the subnet mask defines the host and network identifications. |

| Term | Description |
|------|-------------|
| TCP/IP | The Transmission Control Protocol/Internet Protocol is the networking protocol used on the Internet and is the default protocol in Windows 2000. |
| tunnel | A virtual path through which data travels securely in a VPN. |
| VPN | A Virtual Private Network uses the Internet to transfer information between private networks. |
| WINS | The Windows Internet Naming Service provides name resolution for NetBIOS names. |

# In Brief

| If you want to... | Then do this... |
| --- | --- |
| Meet the needs of a business | Consider the four primary business goals for every network design. The four goals are functionality, security, availability, and performance. |
| Ensure design functionality | Fully understand the protocol or service you plan to implement, and be able to identify the positive and negative aspects of implementation. |
| Meet security needs | Consider how the service changes your network security plan, and adjust as necessary. |
| Build a network that supports all of the Windows 2000 services | Install the TCP/IP protocol. |
| Create a new network for a client | Carefully design the network, implement the design, and manage the network, monitoring for indications that the design needs updating. |

# Lesson 1 Activities

Complete the following activities to better prepare you for the certification exam.

1.  Consider the four business goals. Which one is most important? Why?

2.  This book does not cover Active Directory, and assumes you already have knowledge of the Active Directory directory services. Define Active Directory and explain what other network services are required to run Active Directory.

3.  Some Windows 2000 services are required on every domain, while others provide additional functionality. On a large Windows 2000 domain that contains 1,000 clients (running many different operating systems), which services and protocols are required, and which are optional but highly recommended?

4.  Suppose you plan to take a single-segment network and split it into 3 subnets to reduce network traffic. You propose to use Windows 2000-based routers. What protocols and services does Windows 2000 provide to help you with this task?

5.  There is one business goal that almost always applies, but is not often mentioned in network planning. In addition to providing functionality, security, performance, and availability, what other factor are you likely to contend with when planning and implementing a network?

6.  Explain the differences between the two methods for sharing an Internet connection.

7.  Explain how network support is cyclical.

8.  How will the upgrade from IPv4 to IPv6 change the way you manage your networks?

9.  The RRAS service provides a great deal of functionality on a Windows 2000 network. List some of the network jobs that a Windows 2000 server with RRAS can perform.

10. What is the difference between a hostname and FQDN?

# Answers to Lesson 1 Activities

1.  Functionality is the most important business goal. If the network design is not functional, it does not matter if it is secure, available, or performs well.

2.  Active Directory provides the directory services for Windows 2000 domains. The Active Directory database contains objects that represent every aspect of the network, from user accounts to shared folders. Active Directory is searchable and scalable, simplifying the process of locating objects on any size network. Active Directory requires TCP/IP and DNS.

3.  Since it is a Windows 2000 domain, Active Directory is required. To run Active Directory, you must provide TCP/IP and DNS services. Depending on the clients on the network, you may need to load additional network protocols (for example, AppleTalk is required to support Macintosh clients). WINS is also a required service, assuming some of the clients are using pre-Windows 2000 Microsoft operating systems. On a network this size, DHCP is highly recommended, but is not required.

4.  Every copy of Windows 2000 Server includes Routing and Remote Access, which enables a Windows 2000 computer to act as a router. To simplify management, you can implement either the RIP or OSPF dynamic routing protocol, greatly reducing router administration.

5.  Cost is always an important factor. You may often find that the best solution is not the least expensive, and although companies want the very best solution, they don't want to pay for it. When proposing network plans, you should have at least two plans, one that presents the ideal configuration, and one that presents a less expensive option. You should also be well prepared to explain the differences between the plans, and what the less expensive option lacks.

6.  Connection Sharing is a service included with every copy of Windows 2000, and allows computers on a single network segment to share an Internet connection. ICS requires that all computers use the private IP addresses it allocates, so this is not a good option for any network with more than one subnet. Microsoft Proxy Server is an additional package you can purchase. For the money, Proxy Server provides stronger firewall security, detailed logging options, and control over all Internet traffic (in both directions).

7.   After you design and implement a network, you begin the management stage. While managing and monitoring the network, you will find ways to improve the network, and will design new changes. These changes are then implemented. A good network is dynamic, constantly changing to fit the needs of the company.

8.   If you use DHCP, an upgrade to IPv6 is not likely to change the way you manage the network very much, if at all. You will need to upgrade the DHCP servers to ones that support IPv6, and then re-create IP scopes. But on-going network management will probably not change. If you manually assign IP addresses on the network, you will need to reassign every IP address. Network management will be more difficult, since IP addresses will be much longer, easier to forget, and more difficult to assign to computers without mistyping the address.

9.   RRAS servers can act as internal dynamic or static routers, routers that connect two or more networks across a WAN, demand-dial routers, dial-up remote access servers, VPN servers, RADIUS clients, and security servers (by requiring IPSec on the network).

10.  A hostname is assigned to a single computer, and within any domain, the hostname must be unique. An example of a hostname may be www. An FQDN contains the hostname, appended with the entire DNS domain name. For example, the domain name lightpointlearning.net, appended to the above hostname yields the FQDN www.lightpointlearning.net. By requiring the hostname to be unique within a domain, and each domain name to be unique, you assure that every FQDN in the world is unique.

# Lesson 1 Quiz

These questions test your knowledge of features, vocabulary, procedures, and syntax.

1.    What network service provides automatic assignment of IP addresses?
      A.    TCP/IP
      B.    WINS
      C.    Connection Manager
      D.    DHCP

2.    Which protocol was the default protocol on Windows networks for many years?
      A.    NetBIOS
      B.    NotBIOS
      C.    NetBouys
      D.    TCP/IP

3.    Which of the following is not a primary business goal?
      A.    Functionality
      B.    Security
      C.    Implementation
      D.    Performance

4.    Which of the following is a tunneling protocol? (Choose all that apply).
      A.    L2TP
      B.    PPTP
      C.    T2LP
      D.    TPTT

5.    Which service converts IP addresses to FQDNs?
      A.    WINS
      B.    DHCP
      C.    DNS
      D.    There is no service that converts IP addresses to FQDNs.

6.    Which of the following allows multiple computers to share a single Internet connection? (Choose all that apply).
    A.    IPSec
    B.    Proxy server
    C.    L2TP
    D.    Connection Sharing

7.    What length of IP address will be supported when IPv6 is released?
    A.    32-bit
    B.    64-bit
    C.    128-bit
    D.    2 bits

8.    Which of the following are dynamic routing protocols? (Choose all that apply).
    A.    OPFS
    B.    RIP
    C.    RAP
    D.    L2TP

9.    A DHCP server can issue which of the following to a client? (Choose all that apply).
    A.    IP Address
    B.    Subnet mask
    C.    DNS server address
    D.    WINS server address

10.    What device is used to connect two network segments?
    A.    VPN
    B.    Router
    C.    Proxy server
    D.    Duct tape

# Answers to Lesson 1 Quiz

1.  Answer D is correct. The Dynamic Host Configuration Protocol provides automatic IP address assignments.

    Answer A is incorrect. TCP/IP is a protocol, not a network service.

    Answer B is incorrect. WINS provides name resolution.

    Answer C is incorrect. Connection Manager is used to create connection to servers.

2.  Answer A is correct. All Windows clients support NetBIOS.

    Answers B and C are incorrect. These are fictitious terms.

    Answer D is incorrect. TCP/IP is the default protocol only in Windows 2000.

3.  Answer C is correct. Implementation is one of your concerns, but is not a business goal.

    Answers A, B, and D are incorrect. These are all valid business goals.

4.  Answers A and B are correct. The two tunneling protocols supported by Windows 2000 are L2TP and PPTP.

    Answers C and D are incorrect. These are fictitious terms.

5.  Answer C is correct. The Domain Name System converts IP addresses to FQDNs, and FQDNs to IP addresses.

    Answer A is incorrect. WINS converts NetBIOS names to IP addresses.

    Answer B is incorrect. DHCP provides automatic IP address assignment.

    Answer D is incorrect.

6.    Connection Sharing is a service included with every copy of Windows 2000, and allows computers on a single network segment to share an Internet connection. ICS requires that all computers use the private IP addresses it allocates, so this is not a good option for any network with more than one subnet. Microsoft Proxy Server is an additional package you can purchase. For the money, Proxy Server provides stronger firewall security, detailed logging options, and control over all Internet traffic (in both directions).

7.    After you design and implement a network, you begin the management stage. While managing and monitoring the network, you will find ways to improve the network, and will design new changes. These changes are then implemented. A good network is dynamic, constantly changing to fit the needs of the company.

8.    If you use DHCP, an upgrade to IPv6 is not likely to change the way you manage the network very much, if at all. You will need to upgrade the DHCP servers to ones that support IPv6, and then re-create IP scopes. But on-going network management will probably not change. If you manually assign IP addresses on the network, you will need to reassign every IP address. Network management will be more difficult, since IP addresses will be much longer, easier to forget, and more difficult to assign to computers without mistyping the address.

9.    RRAS servers can act as internal dynamic or static routers, routers that connect two or more networks across a WAN, demand-dial routers, dial-up remote access servers, VPN servers, RADIUS clients, and security servers (by requiring IPSec on the network).

10.    A hostname is assigned to a single computer, and within any domain, the hostname must be unique. An example of a hostname may be www. An FQDN contains the hostname, appended with the entire DNS domain name. For example, the domain name lightpointlearning.net, appended to the above hostname yields the FQDN www.lightpointlearning.net. By requiring the hostname to be unique within a domain, and each domain name to be unique, you assure that every FQDN in the world is unique.

# *Lesson 2*

# Understanding TCP/IP

Transmission Control Protocol/Internet Protocol (TCP/IP) is a protocol suite—a collection of protocols designed to work together to provide network communications. It is the protocol used for all Internet data transmissions and the default protocol of Windows 2000.

The TCP/IP protocol has three advantages. It is reliable, ensuring that data arrives at its intended destination. TCP/IP is an open standard, supported by every major (and most minor) network operating system. Because it is not vendor-specific, a computer running Windows 2000 can communicate as easily with a UNIX-based server or Macintosh client as another Windows 2000 computer. Finally, TCP/IP is a routable protocol, which means that it can be used to transmit data across different network segments.

You will implement TCP/IP in every Windows 2000 network you design. The fundamental services of Windows 2000, including Active Directory, require TCP/IP. In many networks, TCP/IP may be the only protocol you implement, unless you need to support older client computers or proprietary systems that do not use TCP/IP.

After completing this lesson, you should have a better understanding of the following topics:

*   TCP/IP Fundamentals

*   TCP/IP Implementation

*   TCP/IP Management

*   TCP/IP Business Goals

# TCP/IP Fundamentals

TCP/IP is a protocol suite. A protocol is like a language computers use to communicate with one another. A protocol suite is a collection of protocols and applications that are intricately related to one another. In the TCP/IP protocol suite, TCP is one protocol and IP is another. Other members of the TCP/IP protocol suite include Domain Name System (DNS), Dynamic Host Configuration Protocol (DHCP), and Windows Internet Naming Service (WINS).

Windows 2000 relies heavily upon TCP/IP. Used not only as the means of transmitting data from one computer to another, Windows 2000 uses TCP/IP (in part) for user logon authentication, file and print services, and Active Directory replication.

## Understanding IP Addressing

Like all other network protocols, TCP/IP contains a method for identifying each object on a network, called the IP address. Every object or host (a computer or printer, for example) on a network has a unique IP address. An IP address is a 32-bit number that is written as four octets separated by decimals, such as 194.168.25.1. The actual address is a series of 32 bits (binary digits or 0s and 1s). The IP address, 194.168.25.1, looks like this to a computer:

**11000010101010000001100100000001**

These IP addresses are the only way that hosts can be located and accessed on the network. All transactions between computers are based on the IP addresses of the sending and receiving computers. When developing a TCP/IP-based network, you must make sure that a unique IP address is assigned to each host on the network.

---

 **Note:** Each host on a TCP/IP network must have a unique IP address, or network conflicts will occur.

---

These IP addresses are often difficult for people to remember, and are often entered incorrectly. For this reason, hosts can be assigned names (called hostnames). Computers can be referred to by their hostname, and the Domain Name System (DNS) converts these hostnames to the proper IP addresses. It is important to remember that all TCP/IP traffic uses IP addresses. Hostnames exist for no other reason than to make TCP/IP more user-friendly.

# TCP/IP Implementation

As much as this book is about designing a networking strategy, it is about implementing TCP/IP in Windows 2000. Windows 2000 networking without TCP/IP is not reasonable.

 **Note:** You can build a Windows 2000 network without using TCP/IP, but it must be nothing more than a workgroup. A Windows 2000 domain requires Active Directory and DNS, and these services require TCP/IP. For these reasons, it is not reasonable to consider a Windows 2000 network without TCP/IP.

When you implement TCP/IP into your Windows 2000 network scheme, you must consider many variables. Of primary consideration is IP addressing. Every computer on the network must have a unique IP address; and if you are connecting this network to the Internet, special considerations must be made to ensure unique IP addresses.

In addition to deciding on an IP addressing strategy, you must also consider the physical structure of the network—will it be segmented into two or more subnets? If so, how many subnets will you create, and what is the maximum number of hosts on each subnet? Choosing the proper subnet mask for your network will dictate how many subnets can be created, and how many hosts are supported on each.

 **Tip:** When determining the number of subnets and hosts on a network, consider the company's projected growth. Don't let your TCP/IP configuration limit network growth!

# Using an IP Address Scheme

A primary consideration when selecting an IP addressing scheme for your network is determining which computers, if any, will have Internet access. Devices that are connected directly to the Internet must be assigned public IP addresses. Public IP addresses, which are either purchased or leased from an Internet Service Provider, are expensive, but every computer that is connected to the Internet must have one.

Private IP addresses are reserved addresses that do not work on the Internet. Since Internet traffic does not use these IP addresses, you can safely use them on your private network. Table 2.1 lists the four IP address ranges you can use for private IP addresses.

**Table 2.1 Private IP Addresses**

| Starting IP Address | Ending IP Address | Subnet Mask |
|---|---|---|
| 10.0.0.1 | 10.254.254.254 | 255.0.0.0 |
| 169.254.0.1 | 169.254.254.254 | 255.255.0.0 |
| 172.16.0.1 | 172.31.254.254 | 255.255.0.0 |
| 192.168.0.1 | 192.168.254.254 | 255.255.255.0 |

 **Note:** Windows 2000 uses private IP addresses 169.254.0.1 through 169.254.254.254 for Automatic Private Internet Protocol Assignments (APIPA) configuration on networks without a DHCP server.

## Public IP Addresses

Public IP addresses have the following disadvantages:

**Expensive**—Public addresses must be purchased and leased.

**Insecure**—Public IP addresses potentially allow anyone on the Internet to access the computers on your internal network (intranet).

**Unavailable**—Public IP addresses are becoming difficult to obtain, due to the size limitations of IP version 4 (IPv4). If you need thousands of public IP addresses for your network, you may end up with inconsistent ranges of addresses, increasing the administrative effort needed.

## Private IP Addresses

Since public IP addresses are expensive (and becoming rare), it is generally in your best interest to use private IP addresses for all computers except those few that require a direct connection to the Internet.

Computers with private IP addresses cannot connect to the Internet. However, you can still provide Internet access to these computers by routing the traffic through one or more proxy servers (Figure 2.1). The Web browser on each computer must be configured to use a proxy server.

## Figure 2.1 Private and Public Addressing

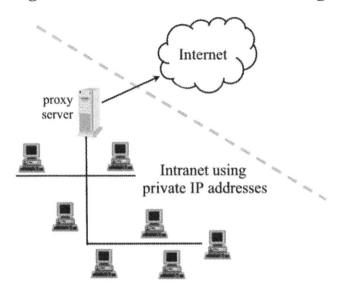

Tip: Using a proxy server to provide Internet access has the added benefit of allowing you to control and monitor all Internet activity.

A proxy server has at least two IP addresses—one private, and one public. The private IP address allows communication between the proxy server and the rest of the internal network (intranet), while the public IP address allows the proxy server to communicate with computers on the Internet (Figure 2.2).

## Figure 2.2 Computer with Private and Public Addresses

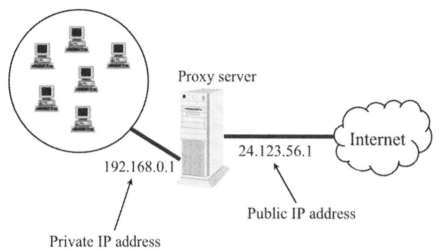

Computers that typically require a public IP address include the following:

*   Proxy servers and other Network Address Translations (NAT) servers

*   Firewalls

*   Remote Access Servers, including Dial-up and Virtual Private Networking (VPN) servers

*   Web Servers, such as computers running Internet Information Services (IIS)

Tip: Using private IP addresses increases network security. By the very nature of private addressing, all network access to and from the Internet must pass through a proxy server and firewall. The firewall or proxy can monitor all traffic and prevent unauthorized accesses.

# Assigning IP Addresses

With Windows 2000, you can assign IP addresses to network clients in three ways. Manual configuration is useful for computers on which you want a persistent IP address. Automatic and dynamic assignments make administration much easier, but may lead to a computer having a different IP address every time it boots.

## *Manual IP Assignment*

Manual assignment of IP addresses requires you to configure each computer on the network, providing each computer with its own unique IP address. You must also configure the subnet mask, default gateway, and all other TCP/IP settings.

Manual configuration often results in network errors—one small mistake when entering an address, and one or more computers will not be able to participate on the network until the error is found and corrected. Furthermore, you must keep track of every IP address used so that you do not assign the same address to two or more computers.

Despite the disadvantages to manual IP configuration, there are a few computers that require a static (unchanging) address. These computers are all servers that provide essential TCP/IP information to the network. Servers providing the following services must have static IP addresses:

*   Dynamic Host Configuration Protocol (DHCP)

*   Domain Name System (DNS)

*   Windows Internet Naming Service (WINS)

## *Dynamic Host Configuration Protocol (DHCP)*

An alternative to manually assigning IP addresses to each computer is to use the DHCP service. You configure the client computers to automatically receive their TCP/IP information during the boot process. As a client computer boots, it broadcasts a request on the network for a DHCP server. If a DHCP server is available, the server will issue an IP address, subnet mask, and other TCP/IP information to the client.

You configure DHCP to issue a range of IP addresses (called a scope). When the DHCP server receives a request, it selects the next available IP address from the scope and leases it to the client.

Note: When an IP address is assigned to a client, it includes a lease duration. When half of the lease time has expired, the client requests a renewal of the IP address lease. Assuming a DHCP server is available for this request, the client will maintain the same IP address.

When the client computer is shut down or rebooted, the IP address is released and returned to the pool of available IP addresses. It is possible, then, that a DHCP client will receive a different IP address the next time it boots.

 Note: When a DHCP client is rebooted or restarted, it will request its previously assigned IP address from the DHCP server. If the address is still available, the DHCP server will reissue the address to the client.

### Automatic Private IP Assignment (APIPA)

Windows 2000 provides an additional method for automatic IP assignment, called Automatic Private IP Addressing (APIPA). APIPA provides an IP address and subnet mask for computers when no DHCP server is available on the network. APIPA works independently on each client computer. If a requesting computer fails to receive TCP/IP information from a DHCP server, it assigns itself an IP address from the private range 169.254.0.0–169.254.254.254 (after verifying no other computer is using the selected IP address).

On small, single-segment networks, APIPA provides an inexpensive and easy method of automatic IP assignments. However, because no default gateway is issued, APIPA cannot be used on multi-segmented networks. If APIPA is used on a network with two or more subnets, computers will only be able to communicate with other computers on the same subnet.

Note: Windows 2000 clients are configured by default to automatically obtain TCP/IP information. Unless you wish to manually assign IP information, you do not need to change the default Windows 2000 TCP/IP configuration.

## Using Subnet Masks

The subnet mask defines the subnet (segment). TCP/IP uses the subnet mask to divide an IP address into the host ID and network ID. The network ID defines the subnet and is used to route information. When a computer sends information, TCP/IP first determines whether the destination computer is on the same segment as the source computer (local) or on a different network segment (remote). If the destination is local, the data is sent directly to that computer. If the destination is remote, the data is sent to the default router (known as the default gateway in TCP/IP configuration). The router then forwards the message as necessary.

 Note: Network segmentation reduces network traffic. All local data and broadcast messages are prevented from passing through routers to other segments.

While the subnet mask is used to determine the portion of the IP address that defines the subnet (the network ID), it also defines how many subnets can be created, and how many hosts can exist on each subnet. TCP/IP uses the subnet mask to determine how many of the 32 bits in the IP address define the network ID. The more bits used for the network ID, the fewer bits available for hosts on each subnet (Figure 2.3).

## Figure 2.3 Hosts and Subnets

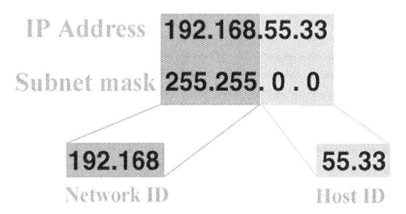

The number of hosts and subnets offered by subnet masks is determined by counting the number of bits used for either. If a subnet mask uses 10 bits for the network ID, a total of $2^{10}$ (1024) subnets are possible. This also means that 22 bits are available for host IDs, and so $2^{22}$ (4,194,304) hosts are possible on each subnet. Table 2.2 provides examples of several subnet masks and the number of subnets and hosts supported by each.

## Table 2.2 Subnet Mask Examples

| Subnet Mask | Bits Used for Network ID | Bits Used for Host ID | Subnets Supported | Hosts Supported |
|---|---|---|---|---|
| 255.0.0.0 | 8 | 24 | 254 | 16,777,216 |
| 255.255.0.0 | 16 | 16 | 65,536 | 65,536 |
| 255.255.128.0 | 17 | 15 | 131,072 | 32,768 |
| 255.252.0.0 | 14 | 18 | 16,384 | 262,144 |
| 255.255.248.0 | 21 | 11 | 2,097,152 | 2,048 |
| 255.255.255.0 | 24 | 8 | 16,777,216 | 254 |

When planning your IP addresses strategy, consider the size of the network and the anticipated growth of the company. For example, if a network currently contains 14 subnets, each with 250 computers, a subnet mask of 255.255.255.0 will work, since there are fewer than 254 computers on each subnet. However, this doesn't leave much room for growth. If the company grows even slightly, the subnet mask will be inappropriate. Furthermore, it is unlikely the company will use the more than 16 million available subnets.

If you are building a new network and must determine how many hosts you want on each subnet, consider the following variables:

**Router support**—Consider the number of hosts supported by the routers you plan to use.

**Performance**—Consider the performance expectations of the company. The more hosts on a subnet, the more network traffic on that segment. Conversely, the more traffic that must pass through routers, the slower the network performance.

## Implementing Subnets

Standard subnet masks use complete bytes (8-bit segments) of the IP address to define the network and host IDs. In other words, a standard subnet mask uses only the numbers 255 and 0. Using standard subnet masks often results in wasted host or network IDs. For example, the subnet mask 255.0.0.0 provides for over 16 million host IDs, far more than most companies need. Likewise, the subnet mask 255.255.255.0 provides for over 16 million segments, but only 254 hosts on each segment.

You can overcome the limitations of standard subnet masks in two ways. You can customize the subnet masks to be variable lengths, so that the network design more closely matches your needs. You can also combine two or more IP ranges by supernetting. Supernetting combines multiple addresses to act as one address range.

 **Note:** The Classless Inter-Domain Routing (CIDR) specification supports supernetting, as does the Windows 2000 implementation of DHCP.

In order to use variable length subnetting or supernetting, the routers on your network must support one or more of the following protocols:

*   Routing Information Protocol for IP version 2 (RIP for IPv2)

*   Open Shortest Path First (OSPF)

*   Border Gateway Protocol (BGP)

## Subnetting Remote Networks and Users

When implementing remote access to your intranet, you must consider special subnetting and addressing requirements.

### Virtual Private Networks (VPNs)

For access to the network through a Virtual Private Network (VPN), each client computer will participate on the intranet as if connected directly. Therefore, you do not need to create a separate subnet for VPN access. However, you must take into account the number of IP addresses that will be assigned to these remote computers.

### Connecting Remote Networks

When you connect two networks through a point-to-point permanent connection, such as a leased line or T1 connection, each connection must have its own subnet, and each connection point (computer or router) must have two IP addresses, one for the network and one for the point-to-point connection.

For packet-switching networks and other multi-port connections (like X.25), one subnet can be used for all connections. Rather than using a separate subnet for each connection, you assign an IP address to each.

## Filtering Network Traffic

The Windows 2000 implementation of TCP/IP supports IP filtering. When you filter TCP/IP information, you prevent certain data from entering your intranet from the Internet. Every IP packet that enters your network must meet your specified criteria or is rejected and discarded.

Note: TCP/IP filtering blocks all network traffic except that which meets your criteria. You must carefully plan a TCP/IP filtering scheme before implementation to ensure important data is not blocked.

## Configuring TCP/IP Filtering

You can configure TCP/IP filtering to block packets based on their TCP port number, UDP port number, or IP protocol number. To configure TCP/IP filtering, follow these steps:

1. From the Start menu, choose Settings, and then select Network and Dial-up Connections. Alternately, from the desktop, right-click My Network Places and choose Properties.

2. Right-click **Local Area Connection**, and then choose **Properties**. Then, **Local Area Connection Properties** will display (Figure 2.4).

## Figure 2.4 Local Area Connection Properties

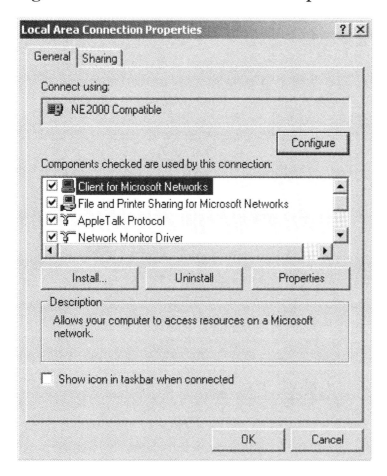

3.   Choose Internet Protocol (TCP/IP), and then select Properties.

4.   From the **General** property page, choose **Advanced**.

5.   From **Advanced TCP/IP Settings**, choose the **Options** property page (Figure 2.5).

# Figure 2.5 Options Property Page

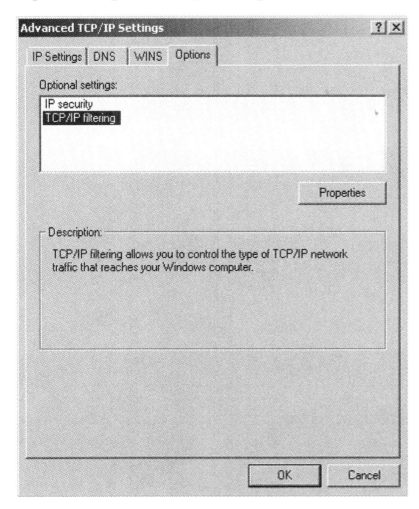

6.  Choose TCP/IP filtering, and then select Properties.

7.  From **TCP/IP Filtering**, choose **Enable TCP/IP Filtering (All adapters)** (Figure 2.6).

## Figure 2.6 Enable TCP/IP Filtering

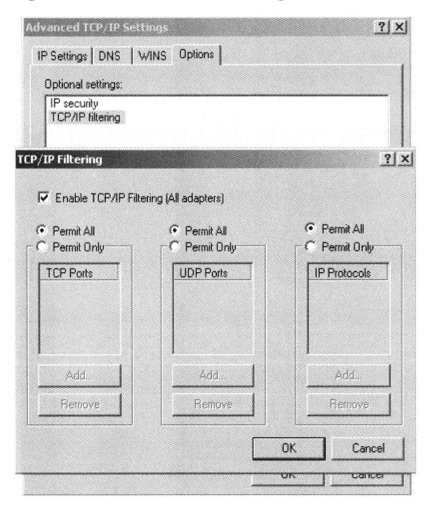

8.  Choose Permit Only for the variable(s) you wish to filter. For example, if you wish to limit traffic to only that carried on TCP/IP port 21, choose Permit Only under TCP Ports, and then select Add.

9.  In **Add Filter**, type **21**, and then click **OK** (Figure 2.7).

## Figure 2.7 Add Filter

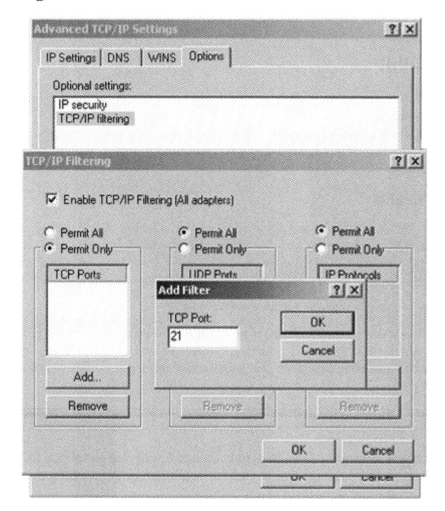

10. Click **OK** in each open window to save the changes and implement the TCP/IP filtering.

### *Testing TCP/IP Filtering*

To test your TCP/IP filters, attempt to send information using several filtered ports. For example, if you filtered all traffic except for TCP port 21, attempt to receive data through a Web browser. Web browsers receive information using the HyperText Transfer Protocol (HTTP), and the default port for HTTP is TCP port 80. If you receive the requested information, your filter is not working properly.

# TCP/IP Management

Once you have planned and implemented the TCP/IP configuration for a network, you manage the network to ensure the plan is appropriate for the network and that it is implemented properly. You must be able to detect and correct problems early, and anticipate the changing needs of your company. Furthermore, you should test the TCP/IP configuration on a regular basis.

## Detecting TCP/IP Problems

Using the Event Viewer and Performance Logs and Alerts tools, you can monitor TCP/IP performance and often detect problems before they cause a total network failure. On larger networks, you cannot expect to have the time to monitor TCP/IP on a regular basis. However, you can configure Performance Logs and Alerts to send an administrative alert when particular thresholds are exceeded.

Common TCP/IP problems you should monitor include the following:

**Reduced network performance**—When too many hosts are attached to one segment, network productivity drops. Configure your network monitor to generate an administrative alert when network utilization on any segment exceeds an acceptable limit. This limit is determined by the expectations of the company and the baseline you created when implementing the network.

**Tip:** Correcting problems takes some time. Be sure to configure your alert thresholds to a low enough point so that you have time to correct the problem before a total system failure occurs.

**Segment or WAN link failure**—Although users will likely notify you when a network segment failure occurs, some failures may go undetected. For example, if you have a redundant WAN link and one of the two links fails, users may not know that the backup link is down. Configure your monitoring software to generate an alert when any link or segment fails.

**Router overload**—Monitor the routers on your network to ensure that they are capable of handling the amount of inter-subnet traffic generated. If a great deal of traffic is traveling through the routers, they can become the slowest link on the network. Configure the routers to generate alerts if an appropriate threshold is exceeded.

**Duplicate IP addresses**—If you manually configure IP addresses, you may inadvertently assign the same IP address to two different computers. You will know immediately if this has occurred and can quickly correct the situation. However, if you are using DHCP on your network and are receiving duplicate IP address errors, you must check the DHCP servers. The DHCP service may be failing on one of the servers, or you may have assigned the same scope of IP addresses to two different servers.

**Network growth**—If you properly planned the TCP/IP network, you should not be concerned by network growth and with having too many hosts on any given subnet. Log every addition to (and removal from) the network, so you will have an up-to-date list of the number of hosts per subnet. Confer with this list before adding any hosts.

## Anticipating Network Changes

Most often, the need to change your TCP/IP configuration is indicated by the current usage of the network. To anticipate needed changes before they become an issue, you should monitor the current network usage. Some of the items you monitor for failure also provide a good indication of the need to change configuration. Consider the following variables on your TCP/IP network:

**Segment and WAN link utilization**—Network utilization is a prime indicator of network demands and needs. If a WAN link is only seeing 15% utilization, you do not need to invest in a faster connection or redundant link. However, if a particular segment is seeing an average of 75% utilization, you should consider breaking the segment into two separate subnets, or moving some of the hosts to a less-used subnet.

**WAN link downtime**—If a WAN link is frequently unavailable to users, you should consider the addition of one or more redundant connections.

**Overburdened router**—Router saturation, which is when a router cannot process the network demands quickly enough, results in many data retransmissions, further exasperating a network slowdown. If a router is handling too much network traffic, add a redundant router or replace the router with one that can handle higher traffic demands.

## Simulating a Failure

Some pieces of a TCP/IP network cannot be readily tested until failure occurs. As the administrator, you should be confident that all portions of the network, including these seemingly untestable aspects, are fully functional. To test certain parts of the TCP/IP network, you need to simulate a network failure.

For example, suppose you have a series of TCP/IP subnets, interconnected by a mesh configuration, so that every subnet has at least one redundant connection to the remaining segments (Figure 2.8).

### Figure 2.8 Mesh Network

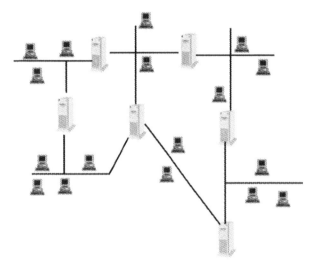

The only way to verify that each of the redundant links is fully functional is to disable several links and ensure that data still arrives at its intended destination. When doing this, you should only disable one link at a time, and you should schedule this failure session to occur during a time of reduced network need.

# TCP/IP Business Goals

For each lesson in this book, we will analyze the protocol or service discussed in the lesson in the light of the four business goals: functionality, security, availability, and performance. You will then be presented with a business scenario to help you apply some of the concepts and to prepare for the Microsoft exam.

## Meeting Business Needs

TCP/IP meets the four business goals as follows:

**Functionality**—TCP/IP is the most functional network protocol for all but the smallest and most homogenous networks. In any network that has more than one segment, TCP/IP is one of the few protocols that will work at all. You can add to the functionality of TCP/IP in Windows 2000 by implementing DHCP to automatically handle IP addressing.

**Security**—When using TCP/IP, you can increase network security by using private IP addresses and implementing a proxy server and firewall. Furthermore, you can implement TCP/IP filtering and data encryption to increase security. For added security for remote network connections, you can establish VPNs and require encrypted logon information.

**Availability**—Network availability should be monitored continually to ensure that users are able to send and receive data in a timely fashion. If availability begins to decline, consider adding redundant links, routers, and servers.

**Performance**—TCP/IP performance depends in part on the amount of network traffic and the capacity of the network to carry that traffic. If network performance declines, you may need to segment the network to reduce traffic, or upgrade the connection media. For example, if a 56-Kbps wide area network (WAN) link can no longer handle the demands of the remote users, consider upgrading the link to an Integrated Services Digital Network (ISDN), T1, or other faster connection medium.

## Business Scenario

Use the following business scenario to help you understand TCP/IP planning and implementation. Questions and answers pertaining to this scenario are found in the Activities section near the end of this lesson.

Woody's Chiropractic Association (WCA) is a national chain of chiropractic doctors' offices throughout the United States. The doctor independently owns each office, but all offices are connected to a regional center through dial-up network connections. Each regional center is connected to the national center in Raleigh, North Carolina, by an ISDN connection, except for the Seattle and Los Angles regional centers, which are connected to the Denver office by 56 Kbps leased lines (Figure 2.9).

## Figure 2.9 Business Scenario

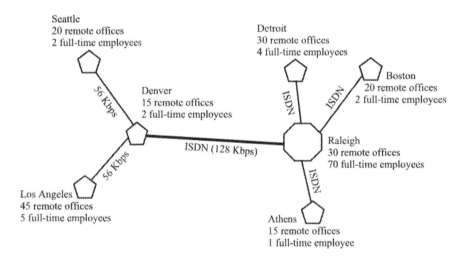

Using the network, doctors can share the latest medical information with other members of the network. The national center maintains a large database of medical resources and contact information, as well as an extensive on-line medical library.

Currently, the servers at each regional center are running Novell NetWare, and communication between the regional centers and the national center uses the IPX/SPX protocol. The dial-up servers to which local offices connect are running UNIX, but there is no standard in place for handling the IP addresses needed for the dial-up connection, and connection failures are common.

WCA has decided to implement Windows 2000 on all their servers and hired you to help plan and implement upgrades to their network. Table 2.3 outlines the needs and expectations of the WCA CEO and staff.

**Table 2.3 Network Expectations**

| General Needs | Expectations |
|---|---|
| Standardization | All servers should be running the same operating system (Windows 2000), and using only 1 protocol. |
| Minimal Configuration | Whichever protocol is used, WCA administration does not want to have to reconfigure frequently. |
| Security | Currently, the connections between the local offices and the regional centers are not secure. The dial-up connections send passwords as clear text, and the data is not encrypted. The connections between regional centers and the national center are private, but the data is not encrypted. WCA wants to protect their data more carefully. |
| Web Integration | To minimize doctor training with specialized software, WCA wants to implement a secure Web site that the doctors can use to browse and share information. This Web server will be located in Raleigh. |
| Internet Connectivity | Full-time employees at the national center require Internet access. Access should not be limited, but should be monitored. |

# Vocabulary

Review the following terms in preparation for the certification exam.

| Term | Description |
|------|-------------|
| Active Directory | The directory database that provides the foundation of every Windows 2000 network. |
| APIPA | Automatic Private Internet Protocol Addressing, supported by all Windows 2000 computers, allows computers to assign themselves an IP address if a DHCP server is unavailable. |
| BGP | Border Gateway Protocol is a routing protocol used by routers on a TCP/IP network to transmit information between autonomous systems. |
| byte | 1 byte is equal to 8 bits. |
| CIDR | Classless Inter-Domain Routing is a way of customizing IP addresses and subnet masks. |
| DHCP | Dynamic Host Configuration Protocol provides automatic TCP/IP client configuration. |
| DNS | The Domain Name System resolves hostnames and FQDNs to IP addresses. |
| domain | A logical grouping of computers, a domain is the basic unit of organization in a Windows 2000 network. |
| firewall | A hardware or software device that separates an internal network from the Internet. |
| FQDN | The Fully Qualified Domain Name includes the hostname and the full domain name for a host. |
| FTP | File Transfer Protocol is a high-speed protocol used to copy files to and from remote computer systems. |

| Term | Description |
|------|-------------|
| host | Any object on a TCP/IP network. |
| host ID | The part of an IP address that specifies the host. |
| hostnames | A TCP/IP name given to each host on a network. DNS resolves hostnames to IP addresses. |
| HTTP | HyperText Transfer Protocol is part of the TCP/IP protocol suite, and is used to transfer Web pages from servers to clients. |
| IIS | Internet Information Server is a Windows 2000 service that provides Web hosting and FTP services. |
| IP filtering | Filtering prevents information from traveling on the network, based on specific TCP/IP information (such as the originating computer's IP address). |
| lease duration | The amount of time a DHCP-assigned IP address remains valid on a client. |
| local | A host that is on the same network segment as your computer is said to be local. |
| NAT | Network Address Translators work like proxy servers to provide Internet connection sharing. |
| network ID | The part of the IP address that defines the subnet on which a host is connected. |
| OSPF | Open Shortest Path First is one of the routing protocols supported by Windows 2000-based routers. |
| private IP addresses | IP addresses that cannot be used on the Internet, and so are suitable for use on intranets. |
| protocol suite | A collection of protocols designed to work together. TCP/IP is an example of a protocol suite. |

| Term | Description |
| --- | --- |
| proxy server | A computer that allows many computers to share a single internet connection. |
| public IP addresses | IP addresses that are valid on the Internet. |
| redundant server | A server that provides the same service as another, and is primarily used in case the first server fails. |
| remote | A host attached to a different network segment from your own is said to be remote. When you send data to a remote host, it must pass through at least one router. |
| RIP for IPv2 | Routing Information Protocol for IP version 2 is one of the routing protocols supported by Windows 2000 routers. |
| router | A hardware or software device that connects two or more network segments and passes information between them. |
| router saturation | When too many network packages need to be routed simultaneously, the router may become saturated. |
| scope | A range of IP addresses from which DHCP will assign addresses to requesting clients. |
| segment | Synonymous with subnet, a segment is one portion of a TCP/IP network and is connected to other segments with routers. |
| static | Does not automatically change; must be configured manually. |
| subnet mask | A 32-bit number always used in association with an IP address to determine the host ID and network ID. |
| subnet | Synonymous with segment, a subnet is one portion of a TCP/IP network, connected to other subnets with routers. |
| supernetting | Combining two or more IP address ranges into one range that can be used on a single network subnet. |

| Term | Description |
|------|-------------|
| TCP | Transmission Control Protocol is one of many protocols in the TCP/IP protocol suite. |
| TCP port | TCP directs information based on a port number. Some services have default ports, like port 80 for HTTP. |
| VPN | Virtual Private Networks use tunneling protocols to securely transmit data across the Internet. |
| WINS | The Windows Internet Naming Service resolves NetBIOS names to IP addresses. |
| X.25 | One of many packet switching, high-speed WAN technologies. |

# In Brief

| If you want to... | Then do this... |
| --- | --- |
| Automate IP assignments | Use DHCP. |
| Determine the best subnet mask to use | Consider the number of network segments needed, and the number of hosts on each segment. |
| Prevent certain network traffic from entering your network | Use IP filters. |
| Determine the number of hosts supported on a segment | Use the subnet mask to determine the number of bits used for the Host ID. |
| Increase TCP/IP functionality | Implement DHCP, DNS, and WINS. |
| Determine whether two computers are local or remote with respect to one another | Use the subnet mask to compare the Network IDs for both computers. |

# Lesson 2 Activities

Complete the following activities to better prepare you for the certification exam.

1.  Based on the business scenario presented, what protocol(s) will you use on the WCA network?

2.  In what ways can you minimize IP address administration?

3.  When deciding an IP addressing scheme, which business needs (as listed in Table 2.3) are important?

4.  Will you suggest using private or public IP addresses for this network? Why?

5.  Given the expectations of adding an internal Web server to the network, does your selection of an IP addressing scheme change?

6.  How many subnets will you create on the WCA network?

7.  What subnet mask do you think is most appropriate?

8.  Suppose WCA is expecting to double in size within the next 15 months. What subnet mask would you use now to accommodate that growth?

9.  How will you provide Internet connectivity to the full-time employees of WCA?

10. What is the minimum number of public IP addresses you must obtain for WCA to provide internet access to all full-time employees?

# Answers to Lesson 2 Activities

1.  WCA wants only one protocol on the entire network, and wants to upgrade their servers to Windows 2000. In order to support the full functionality of Windows 2000, your only choice for a single protocol is TCP/IP.

2.  To minimize IP management, you should implement DHCP to handle all IP address assignments. Replace the UNIX remote access servers with Windows 2000 servers, and configure them to use DHCP to assign IP addresses to dial-up users.

3.  When deciding whether to use public or private IP addresses, consider the need for security. Private IP addresses on an intranet ensure that resources on the internal computers cannot be directly seen on the Internet. The need to minimize configuration also suggests the use of private addresses. Private addresses can be added at any time, whereas additional public addresses must be leased or purchased.

4.  Private addresses make more sense. The cost of providing every computer with a public address is prohibitive and unnecessary. The requirement of Internet connectivity can be handled using private IP addresses.

5.  No. An internal Web server will work with any IP addresses, whether private or public. If the server is to be accessed from the Internet as well, it needs a single public IP address.

6.  Without additional information on the ability of the routers to handle network traffic and the maximum number of computers attached to each subnet, creating seven subnets is a logical decision. Each location will have its own subnet, and dial-up users will become members of these subnets.

7.  You need to choose a subnet mask that allows for AT LEAST seven subnets and supports up to 70 computers on any subnet (since Raleigh currently has 70 employees). Although there are many correct answers, an appropriate choice may be 255.255.255.0, which supports up to 254 subnets, each with 254 computers.

8.  Even if WCA doubles in size, the subnet mask 255.255.255.0 will support their needs. However, if that type of growth is expected to continue, they will outgrow the subnet mask in a few years.

9.    Since you are using private IP addresses on the WCA network, you will need to use a proxy server to provide Internet connectivity for full time employees. The proxy server will need a single public IP address. To optimize connections, you may wish to install proxy servers at several regional offices, so that not all Internet traffic must first pass through Raleigh.

10.   You only need one public IP address to connect everyone at WCA to the Internet. However, if you install multiple proxy servers (one for each regional office, for example), you will need a public IP address for each.

# Lesson 2 Quiz

These questions test your knowledge of features, vocabulary, procedures, and syntax.

1.    What does the subnet mask do?
      A.    Hides the IP address from public view.
      B.    Separates the network servers from clients.
      C.    Determines the Host ID and Network ID in an IP address.
      D.    Separates the subnet from the segment.

2.    Which of the following is NOT a valid private IP address?
      A.    169.254.32.200
      B.    192.168.10.1
      C.    10.2.5.33
      D.    24.52.125.91

3.    If a Windows 2000 computer is configured to receive an IP address automatically, and a DHCP server is unavailable, what happens?
      A.    The computer crashes.
      B.    An error is generated.
      C.    Nothing. The computer will use its old IP address.
      D.    The computer will assign itself an IP address using APIPA.

4.    What is the range of IP addresses that a DHCP server uses called?
      A.    Scope
      B.    IPRange
      C.    DNS
      D.    IP Pool

5.    A user complains that she cannot browse the Web using Internet Explorer. The network is configured to use private IP addresses and a proxy server to provide Internet Access. Which of the following is a possible reason?
    A.    The Internet is not working.
    B.    Her browser is not configured to use a proxy server.
    C.    TCP/IP filtering is blocking all traffic on TCP port 30.
    D.    The proxy server is also the DHCP server.

6.    You are using non-standard (classless) subnet masks on your network. Which of the following routing protocols support these subnet masks? (Choose all that apply).
    A.    RIP version 1
    B.    RIP version 2
    C.    OSPF
    D.    UDP

7.    A company has hired you to upgrade their entire network to a Windows 2000 domain, but they don't want to use TCP/IP. What other choice can you offer?
    A.    Use NetBIOS
    B.    Use NWLink (IPX/SPX)
    C.    Use DNS
    D.    They have no choice. Windows 2000 domains require TCP/IP.

8.    One computer is not seeing other computers on the network. Using IPCONFIG, you see that it has an IP address of 169.254.0.32. What's wrong?
    A.    The computer could not find a DHCP server.
    B.    The NIC has failed.
    C.    The network cable is unplugged.
    D.    Windows 2000 needs to be reloaded.

9.    Which of the following computers must have a static IP address (Choose all that apply).
    A.    All non-Windows 2000 computers
    B.    WINS servers
    C.    Windows 2000 computers with two hard drives
    D.    None. Every computer can use automatic IP assignments.

10.    When does a client first attempt to renew a DHCP-assigned IP address?
    A.    When the lease duration ends.
    B.    When the lease duration is half over.
    C.    Randomly, when network traffic is low.
    D.    Never. It waits for DHCP to renew it.

# Answers to Lesson 2 Quiz

1.    Answer C is correct. The subnet mask divides the IP address into a Host ID and a Network ID.

      Answer A is incorrect. A firewall or proxy server hides an IP address from public view.

      Answer B is incorrect. In TCP/IP, servers and clients are the same thing. They are both hosts on the network.

      Answer D is incorrect. The terms subnet and segment are synonymous.

2.    Answer D is correct. 24.52.125.91 is a public IP address.

      Answers A, B, and C are incorrect. These are all valid private IP addresses.

3.    Answer D is correct. A Windows 2000 computer will generate its own IP address if a DHCP server is unavailable on the network. The APIPA service provides this functionality.

      Answer A is incorrect. A Windows 2000 computer will not crash just because it does not have an IP address.

      Answer B is incorrect. Windows NT 4.0 computers generate an error if they cannot contact a DHCP server, but Windows 2000 computers do not.

      Answer C is incorrect. A computer will try to renew its old address with the DHCP server, but if the server is unavailable, the computer cannot use that address.

4.    Answer A is correct. The Scope is the range of IP addresses configured in DHCP.

      Answers B and D are incorrect. These are fictitious terms.

      Answer C is incorrect. The Domain Name System provides name resolution.

5.    Answer B is correct. Each Web browser must be configured to use a proxy server.

Answer A is incorrect. The Internet is never "not working."

Answer C is incorrect. TCP port 30 is not used for Web browsing (HTTP uses port 80).

Answer D is incorrect. Although it may be a bit unconventional, there is nothing wrong with having the proxy server also run the DHCP service.

6.    Answers B and C are correct. To support CIDR, the routers on your network must use RIP version 2 or OSPF.

Answer A is incorrect. The original version of RIP (version 1) does not support classless subnets.

Answer D is incorrect. UDP is not a routing protocol.

7.    Answer D is correct. This is one time where you cannot offer the customer a choice—Active Directory, the foundation of every Windows 2000 domain, requires TCP/IP.

Answers A and B are incorrect.

Answer C is incorrect. DNS is part of the TCP/IP protocol suite.

8.    Answer A is correct. If a computer cannot contact a DHCP server, it will generate an IP address in the 169.254.x.y range.

Answers B and C may be correct. If the NIC has failed or the cable is unplugged, the computer cannot contact a DHCP server, and so will generate the IP address listed.

Answer D is incorrect.

9.    Answer B is correct. WINS, DNS, and DHCP servers must have static IP addresses.

Answer A is incorrect. Many non-Windows 2000 computers can use DHCP.

Answer C is incorrect. The number of hard drives in a computer has nothing to do with IP addressing.

Answer D is incorrect. Some computers must have unchanging IP addresses.

10.    Answer B is correct. A DHCP client will attempt to renew its address when the lease duration is half through, or whenever the computer is booted.

Answers A, C, and D are incorrect. A DHCP client only attempts to renew its address half through the lease duration, or when the computer boots.

# Lesson 3

# Dynamic Host Configuration Protocol (DHCP)

Every computer on a TCP/IP-based network requires a unique IP address and a properly configured subnet mask. On segmented networks, each computer also needs to know the IP address of the default gateway (the default router). On most networks, which use many different TCP/IP-related services, clients also need to know the IP addresses of Domain Name System (DNS) and Windows Internet Naming Service (WINS) servers.

The Dynamic Host Configuration Protocol (DHCP) handles the automatic assignment of IP addresses and the other TCP/IP information to requesting clients. On all but the smallest networks, the Windows 2000 DHCP service is a vital part of TCP/IP networking.

After completing this lesson, you should have a better understanding of the following topics:

- DHCP Overview
- DHCP Implementation
- DHCP Management
- DHCP Business Goals

# DHCP Overview

One of the most time-consuming administrative tasks on a TCP/IP-based network is the configuration of TCP/IP information on client computers. For each client attached to the network, you must assign a unique IP address, subnet mask, default gateway, DNS server addresses, and WINS server addresses. DHCP automates this process, so that all information is sent to each client as it boots.

## Using DHCP

To use DHCP on a Windows 2000 network, you install the service on one or more Windows 2000 servers, and then create scopes. A scope is a range of IP addresses from which the DHCP server obtains addresses to assign to clients. You can associate the following TCP/IP configuration settings with a scope:

- IP Address

- Subnet mask

- Default gateway

- DNS server addresses

- WINS server addresses

When a client boots, it broadcasts a message on its local subnet requesting TCP/IP configuration information. The DHCP server responds, selecting an IP address from the scope and sending it and the associated settings to the client.

A major advantage of using DHCP is its centralized nature. When a network configuration change is made—say, for example, the WINS server IP address is changed—you make the change once, in the DHCP scope. When each client computer is rebooted, it receives the new configuration information. Thousands of client computers can be reconfigured effortlessly.

## Installing and Configuring DHCP

DHCP, like all other Windows 2000 services, is installed during the initial installation of Windows 2000, or from the Control Panel after Windows 2000 is installed. To install DHCP from the Control Panel, follow these steps:

1.  From the **Start** menu, choose **Settings**, and then select **Control Panel**.

2.  Double-click **Add/Remove Programs**.

3.  Choose **Add/Remove Windows Components**.

4.  From **Windows Components**, choose **Networking Services** and then select **Details**.

5.  From the **Subcomponents** list, choose the box next to **Dynamic Host Configuration Protocol (DHCP)**, and then select **OK**.

6.  Choose **Next** to begin the installation process.

7.  When Windows 2000 is finished installing the software, choose Finish.

8.  Close the **Add/Remove Programs Control Panel**.

Installation of the DHCP service does not require a reboot of the server.

### Creating and Configuring a DHCP Scope

To configure a scope in DHCP, follow these steps:

1.  From the **Start** menu, choose **Programs**, **Administrative Tools** and then select **DHCP**.

2.  From **DHCP**, right-click the server and then choose **New Scope** (Figure 3.1).

## Figure 3.1 New DHCP Scope Creation

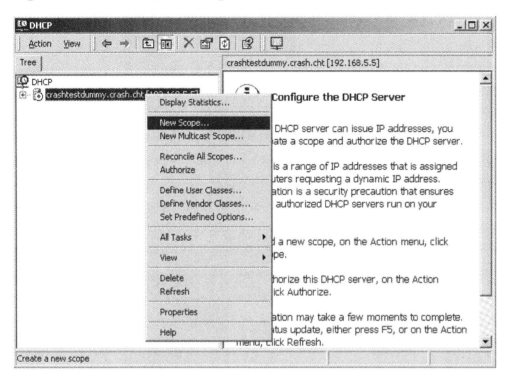

3. Choose **Next** to begin the **New Scope** wizard.

4. Type a name and description for the scope, and then choose **Next**.

5. Type the **Start** and **End IP** addresses for the range that the scope includes, type a subnet mask (or a length, in bits) and then choose **Next** (Figure 3.2).

## Figure 3.2 Scope Range Configuration

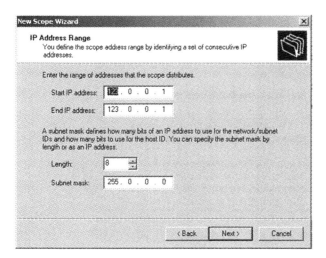

6.  To exclude any IP addresses from the range you created, type the **Start** and **End IP** addresses of the excluded range, choose **Add**, and then select **Next**.

7.  Type the lease duration and then choose **Next**.

 **Note:** The default lease duration is 8 days.

8.  To configure additional DHCP settings, choose **Yes, I want to configure these options now**, and then select **Next**. If you do not wish to configure additional options, choose **No, I will con-figure these options later**, and then select **Next**.

9.  Type the IP address for the default gateway (router) DHCP clients will use, choose **Add** and then select **Next**.

10. Type the name of the parent domain for the clients, type the IP address of the DNS servers the clients will use, choose **Add** and then select **Next** (Figure 3.3).

 **Note:** If you do not know the IP address for a DNS server, you can enter the server name and choose **Resolve**. The DNS service resolves the IP address for you, and automatically enters it in the IP address box.

## Figure 3.3 DNS Settings in the DHCP Scope

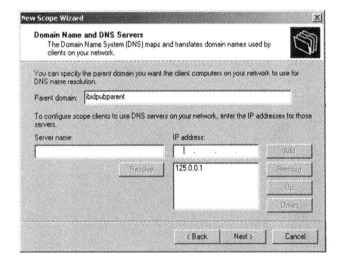

11. Type the name or IP address of any WINS servers on the network. If you type the name, choose **Resolve** to have DNS determine the IP address for you. Choose **Add** and then select **Next**.

12. To activate the scope immediately, choose **Yes, I want to activate the scope now** and then select **Next**. Otherwise, choose **No, I will activate this scope later** and then select **Next**.

13. Choose **Finish** to close the wizard.

# DHCP Implementation

When planning the implementation of DHCP, you must take into consideration the physical layout of the network. DHCP relies upon broadcast messages, and broadcast messages are not passed through routers by default. To overcome this obstacle, you must consider the type of routers used and the placement of DHCP servers.

## Using DHCP on Segmented Networks

DHCP clients rely on broadcast messages to obtain their TCP/IP configuration information. Since a new client computer does not yet have an IP address, it cannot send directed information to a DHCP server. Rather, it broadcasts a message and all computers on the segment receive the data. Only a DHCP server responds to the broadcast (Figure 3.4).

## Figure 3.4 Broadcast Request for DHCP Information

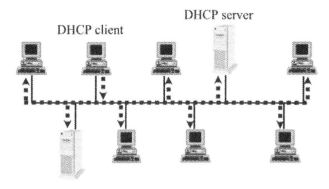

Although the broadcast method is necessary when first obtaining an IP address, broadcast messages are not routable. On a segmented (routed) network, when a router receives a broadcast, it does not forward the broadcast to other network segments.

 **Note:** Routers greatly reduce overall network traffic by preventing broadcast messages from reaching other segments. Unfortunately, this typically includes broadcast messages from DHCP clients requesting TCP/IP information.

When implementing DHCP on a segmented network, you have the following options:

**Use Multiple DHCP servers**—Place a DHCP server on each subnet so that a DHCP server receives all broadcast messages. This method is expensive but effective (Figure 3.5).

## Figure 3.5 Multiple DHCP Servers

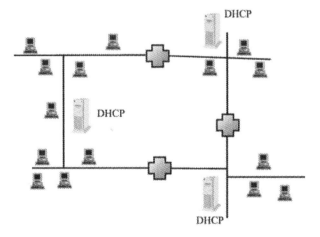

**Enable Broadcast Forwarding on the routers**—You can configure routers that support DHCP and the Bootstrap Protocol (BOOTP) to forward DHCP broadcast messages. These routers will still prevent other broadcast messages from crossing to other subnets, but do allow DHCP requests.

 **Note:** DHCP uses User Datagram Protocol (UDP) ports 67 and 68 for IP lease assignments. These are the same UDP ports used by BOOTP, which is why routers that support BOOTP can support DHCP.

If all routers on your network support BOOTP or DHCP, this method provides the least expensive method for using DHCP on a segmented network.

**Configure a DHCP relay agent on each subnet**—A DHCP relay agent is a Windows 2000 or Windows NT 4.0 computer that passes DHCP broadcast messages through the router. When a DHCP relay agent receives a broadcast request, it repackages the message and directs it to the DHCP server. Upon receipt of information from the DHCP server, the relay agent forwards the information to the requesting client (Figure 3.6).

## Figure 3.6 DHCP Relay Agent

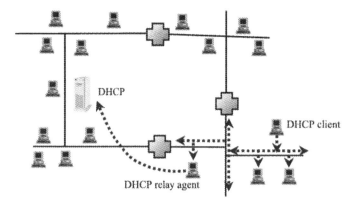

Note: The DHCP relay agent is transparent to the DHCP client. As far as the client knows, the DHCP server responds directly to broadcast requests.

**Create a multihomed DHCP server**—A multihomed server is one in which multiple Network Interface Cards (NICs) are installed. The DHCP server simultaneously participates on multiple segments (Figure 3.7).

## Figure 3.7 Multihomed DHCP Server

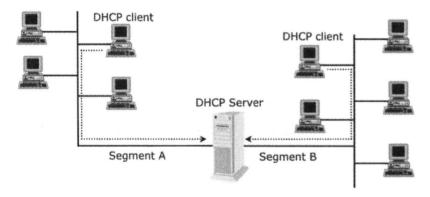

 Tip: You can also create multihomed DHCP relay agents. A multihomed relay agent will receive broadcast requests on several segments, and then forward the requests to a single DHCP server.

## Using DHCP with Wide Area Networks (WANs)

When you have one or more remote locations connected to your intranet through Wide Area Network (WAN) connections, consider the bandwidth usage and speed when planning DHCP server placement. For slower connections, it is typically more cost-effective to place a DHCP at each remote location. The benefits of implementing a remote DHCP server are three-fold:

**Increased speed**—DHCP requests can be handled at the speed of the Local Area Network (LAN), rather than the speed of the much slower WAN.

**Reduced network traffic**—Broadcast messages use significant bandwidth, and you should always strive to reduce bandwidth over slower WAN links. By reducing DHCP requests across the WAN, you make more bandwidth available for data transmissions.

**Reduced Cost**—Although the addition of a server may be costly, the time and bandwidth savings often more than compensate for the cost of a server. This holds true especially on those WAN links for which you are billed by time or data usage.

## Authorizing DHCP Servers

Since DHCP provides the configuration information for all requesting clients, you must ensure that no unauthorized DHCP exist on the network. In Windows NT 4.0, anyone with access to a computer and Windows NT 4.0 Server could install a DHCP server on the network, and have this server issue spurious TCP/IP information. Within a few hours or days, all clients on a network segment could have incorrect configuration information, and be rendered useless on the network.

In Windows 2000, each DHCP server must be authorized in the Active Directory before it can begin issuing DHCP information. Each time the DHCP service is started, the DHCP server queries a domain controller. The domain controller checks the Active Directory for a match in the list of authorized DHCP servers. If a match is found, the DHCP service starts. If no match is found, the DHCP service generates a system error and fails to start.

Tip: If the DHCP service fails to start, it will periodically re-query the Active Directory for authorization.

# Optimizing DHCP Performance

If you are using automatic IP assignment on your network, almost every computer must contact a DHCP server before that computer can participate in network activity. The performance of the DHCP service directly influences the performance of your network.

There are three things you can do to increase DHCP performance on a network. Most performance enhancements involve adding more DHCP servers to the network. Your options include the following:

## *Distributed Scopes*

You can distribute the network and processing demands on a DHCP server by adding a second server and splitting the DHCP scope equally between them. For example, suppose you have one DHCP server handling a scope of over 500 addresses (say, the IP address range 192.168.1.1 through 192.168.2.254). DHCP performance is low. When you add a second DHCP server, you assign the scope 192.168.1.1 through 192.168.1.254 to one server and 192.168.2.1 through 192.168.2.254 to the second. The demands are now evenly distributed between the two servers (Figure 3.8).

## Figure 3.8 Distributed Scopes

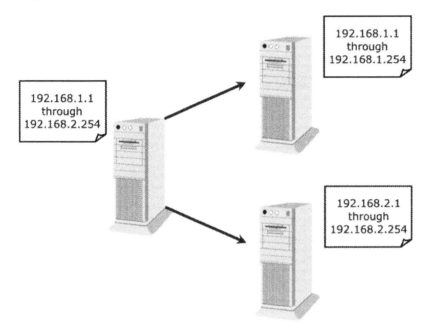

### *Server Clustering*

Windows 2000 supports clustering, which is a service that combines two or more servers into one virtual server. Computers on the network see only one DHCP server, but the network and processing demands are equally distributed among several servers (Figure 3.9). All servers in a cluster share the same DHCP scope.

# Figure 3.9 Server Clustering

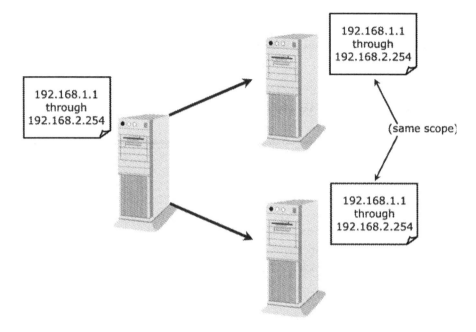

Server clustering requires more system resources than distributed scopes, but provides two benefits. Clustering provides fault-tolerance, so that—if one server fails—the entire DHCP scope is still available. Also, when you recover a failed server, you do not need to recreate the lost scope.

## *Lease Duration*

The lease duration defines how long a client can use an IP address before it is released and becomes available to other requesting clients. Adjusting the lease duration can help with DHCP performance, but you must weigh all consequences.

Consider the following examples:

**Increased lease duration**—You have increased the DHCP lease duration to

24 days. This increase results in fewer requests to the DHCP server for IP address renewals. However, a client computer crashes and is removed from the network. The IP address that computer was using is unavailable to other computers for 24 days, rather than the default 8 days.

**Decreased lease duration**—You decrease the lease duration because computers on your network are constantly moved from one subnet to another, and you do not want to tie up IP addresses. However, the shorter lease duration results in more frequent requests to the DHCP server.

**Tip:** You should manually release an IP address before taking a computer offline. From a command prompt, type **IPCONFIG /RELEASE**.

## Using DHCP with Other Services

The DHCP service integrates with other Windows 2000 services to provide a more stable network. In particular, Windows 2000 supports integration between DHCP and the Domain Name System (DNS), Active Directory, and remote access servers.

### Dynamic DNS

The Domain Name System (DNS) service provides name resolution from hostnames (friendly names) to IP addresses on a TCP/IP-based network. One of the drawbacks to using DNS on older networks (including those based on Windows NT 4.0) is that DNS is not a dynamic service. As IP addresses change, the DNS database needs to be manually updated. Using DHCP—by its very nature—means that IP addresses may change frequently. DHCP and DNS seem to be at odds with one another, but both are very important services.

With Windows 2000, the DHCP and DNS services support dynamic updates. When a DHCP client receives a new or different IP address from a DHCP server, either the client or the DHCP server itself will notify the DNS server. In this way, the IP address for every computer on the network is automatically updated in the DNS database.

**Tip:** Although you can rely on dynamic DNS to update all IP addresses, including those for servers, it is still a good practice to assign static (unchanging) IP addresses to servers. If the DHCP or DNS services fail, you want to know the IP addresses for other crucial servers.

To configure DHCP for DNS integration, follow these steps:

1.  From the **Start** menu, choose **Programs**, **Administrative Tools**, and then select **DHCP**.

2.  From **DHCP**, right-click the server, and then choose **Properties**.

3.  From **Properties**, choose the **DNS** property page (Figure 3.10).

## Figure 3.10 Dynamic Update Options

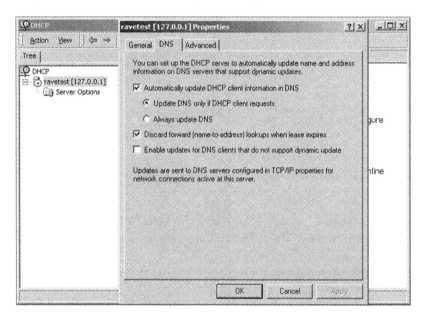

4.  Choose **Automatically update DHCP client information in DNS**. You may then select any of the following options (Table 3.x). After making your selections, click **OK**.

## Table 3.1 Dynamic DNS Update Options

| Option | Description |
|---|---|
| Update DNS only if DHCP client requests | Updates the DNS database only if the client computer requests the update. This requires a client computer that supports dynamic updates. |
| Always update DNS | Updates the DNS database regardless of what the client computer does. |
| Discard forward (name-to-address) lookups when lease expires | Removes client records from the DNS database when an IP address lease expires. |
| Enable updates for DNS clients that do not support dynamic update | Handles all aspects of the dynamic update for clients that do not support dynamic updates. |

5.  Close **DHCP**.

**Tip:** By default, the client computer updates the host (A) resource record and DHCP updates the PTR resource record in the DNS database.

### *Active Directory Integration*

DHCP works with Active Directory to ensure that no rogue DHCP servers are operating on the network. A domain controller must verify every DHCP before it can issue an IP address.

### *Routing and Remote Access Service (RRAS) Integration*

RRAS is the service that provides dial-up and Virtual Private Network (VPN) connections to your network. One of the functions of an RRAS server is to assign a temporary IP address and subnet mask to dial-up clients so that they can connect to the network. With RRAS and DHCP integration, RRAS does not need its own IP address scope. Rather, it obtains IP addresses for dial-up clients.

 **Note:** When an RRAS server initializes, it immediately requests 11 IP addresses from the DHCP server. If the number of dial-up connections exceeds 11, the RRAS server requests more addresses, in blocks of 10 addresses.

You can also configure the RRAS server to be a DHCP relay agent. When the RRAS server acts in this capacity, the DHCP server issues not only an IP address and subnet mask, but all of the other TCP/IP information in the scope as well.

To configure RRAS to use DHCP for IP address allocation, follow these steps:

1. From the **Start** menu, choose **Programs**, **Administrative Tools**, and then select **Routing and Remote Access**.

2. From **Routing and Remote Access**, right-click the server and then choose **Properties**.

3. From **Properties**, choose the **IP** property page (Figure 3.11).

## Figure 3.11 IP Property Page

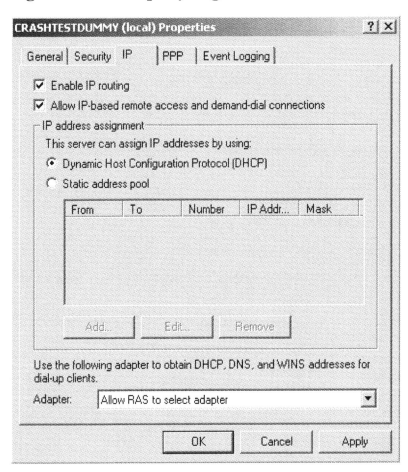

4.  From the **IP** property page, choose **Use DHCP** to assign remote IP addresses, and then select **OK**.

# DHCP Management

DHCP, if initially configured properly, rarely causes problems on the network. However, errors can occur, and DHCP servers can become overloaded as the network grows. To manage DHCP on a larger network, you should monitor DHCP and send administrative alerts when errors occur.

In addition to monitoring the DHCP service, you must anticipate changes in the DHCP configuration and implement changes before network problems occur. Testing the DHCP service is one way to help anticipate needed changes.

## Detecting DHCP Errors

Some of the DHCP errors you may encounter include the following:

**DHCP server failure**—If a DHCP server or relay agent fails, client computers may not be able to receive IP information. If you have designed redundancy into your network (using Windows clustering, for example), you may not immediately know that a server has failed. You should implement alerts on all DHCP servers and relay agents so that failure is immediately know and can be promptly fixed.

**Overloaded routers**—Routers can become saturated when too much network traffic tries to pass through them. If you are using a central DHCP server and routers with BOOTP or DHCP forwarding enabled, the routers may become saturated with DHCP requests. The routers should be continually monitored, and an alert should be generated before a router reaches its saturation point.

If router saturation occurs, you can replace the router with one that can handle more network traffic, or place an additional DHCP server on the other side of the router. This second DHCP server would effectively eliminate all DHCP traffic across the router.

**Rogue DHCP servers**—If a domain controller detects an unauthorized DHCP on the network, an administrative alert should be generated so that the unauthorized server can be found and removed from the network.

## Preparing for DHCP Changes

The best way to anticipate changes to the DHCP configuration is to monitor how DHCP is performing. The error detection strategies discussed in the previous section can aid in determining when the DHCP infrastructure needs to change. In addition to these strategies, you should also monitor the following:

**DHCP Uptime**—You should monitor individual DHCP servers and the DHCP service as a whole for uptime. Uptime measures the availability of the DHCP server (and service overall) to handle DHCP requests. If the availability of the DHCP service drops below a pre-determined level, consider adding additional DHCP servers, either by sharing a scope or creating one or more DHCP clusters.

**Low address availability**—You should monitor the number of available IP addresses carefully. If you chose a proper IP addressing scheme, you should have planned enough IP addresses for the anticipated network growth. However, plans change. If a DHCP server runs out of available IP addresses, it fails to serve the needs of the network.

If the DHCP has no more available IP addresses, consider the following remedies:

- Reduce the lease duration, so that unused IP addresses are made available more quickly
- Add more IP addresses to the scope
- Add an additional scope with a new range of IP addresses

**Router uptime and saturation**—You should monitor the availability of the BOOTP/DHCP-enabled routers. If the routers are saturated, replace the routers or add a redundant router to handle half of the requests.

# Testing DHCP

You should test your DHCP installation and configuration at regular intervals to ensure that the system is working as expected, and to ensure that you have provided redundancy and fault tolerance.

## Testing Redundancy

For redundant DHCP systems, you should intentionally take one or more DHCP servers offline temporarily and verify that clients are still able to receive TCP/IP information. You may notice a general decrease in network performance during these tests, which is expected, but DHCP servers should still be able to handle requests successfully.

## Testing Authorization

To test whether rogue DHCP servers are denied network service, load the DHCP service on a server that is not authorized in the Active Directory. After loading and configuring DHCP, the service should attempt to start, and then fail. An error message will be listed in the Event Log. If the service does not fail to start, check the Active Directory list of authorized DHCP servers.

# DHCP Business Goals

As with other Windows 2000 services and protocols, you should consider the use of DHCP from a business perspective. The four business goals (functionality, security, availability, and performance) are analyzed below, and you are presented with a business scenario using the DHCP service.

## Meeting Business Needs

Using DHCP with Windows 2000, you can meet the four business goals as follows:

**Functionality**—DHCP itself provides automatic TCP/IP configuration, reducing administrative over-head. Furthermore, the Windows 2000 implementation of DHCP provides additional functionality by:

* Supporting DHCP/BOOTP-enabled routers

* Supporting DHCP relay agents

* Adhering to the latest DHCP specifications, as defined by the Internet Engineering Task Force (IETF).

**Security**—The Windows 2000 implementation of DHCP prevents unauthorized DHCP servers from operating on the network. By preventing rogue DHCP servers, Windows 2000 ensures that only valid TCP/IP information is issued to requesting clients. You should establish a network requirement that all DHCP servers run Windows 2000, so that full integration with Active Directory is obtained.

**Availability**—Using DHCP on Windows 2000 servers, you can increase DHCP server availability in two ways. First, you can have multiple DHCP servers sharing a distributed DHCP scope. Second, you can use Windows Clustering to create a DHCP server cluster.

**Performance**—Using multiple DHCP servers sharing a distributed scope enhances DHCP server performance.

## Business Scenario

Woody's Chiropractic Association (WCA), a national chain of doctor's offices and regional centers, has a network of computers that allows members of the association to share information. The national center, in Raleigh, North Carolina, is connected to regional centers in Boston, Detroit, Athens, and Denver. The Denver regional office is connected to two west-coast regional centers, one in Los Angeles, and the other in Seattle (Figure 3.12).

### Figure 3.12 Business Scenario

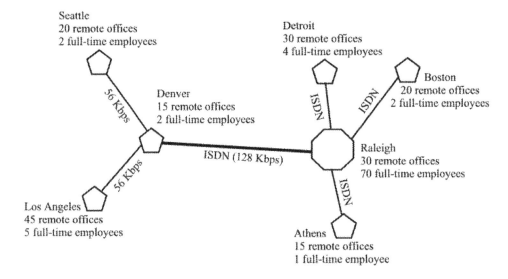

Each of the regional centers and the national center provides dial-up access to numerous doctors' offices. However, there has been little control over the IP addresses assigned to these dial-up connections, and many doctors are reporting an inability to reach resources on the network. Figure 3.13 shows the network structure of the national center, Figure 3.14 illustrates the network structure of the Denver regional center, and Figure 3.15 illustrates the general network structure of each of the other regional offices. All routers used in this network support BOOTP/DHCP forwarding.

# Figure 3.13 National Center Structure

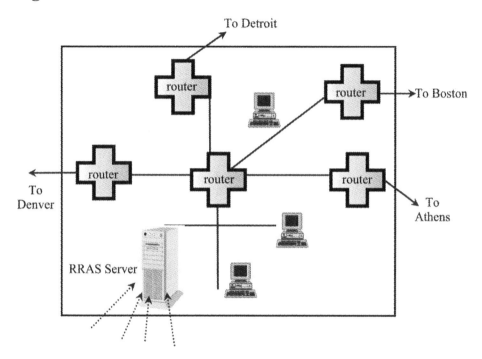

## Figure 3.14 Denver Regional Center

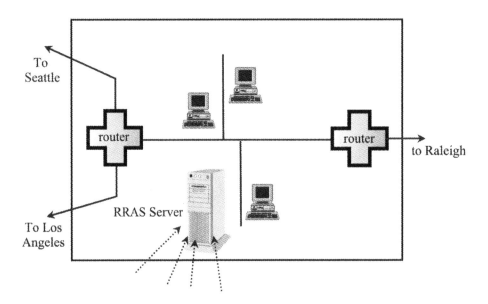

## Figure 3.15 Regional Offices Network Structure

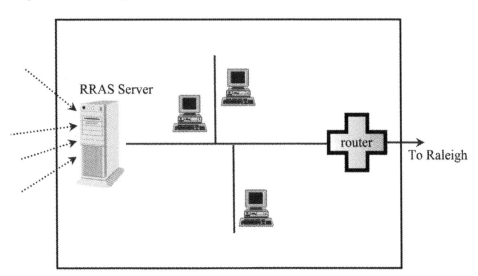

WCA has hired you to implement IP addressing throughout the network, so that communication can occur between all permanent computers and dial-up clients. The administrative staff wants to automate the process as much as possible. Since the entire network depends upon the TCP/IP protocol, reliability and availability of the DHCP servers is paramount.

Questions and answers regarding this scenario are found in the Activities section near the end of this lesson.

# Vocabulary

Review the following terms in preparation for the certification exam.

| Term | Description |
|---|---|
| Active Directory | The directory database used in Windows 2000 networks. |
| BOOTP | Routers use the Bootstrap Protocol to forward DHCP broadcast messages. |
| broadcast forwarding | The ability of routers to pass certain broadcast messages on to other network segments. |
| broadcasts | TCP/IP data messages sent to every computer on the network without a destination IP address specified. |
| client | A computer requesting information from a server (like a DHCP server). |
| clustering | The combining of two or more servers into one logical server. |
| default gateway | A TCP/IP configuration setting that defines the IP address of the default router used on a segment. |
| DHCP | The Dynamic Host Configuration Protocol performs automatic assignment of TCP/IP information. |
| DHCP relay agent | A computer that forwards DHCP broadcast messages directly to a DHCP server. |

| Term | Description |
|------|-------------|
| distributed scope | A DHCP scope that has been divided into two or more parts and placed on several DHCP servers. |
| DNS | The Domain Name System resolves IP addresses to hostnames, and hostnames to IP addresses. |
| DNS integration | The Windows 2000 implementation of DNS and DHCP are designed to work together so that DHCP can update the DNS database when IP address changes occur. |
| dynamic updates | When the IP information changes on a DHCP client, the client or DHCP updates the DNS database. |
| fault tolerance | The ability of a network or computer to recover from a single failure. |
| hostname | A user-friendly name assigned to each host on a TCP/IP network. |
| IP address | A 32-bit Internet Protocol number assigned to each host on a TCP/IP network, the IP address uniquely identifies each computer. |
| **IPCONFIG** | The **IPCONFIG** command displays information about the current TCP/IP configuration information on a computer. |
| LAN | A Local Area Network is a collection of computers in a single location, connected by a cable. |
| lease duration | The length of time that a DHCP-issued IP address is valid. |
| multihomed | Any computer with two or more NICs and attached to two or more subnets. |
| NetBIOS | Network Basic Input/Output System provides an application programming interface for computer programs to communicate with other network protocols. |

| Term | Description |
| --- | --- |
| NIC | The Network Interface Card connects a computer to the network medium (cable). NICs may also be called network cards and network adapters. |
| query | A client computer queries (sends a request to) DHCP for TCP/IP configuration information. |
| redundancy | Providing one or more additional servers to a network to distribute network demands and to provide fault tolerance. |
| rogue server | A DHCP server that is not authorized to be on the network. |
| routable | A protocol or network message that can be passed on by routers from one subnet to another. |
| router | A device that connects two or more subnets. |
| RRAS | The Windows 2000 Routing and Remote Access Service provides remote network access and routing services on the network. |
| saturated | The state of a router or server that has received more requests for service than it can handle. |
| scope | The range of IP addresses DHCP uses to issue configuration information to clients. |
| subnet | A single section of a TCP/IP network, connected to other subnets with routers. |
| subnet mask | A 32-bit number used in conjunction with the IP address to determine the host ID and network ID. |

| Term | Description |
|------|-------------|
| UDP | The User Datagram Protocol is one protocol in the TCP/IP protocol suite. |
| VPN | Virtual Private Networks create virtual tunnels through which data travels securely from one network to another across the Internet. |
| WAN | Wide Area Networks consist of two or more LANs connected over large distances by leased lines or VPNs. |
| WINS | The Windows Internet Naming System resolves NetBIOS names to IP addresses. |

# In Brief

| If you want to... | Then do this... |
| --- | --- |
| Increase DHCP availability | Add a DHCP server at each remote network location. |
| Further increase DHCP availability | Add a DHCP on each network segment. |
| Create a distributed scope | Divide a scope into two parts (with no overlap), and place each of the new scopes on a separate DHCP server. |
| Reduce DHCP traffic across a WAN link | Place a DHCP server at the remote WAN location and on the main network. |
| Provide DHCP on a segmented network | Ensure the routers support BOOTP/DHCP forwarding. |
| Provide DHCP service on a segmented network with routers that do not support BOOTP/DHCP forwarding | Implement two DHCP relay agents on each subnet. |

# Lesson 3 Activities

Complete the following activities to better prepare you for the certification exam.

1. What is the minimum number of DHCP servers required in the WCA scenario?

2. How many relay agents are required in the WCA scenario?

3. Given WCA's expectation of reliability and availability, how many DHCP servers would you recommend?

4. Given the expectations of the company, how many relay agents will you recommend?

5. How many DHCP scopes must you create for the number of subnets represented?

6. As the Denver regional office continues to grow, WCA wants to consider adding another network segment within that office to alleviate some network traffic. How will that affect the number of DHCP servers needed?

7. You want the dial-up clients to receive the IP address of the DNS servers when they connect. To provide this service, how many RRAS servers must be configured as DHCP relay agents?

8. The network traffic on the link between Denver and Raleigh is very high, and the routers are close to saturation. WCA does not want to pay for a new, faster connection. The WCA CEO suggests placing a relay agent in the Denver office. Will this solution help? Why or why not?

9. In order to reduce the network traffic between Denver and Raleigh, the WCA chief custodian suggests placing a DHCP server in the Denver office. Does this solution help? Why or why not?

10. The router connecting the Denver center to the Seattle and Los Angeles centers has failed and been replaced with an older router. Now, several days later, employees at the Los Angeles and Seattle centers complain that they are getting boot-up errors and can no longer "see" any computers outside their regional office. What is the likely reason?

# Answers to Lesson 3 Activities

1.    Only one DHCP server is required on the network, although adding more servers may be a better plan.

2.    No relay agents are needed, since all of the routers on the network support BOOTP/DHCP forwarding.

3.    Since the availability of the DHCP servers is very important to WCA, you should consider placing a DHCP server at each regional office, and at least two servers at the Raleigh center. You may consider placing a DHCP server on each subnet in the Raleigh LAN if costs and demands dictate this.

4.    Again, because the routers all support BOOTP/DHCP forwarding, you do not need any relay agents. Adding relay agents will not increase the availability of the DHCP service, and will only complicate network administration.

5.    There are 11 subnets in the network (five in Raleigh, and one at each regional location). Each subnet needs its own DHCP scope.

6.    Adding an additional segment does not necessarily change the number of DHCP servers needed, since the routers can forward BOOTP/DHCP requests. For availability, you may consider adding an additional DHCP server on the Denver subnet.

7.    Dial-up clients receive an IP address and subnet mask, WINS and DNS information without the RRAS servers being configured as DHCP relay agents.

8.    This solution will not help. The relay agent does not handle DHCP requests. In fact, the relay agent will forward DHCP requests across the WAN link, adding more network traffic.

9.    Placing a DHCP server in the Denver regional office will significantly reduce traffic across the Denver-Raleigh WAN link. All DHCP clients from Denver, Seattle, and Los Angeles will receive their DHCP information from the Denver DHCP server, and so this traffic will no longer travel to Raleigh.

10.   The router used to replace the failed router does not support BOOTP/DHCP forwarding. The clients in Seattle and Los Angeles can no longer contact a DHCP server, and so are not receiving IP addresses. You could solve this problem by replacing the router or adding a DHCP relay agent in Seattle and Los Angeles.

# Lesson 3 Quiz

These questions test your knowledge of features, vocabulary, procedures, and syntax.

1.  What is the ability of DNS to update its database when DHCP clients receive new IP addresses called?
    A.   DHCP Updater
    B.   DNS-DHCP Chat
    C.   Dynamic DNS
    D.   DNS Updater

2.  Which command removes an IP address from a client computer?
    A.   **IPRELEASE**
    B.   **IPCONFIG / REMOVE**
    C.   **LEASE END**
    D.   **IPCONFIG /RELEASE**

3.  You add a new DHCP server to you Windows 2000 network, but it isn't issuing IP addresses. What is a possible reason? (Choose all that apply).
    A.   The DHCP service is improperly configured.
    B.   The DHCP server is not authorized in Active Directory.
    C.   You already have a DHCP server on the network.
    D.   The DHCP server is multihomed.

4.  When RRAS uses DHCP for IP assignment for dial-up connections, how many IP addresses does RRAS first reserve?
    A.   None. It requests an address when a connection is made.
    B.   10
    C.   11
    D.   12

5.  A DHCP scope contains what information?
    A.   The IP address of the DHCP server.
    B.   The Active Directory domain controller IP address.
    C.   The hostname of the client.
    D.   The subnet mask for the client.

6.    What is the default lease duration for an IP address assignment?
      A.    8 minutes
      B.    8 hours
      C.    8 days
      D.    8 weeks

7.    What is the default gateway?
      A.    The portal to the Internet.
      B.    The router used to forward IP packets to other segments.
      C.    The location of the DHCP server.
      D.    The location of the domain controller.

8.    What does a DHCP relay agent do? (Choose all that apply).
      A.    Issues broadcast messages on all network segments.
      B.    Converts DHCP broadcast requests to directed messages.
      C.    Prevents DHCP messages from reaching a router.
      D.    Provides IP addresses from a DHCP server to clients.

9.    How is security increased when using DHCP?
      A.    Through DHCP server authorization.
      B.    By preventing clients from contacting the DHCP server.
      C.    By hiding the DHCP server behind a firewall.
      D.    By using a subnet mask.

10.   Which of the following increases DHCP performance? (Choose all that apply).
      A.    Using distributed scopes
      B.    Using Windows clustering
      C.    Increasing the lease duration
      D.    Removing the DHCP service.

# Answers to Lesson 3 Quiz

1.    Answer C is correct. Dynamic DNS is the service that allows DHCP and DHCP clients to update DNS with changes.

      Answers A, B, and D are incorrect. These are all fictitious terms.

2.    Answer D is correct. The IPCONFIG /RELEASE command releases the DHCP-assigned IP address and adds it to the scope of available addresses.

      Answers A, B, and C are incorrect. These are all fictitious commands.

3.    Answers A and B are correct. If the DHCP service is not properly configured, or if the DHCP server is not in the list of authorized DHCP servers in Active Directory, the server will not issue IP addresses.

      Answer C is incorrect. You can have multiple DHCP servers on a network without a problem.

      Answer D is incorrect. A multihomed DHCP server serves two or more networks simultaneously.

4.    Answer C is correct. RRAS reserves 11 addresses for dial-up connections. If more are needed, RRAS reserves them in blocks of 10 addresses.

      Answers A, B, and D are incorrect.

5.    Answer D is correct. The DHCP scope contains the IP address and subnet mask for the client, and may also contain the IP addresses for the DNS and WINS servers and the default gateway.

      Answer A is incorrect. Clients learn the IP address of the DHCP server after receiving the scope information from the server. This information is not included in the scope.

      Answer B is incorrect. The IP address of the domain controllers is not included in the scope information.

      Answer C is incorrect. The DHCP server does not include hostnames in the scope information.

6.     Answer C is correct. By default, an IP lease lasts 8 days.

       Therefore, answers A, B, and D are incorrect.

7.     Answer B is correct. In IP configuration, the default gateway address indicates the IP address of the router used to forward data to other network segments.

       Answer A is incorrect. The connection to the Internet may be a proxy server or firewall, but not the default gateway.

       Answers C and D are incorrect. The locations of the DHCP and Active Directory servers are not indicated in the IP configuration.

8.     Answers B and D are correct. When a DHCP relay agent receives a broadcast message, it repackages the message and directs it to a DHCP server. When it receives a response from the server, it sends the response back to the requesting client.

       Answer A is incorrect. No standard device is capable of sending broadcast messages on all network segments.

       Answer C is incorrect. A broadcast message will still reach a router, but the router will prevent it from propagating to other subnets.

9.     Answer A is correct. By requiring DHCP servers to be authorized by Active Directory, rogue DHCP servers are prevented form shutting down the network.

       Answer B is incorrect. If clients cannot contact the DHCP server, there is no point in having a DHCP server.

       Answer C is incorrect. Placing a DHCP server behind a firewall does not increase network security.

       Answer D is incorrect. The subnet mask is part of the TCP/IP configuration information.

10.    Answers A, B, and C are correct. By adding additional servers and either distributing the scope or creating a server cluster, you increase the ability of each server to handle network demands. Increasing the lease duration will cause fewer requests to the DHCP server and reduce network demands.

       Answer D is incorrect. Removing the DHCP service does not increase DHCP performance.

# Name Resolution Services

The Transmission Control Protocol/Internet Protocol (TCP/IP) provides a means of reliably transmitting data on any size of network. TCP/IP is the protocol of the Internet because it is routable and reliable.

TCP/IP uses IP addresses to identify each computer on a network. People do not easily remember IP addresses, and they are often incorrectly typed or forgotten. To make TCP/IP easier for people to use, the Domain Name System (DNS) converts IP addresses to hostnames, which are friendly names people can more easily remember.

Before Windows 2000 and the prominence of the Transmission Control Protocol/Internet Protocol (TCP/IP) in Windows networking, many Windows networks used the Network Basic Input/Output System (NetBIOS) protocol. Each computer on a NetBIOS-based network identifies itself with a NetBIOS name. For each network, every NetBIOS name must be unique.

As connectivity to the Internet has become commonplace, and TCP/IP has become the default Windows networking protocol, the need for NetBIOS names has diminished. TCP/IP uses hostnames to identify computers on a network.

Despite the diminished use of NetBIOS, NetBIOS names are still used on    Windows-based networks, mainly to provide support for older Microsoft operating systems and older applications. NetBIOS now runs in association with TCP/IP (often referred to as NetBIOS over TCP/IP, or NBT), and so there is need to resolve NetBIOS names to IP addresses. The Windows Internet Naming Service (WINS) provides this conversion service.

After completing this lesson, you should have a better understanding of the following topics:

• DNS Overview

• DNS Implementation

• DNS Management

• DNS Business Goals

- WINS Overview
- WINS Implementation
- WINS Management
- WINS Business Goals

# DNS Overview

The Domain Name System (DNS) allows you to assign a name to each host computer on a TCP/IP-based network, and then use these names to transfer data. The names you assign are called hostnames. In the background, TCP/IP uses IP addresses to identify the source and destination hosts, so a method must be in place to convert the hostnames to IP addresses. DNS provides that system of name conversion.

## Understanding the DNS Namespace

DNS converts (resolves) a hostname to an IP address, or an IP address to a hostname. More specifically, a name server (a computer running the DNS service) translates IP addresses into Fully Qualified Domain Names (FQDNs). An FQDN is the hostname plus the full name of the domain in which the computer exists. The full domain name is defined by the domain namespace in which a computer is located.

The domain namespace is a hierarchical structure that organizes groups of computers on the Internet. The term domain defines a level within this hierarchical structure. There are three main levels in the domain name system: the root-level domain, top-level domains, and second-level domains (Figure 4.1).

## Figure 4.1 Domain Namespace

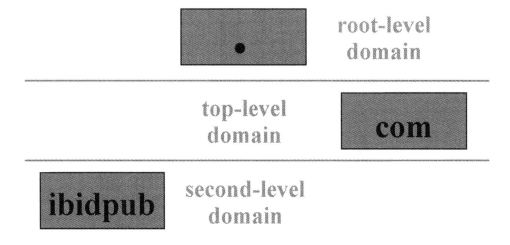

The root-level domain is at the top of the domain namespace hierarchy. It does not have a label but is represented by a period (.). All domains on the Internet are members of the root domain. Below the root domain are a series of top-level domains. These domain names consist of two-or three-letter names that define the type of domain.

Examples of top-level domains including the following:

- **com** = Commercial organizations

- **org** = Non-profit organizations

- **edu** = Educational institutions

- **gov** = Non-military U.S. Government organizations

- **net** = Networks

- **mil** = U.S. military

Some two-letter country abbreviations are:

- **ca** = Canada

- **de** = Germany

Below the top-level domains are second-level domain names. These second-level domains contain hosts and other domains, called subdomains. Second-level domains are typically company, agency, or university names.

## Resolving Hostnames

When you ask for information from a DNS server (for example, when you browse the Internet using FQDNs), your computer (the client) sends a request to the DNS server in your zone that is configured as the default name server.

 Note: The default name server is manually configured within the TCP/IP Properties sheet and can also be assigned dynamically using Dynamic Host Configuration Protocol (DHCP).

The request is called a recursive request. The client computer is saying, "give me an address, or give me an error, but don't give me partial information". The local name server needs to resolve a host name to an IP address, so it first looks for the host name in its own database file. If it finds the host name and IP addresses, the local name server sends this information back to your client.

However, the request for an IP address is frequently beyond the zone of authority of the local name server, which means the information is not in the local DNS database. If this is the case, your default DNS server must find the information for you.

The DNS server performs a forward lookup query to resolve the FQDN. To understand the process of resolving an FQDN through a forward lookup, let's use an example. From your computer, which has an FQDN of admin1.ibidpub.com, you type **http://www.lightpointlearning.com** into your Web browser. The following events occur to resolve that FQDN:

1.  Your computer queries the local DNS server. If www.lightpointlearning.com is in the zone of authority of your local DNS server, or if the address is in the DNS cache, your computer receives the IP address.

2.  If the local DNS server does not know the IP address for www.lightpointlearning.com, the local DNS queries a root-level DNS server.

3.  The root-level DNS returns the IP address of a top-level DNS server. In this case, the address of a DNS server that handles the .com domain is returned.

4.  The local DNS server sends a query to the .com top-level DNS.

5.  The top-level DNS server returns the address of a second-level DNS server. In this case, your local DNS receives the IP address of a DNS server in the lightpointlearning.com domain.

6.  The local DNS sends a request to the second-level DNS.

7.  The second-level DNS sends back the IP address of the computer. In this case, the computer with a hostname of www is resolved.

8.  The local DNS sends the IP address of www.lightpointlearning.com to your computer.

9.  Your computer sends a request for information directly to the target computer (in this case, it asks for a Web page from the computer www).

10. The target computer returns the requested information.

## Installing DNS

You can install the DNS service during the initial installation of Windows 2000, or after the Windows 2000 setup.

 **Note:** Before installing the DNS service on a Windows 2000 computer, you must config-ure the server. For DNS to install properly, the server must have a static IP address (it cannot be a DHCP client).

To install DNS on a Windows 2000 server, follow these steps:

1. From the **Start** menu, choose **Settings**, and then select **Control Panel**.

2. Double-click **Add/Remove Programs**.

3. Choose **Add/Remove Windows Components**.

4. From **Windows Components**, choose **Networking Services**, and then select **Details**.

 **Tip:** You can also view the Details by double-clicking the component.

5. From the **Subcomponents** list, choose the box next to **Domain Name System (DNS)**, and then click **OK** (Figure 4.2).

## Figure 4.2 Domain Name Selection

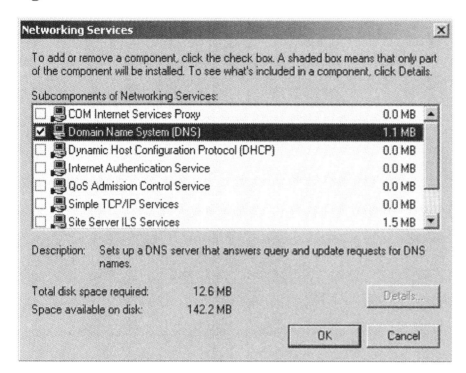

6. Choose **Next** to begin the installation process.

7. When Windows 2000 is finished installing the software, choose **Finish**.

   Close the **Add/Remove Programs Control Panel**.

# DNS Implementation

Installation and configuration of DNS requires a significant amount of planning. Although all services require planning, DNS has perhaps the greatest number of decisions. Furthermore, once DNS is installed, it is difficult to make changes. In a Windows 2000-based network, the DNS structure is very closely intertwined with your Active Directory domain structure.

# Choosing a DNS Infrastructure

You can install DNS to be an integral part of your Active Directory structure or as an independent (standard) DNS configuration. If you are using a Windows 2000-based network, there are many advantages to integrating DNS with the Active Directory. If you are adding a Windows 2000-based DNS server to an existing network, you cannot integrate DNS with Active Directory (since there is no Active Directory).

### Integration with Active Directory

When you integrate DNS with Active Directory, you gain the following benefits:

- To standard DNS servers, an Active Directory-integrated DNS server acts as a standard DNS server, with a primary DNS zone

- Active Directory-integrated DNS servers are authorized by Active Directory, reducing the possibility of rogue DNS servers on the network

- Every Active Directory-integrated DNS server contains a read-and-write copy of the zone information, providing fault-tolerance in the event of a single DNS server failure

### Standard DNS Configuration

If you are installing DNS on a Windows 2000 server and adding it to an existing DNS infrastructure, you configure standard DNS zones. The Windows 2000 implementation of DNS provides the following features:

- Adheres to the International Engineering Task Force (IETF) specifications

- Supports standard primary and secondary zone creation

- Supports caching-only servers

If you are installing DNS on a Windows 2000-based network, it is to your advantage to integrate DNS with Active Directory. There are many disadvantages to using a standard DNS configuration, including the following:

- Only Active Directory-integrated DNS allows incremental zone transfers, thus reducing overall network traffic

- Standard DNS does not support DNS zone database updates when the primary zone server fails

- Active Directory-integrated DNS provides a central, single administrative infrastructure for both DNS and Active Directory

- Standard DNS does not support Active Directory authorization, thus slightly reducing network security

## Using DNS Servers on Routed Networks

Unlike requests to DHCP servers, queries sent to DNS servers are directed. The DNS service does not rely upon broadcast messages to resolve hostnames. Therefore, implementing DNS on a segmented network is not of great concern. Routers forward DNS requests just as any other directed data transmission.

When planning the DNS implementation on a complex network, you should consider whether you want to create a hierarchical DNS structure or a flat design. A hierarchical structure is appropriate when your company has a large number of locations and hosts, and most DNS queries are for hostnames within the same location. A hierarchical structure is also useful if you want to delegate administrative control over local DNS databases.

A flat DNS design is more useful in smaller organizations, or when DNS queries are often for resources in different locations. A flat DNS design allows you to administer the DNS database in a central location.

The decision to use Active Directory-integrated DNS or standard DNS does not significantly change the way you implement DNS on a routed network. With Active Directory-integrated DNS, at least one DNS server must support the Active Directory-integrated DNS database. With standard DNS, one server must contain the standard primary zone database.

**Tip:** As a rule, you should minimize the number of DNS servers on the network. Only add servers when the demand requires the addition. A single DNS server can potentially handle tens of thousands clients.

Additional DNS servers are added to a network when one of the following situations arises:

*   You need to provide fault-tolerance in the event of a DNS server failure

*   To provide more DNS availability as the network grows

*   To reduce traffic across a slower Wide Area Network (WAN) link

## Replicating DNS Zone Information Securely

On small networks, DNS zone replication occurs only on the intranet, and so the information copied among DNS servers is not a great security risk. However, on larger networks and those that include one or more WANs, the DNS zone information may be replicated across public channels, including the Internet. You can increase DNS security by encrypting this data and by requiring authentication of DNS in the Active Directory.

### DNS Encryption

You can use the Routing and Remote Access Service (RRAS) to encrypt the DNS zone replication data with the Internet Protocol Security (IPSec) protocol. For extra security, create a Virtual Private Network (VPN) connection between replication partners.

### DNS Authentication

Data encryption ensures that the zone information—if received by an unauthorized party—cannot be read. To help ensure that the data is not sent to unauthorized computers, implement Active Directory-integrated DNS. Active Directory-based DNS servers must be listed in the Active Directory database, and the identity of each server is verified before zone information is transmitted.

 Note: The Active Directory service stores the Security Identifier (SID) of each DNS server in the Active Directory database. This SID is compared to the SID of the DNS computer before zone replication.

# Optimizing DNS Servers

Although a single DNS server can process DNS queries from tens of thousands of hosts, you do not want to rely on a single server to provide this fundamental service. If DNS is unavailable, many network services will not work properly. Also, if your network includes WAN links, you should consider the addition of more DNS servers to reduce network traffic across these slower links.

## *Zone Replication*

You can add a second DNS server to a network and configure replication between the servers. The second server provides redundancy in case the first DNS server fails and also provides load balancing. If you place a second DNS server on the distant end of a WAN link, you provide DNS support if the WAN link fails and you reduce traffic across the link.

Zone replication characteristics depend on whether you are using Active Directory-integrated DNS or standard DNS, as follows:

**Active Directory-integrated DNS**—Zone information is replicated incrementally between all DNS servers, which reduces the overall network traffic.

**Standard DNS**—Zone information is replicated between primary and secondary DNS servers either incrementally (if all DNS servers support this) or as a complete zone transfer.

## *Clustering Servers*

If you need to provide a higher level of DNS availability than that provided by replicated zone information, you can configure two or more DNS servers as a single DNS cluster. Windows Clustering service combines multiple servers as one server. These servers share one DNS database, so no zone replication traffic is generated. Furthermore, if one of the servers in a cluster fails and is replaced, you do not need to resynchronize the new server. As it joins the cluster, the DNS information is restored.

 **Tip:** All servers joined in a cluster must be connected by a high-speed, reliable link. Therefore, you should not consider Windows Clustering an option when placing a DNS server at a remote WAN location.

## Reducing Name Resolution Time

One way to optimize DNS performance is to reduce the amount of time it takes for DNS to resolve FQDNs to IP addresses. This is perhaps the single most noticeable optimization you can make to DNS. To reduce name resolution time, consider one of the following three methods:

**Add caching-only servers**—Caching-only servers do not contain any zone information, but instead retain a cache of recently resolved FQDNs. When a client requests resolution, the request is sent to the caching-only server, which either returns a result from the cache or forwards the request to a DNS zone server.

**Tip:** Caching-only servers are particularly useful at remote locations, where zone transfers can use up a significant amount of the WAN link bandwidth, and on networks where the DNS information is relatively unchanging.

**Delegate zones**—On larger networks, you can break up the zone of authority for a DNS server so that it does not contain all of the IP addresses for the network. The more IP addresses the DNS server has in its database, the longer hostname resolution takes. By delegating some of the IP addresses to another DNS server, you reduce the time it takes to search the database, and thus reduce the name resolution time.

**Tip:** Delegating DNS zones is most appropriate in hierarchical DNS structures.

**Create redundant zones**—Redundant DNS servers contain copies of the DNS database and provide load balancing. Redundant zones use zone replication to keep the DNS database current on each server.

### Reducing Replication Traffic

While reducing the time to resolve hostnames is paramount in optimizing DNS, reducing the amount of traffic generated by DNS can be equally important, especially on WAN links. You can reduce replication traffic in the following ways:

- Compress the zone replication information using fast zone transfers

- Change the zone replication schedule so that replication does not occur at peak hours

- Use incremental zone replication rather than full zone replication

## Using DNS with Other Services

The DNS in Windows 2000 fully integrates with three other Windows 2000 services to enhance the network. The Windows 2000 implementation of DNS is designed to work with Dynamic Host Configuration Protocol (DHCP), Windows Internet Naming Service (WINS), and Windows 2000 Active Directory.

### DHCP Integration

Dynamic DNS is a feature of Windows 2000 that allows Windows 2000-based DHCP servers and clients to update the DNS database as IP addresses change. Using Dynamic DNS greatly reduces administrative overhead and common configuration errors.

 **Note:** You can find more information about Dynamic DNS in the lesson covering DHCP.

### WINS Integration

When a request for name resolution reaches a DNS server, it first checks its own database. If the requested name is not found in the database, DNS will forward the request to a WINS server, if one is available on the network. Likewise, WINS (which resolves Network Basic Input/Output System (NetBIOS) names to IP addresses) forwards unanswerable requests to DNS for resolution.

Note: Many older Windows clients and programs use NetBIOS names instead of host-names. By integrating DNS and WINS, Windows 2000 provides support for these legacy systems within the DNS infrastructure.

### Active Directory Integration

As you have already seen, DNS servers can be fully integrated into the Active Directory to take advantage of Active Directory replication services and to increase network security. Active Directory uses DNS SIDs to verify each DNS server on the network.

# DNS Management

When managing DNS, you should implement a strategy to monitor DNS errors, overall DNS performance, and availability of the DNS service to meet network demands. Persistent monitoring and testing of the DNS service will enable you to predict and meet future network demands and needs.

## Detecting DNS Errors

The most common DNS error occurs when hostnames are not resolved to IP addresses in a timely fashion. Even if the names are eventually resolved, most software programs have a timeout limit and will report an error before receiving an IP address from the DNS server. To detect and resolve DNS-related problems, you should implement a monitoring plan that sends administrative alerts when DNS name resolution is not occurring or is taking too long.

If you have implemented redundant DNS servers or a server cluster, users may not know about a DNS server failure. Users may complain that network response seems slower, but clients still receive IP addresses. You should implement monitoring of each DNS server, configured so that a DNS server failure immediately alerts administrators.

### Replication Errors

Zone replication ensures that each DNS server contains a current copy of the DNS zone database. If replication is not occurring, some clients may receive outdated and incorrect IP information, making some servers and services unreachable. DNS zone replication should be monitored, and as errors occur, administrative alerts should be automatically generated.

## Preparing for DNS Changes

To anticipate changes to the DNS infrastructure, monitoring is the single-most important tool. By monitoring the DNS servers individually, and the DNS service as a whole, you can implement changes before a network failure occurs. You should monitor the following two things:

**DNS service uptime**—Monitor the amount of time clients receive DNS errors when resolving hostnames. If the number of errors is increasing with time, consider adding a redundant DNS server and implementing zone replication, or creating a server cluster.

**DNS query rate**—If the number of queries reaching a DNS server exceeds the limitations of the server, consider adding a second DNS server for load balancing or replacing the server with one that can handle more queries simultaneously.

## Testing DNS

The people who use the network test the DNS service daily. If DNS is not doing its job of resolving hostnames, the administrative staff will know about the failure. However, if you have redundant DNS servers, your users may not be immediately aware of failure. You can do two things to test DNS beyond what the users of your network do daily.

**Test DNS availability**—at a time of low network use, disconnect redundant DNS servers form the network and ensure that the network is still operational.

Tip: Be sure to disconnect only one DNS server at a time, so that you can pinpoint a failure quickly.

**Test DNS security**—If you have implemented data encryption for the zone replication information, you should use a network analyzer to capture the zone information during replication. Verify that the information is encrypted and unreadable.

# DNS Business Goals

As with other Windows 2000 services and protocols, you should consider the use of DNS from a business perspective. The four business goals (functionality, security, availability, and performance) are analyzed below, and you are presented with business scenario using the DNS service.

## Meeting Business Needs

Using DNS with Windows 2000, you can meet the four business goals as follows:

**Functionality**—DNS provides a fundamental and necessary part of a TCP/IP network. Perhaps more than any other service, DNS makes a TCP/IP network more functional by allowing users to use friendly names to identify computers, rather than relying on confusing IP addresses.

You achieve enhanced DNS functionality by integrating DNS with DHCP, WINS, and Active Directory. By creating Active Directory-integrated DNS zones, you increase performance and security, and reduce administrative overhead.

**Security**—Although the data carried during DNS zone replication is not as vital as much of the information on your network, you can enhance security by implementing IPSec encryption and creating VPNs to carry the data among DNS servers. Also, by integrating DNS with Active Directory, you can verify the identity of each DNS server before it receives zone information.

**Availability**—The availability of the DNS service on the network depends on the number of DNS servers and the number of clients requesting service. The number of DNS servers you implement depends mainly on a cost-benefit analysis. If no user on the network uses a Web browser, demands on the DNS server will be minimal. However, if the company decides to make all employee information available on the corporate intranet Web site, the demands on the DNS servers will suddenly increase. You increase the availability of DNS by adding additional redundant servers or creating a server cluster.

**Performance**—Performance of DNS, like availability, depends on the user needs. To handle increased demands and prevent a decrease in DNS performance, add additional DNS servers.

# WINS Overview

The Windows Internet Naming Service (WINS) provides name resolution for NetBIOS names. NetBIOS names are used by many Windows networking services, and are particularly prevalent in Microsoft operating systems older than Windows 2000. WINS converts these friendly NetBIOS names to IP addresses, so that users can access resources on a TCP/IP-based network by using NetBIOS names.

It is important to separate the roles of the Domain Name Service (DNS) and WINS. DNS resolves hostnames and Fully Qualified Domain Names (FQDNs) to IP addresses. WINS resolves NetBIOS names to IP addresses.

## Using WINS

The primary responsibility of WINS is resolution of NetBIOS names. Name resolution in WINS actually involves three other NetBIOS processes as well. The four processes are as follows:

**Registration**—New network devices are registered with WINS. When a WINS client initializes, it informs the WINS server of its NetBIOS name and IP addresses. In this way, the WINS database remains current.

**Resolution**—When a WINS client requests name resolution, the WINS server resolves the NetBIOS name to an IP address by checking the WINS database of registered computers.

**Renewal**—Entries in the WINS database are set to expire after a configurable amount of time. To prevent registration expiration, a WINS client renews its registration with the WINS server. If a registration expires, the WINS server removes the entry from the WINS database.

**Release**—During a system shutdown, the WINS client releases its NetBIOS name from the WINS database.

# WINS Implementation

On any network that needs to support computers running older Microsoft operating systems, you need to implement a WINS strategy to provide necessary network compatibility. Even on Windows 2000-only networks, a WINS server enhances networking services.

Unlike Active Directory or DNS, which are necessary components of almost all Windows 2000 networks, your use of WINS is dictated by the needs and expectations of the business.

A single WINS server can handle the demands placed on it from tens of thousands of client computers. In many networks, a single WINS server will provide all NetBIOS name resolution without slowing networking. However, when planning and designing the role of WINS in your network, you must consider the physical structure of the network, including the number of segments and Wide Area Network (WAN) links.

## Using WINS Servers on Routed Networks

The original implementation of NetBIOS relied upon broadcast messages to transmit information. There are two problems with broadcast messages: they generate considerable network traffic, and they are not routable. On segmented (routed) networks, the routers prevent broadcast messages from propagating to other network segments. This means that older NetBIOS computers that rely on broadcast messaging can only communicate with other computers on the same segment (Figure 4.3).

## Figure 4.3 NetBIOS Communications

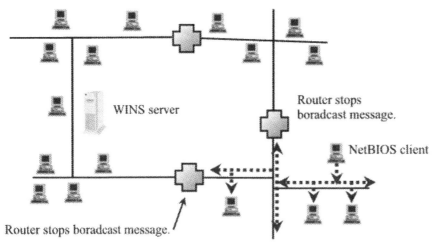

WINS clients and servers, which use NetBIOS over TCP/IP (NBT), do not use broadcasting. WINS computers send information in directed packets. Therefore, WINS queries, like all other directed transmissions, are routable.

You can support communications with older non-WINS client computers using NetBIOS in two ways, as follows:

**WINS server placement**—An expensive remedy, you can place a WINS server on the segments that contain the non-WINS clients. Since the WINS server and clients are on the same segment, the server receives and acts upon the broadcast messages (Figure 4.4).

## Figure 4.4 WINS Server Placement

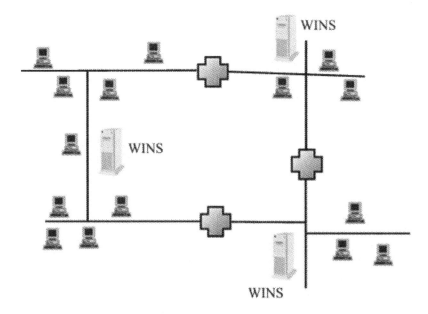

**WINS proxy agent**—Any current WINS client computer can serve as a WINS proxy agent. A WINS proxy agent receives broadcast messages, converts them to directed packets, and sends them to the WINS server. The proxy agent then redirects responses from the WINS server to the non-WINS client (Figure 4.5).

## Figure 4.5 WINS Proxy Agent

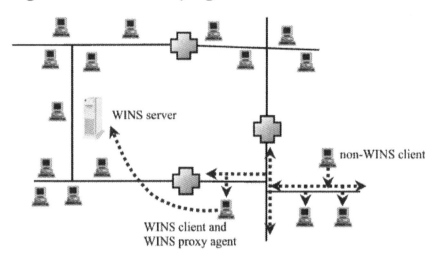

---

**Tip:** When implementing WINS proxy agents, consider the following rule: For every network segment that has non-WINS clients, configure two—and only two—WINS proxy agents. Two agents provide redundancy and fault tolerance. More than two agents produces too much network traffic, since each agent will forward every NetBIOS broadcast message received.

---

## Replicating WINS Information Securely

Replication between WINS servers ensures that all WINS servers have a current copy of the WINS database. If you have WINS servers at remote locations, replication data may be carried over public lines, including the Internet. Although the WINS database information may not contain the most sensitive corporate information, security is always an issue with any data.

You can increase network security by encrypting the WINS replication data. Using the Routing and Remote Access Service (RRAS), create a Virtual Private Network (VPN) between replication partners, or encrypt the data using IP Security (IPSec).

# Optimizing WINS Servers

If the current network configuration demands high availability of the WINS service, you need to consider ways to optimize WINS. You can increase availability and optimize WINS by adding more servers, configuring replication partners, and reducing the response time of the WINS servers.

## *Clustering Servers*

Using the Windows Clustering service, you can add one or more additional servers to your current WINS configuration. All of the servers in a cluster act as a single server, providing a single WINS service. A server cluster provides immediate fault-tolerance if one server fails, and makes failed WINS server recovery much easier.

Windows Clustering is not inexpensive, and should be considered only when availability of the WINS service is of paramount importance to the company.

 Note: Windows Clustering requires a fast, persistent connection among members of the cluster. You cannot use Windows Clustering to place WINS servers at remote locations across WAN links.

## *Using WINS Replication*

An alternative to creating a WINS cluster is to place additional WINS servers on the network and implement replication between servers. The multiple WINS servers provide fault tolerance and load balancing. You can configure WINS replication as either a pull or a push/pull partnership.

**Pull replication**—A pull partner will periodically query its replication partner for changes to the WINS database. Pull partnerships reduce overall network traffic, and are appropriate when replicating across WAN links and other congested network segments.

**Push/pull replication**—In a push/pull partnership, a WINS server will notify its replication partner when changes have occurred in the WINS database. Push/pull partnerships generate more network traffic, but ensure that all WINS servers know about WINS changes as soon as possible.

Note: If you want to schedule WINS replication to occur at specific times, use pull replication. You cannot specify replication times in push/pull partnerships.

## Reducing WINS Response Time

Reducing the time it takes for a WINS server to resolve NetBIOS names increases overall performance of the WINS service. Adding additional servers and implementing replication increases the response time of the WINS service. In addition, you should optimize the individual servers. You can reduce WINS response times by using burst-mode name registration.

If a WINS server simultaneously receives a large number of NetBIOS name registration requests, it can become saturated and fail to process requests. Using burst-mode name registration, the WINS server will issue a lease with a relatively short and randomly-generated time-to-live (TTL) to each WINS client. This forces WINS clients to fully re-register after a period of time, and also spaces out the requests so that the server does not become saturated (Figure 4.6).

## Figure 4.6 Burst-Mode Name Registration

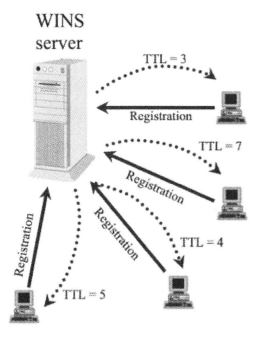

 **Note:** Burst-mode name registration is only helpful in situations where numerous WINS clients request name registration at the same time. For example, if client computers are turned on at the same time each day, burst-mode registration is helpful.

### *Reducing Replication Traffic*

In addition to reducing the response time of servers, you can reduce the amount of network bandwidth used for WINS replication data. The following are three main ways to reduce replication overhead:

*   Implement pull partnerships, and then control the frequency of replication requests

*   Modify the replication schedule to replicate during times of limited network use

*   Use persistent connections between all WINS replication partners

---

Tip: Don't reduce the replication time to the point where WINS servers are failing to properly resolve NetBIOS names. Although you want to reduce replication traffic, you do not want to create WINS errors due to outdated information.

---

## Installing and Configuring WINS

WINS is installed during setup of Windows 2000 or after the operating system is installed. To install WINS after Windows 2000 Server is installed, follow these steps:

1.  From the **Start** menu, choose **Settings**, and then select **Control Panel**.

2.  From **Control Panel**, double-click **Add/Remove Programs**.

3.  From **Add/Remove Programs**, choose **Add/Remove Windows Components**.

4.  From **Windows Components**, choose **Networking Services**, and then select **Details**.

5.  From the list of subcomponents, choose the box next to **Windows Internet Naming Service (WINS)**, and then click **OK** (Figure 4.7).

## Figure 4.7 WINS Selection

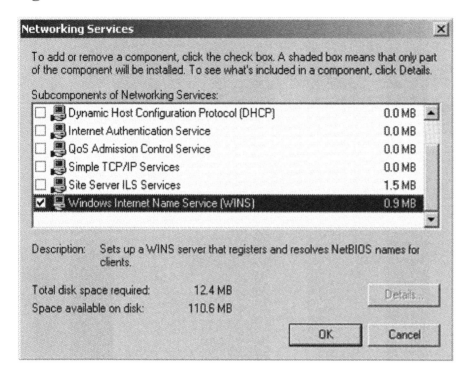

6.  Choose **Next** to begin the installation process.

7.  When installation is complete, choose **Finish**, and then close the **Add/Remove Programs Control Panel**.

### *Configuring WINS Replication Partners*

To configure WINS replication, follow these steps:

1.  From the **Start** menu, choose **Programs**, **Administrative Tools**, and then select **WINS**.

2.  From the **Tree** pane of **WINS**, expand the server container (Figure 4.8).

## Figure 4.8 WINS Server Display

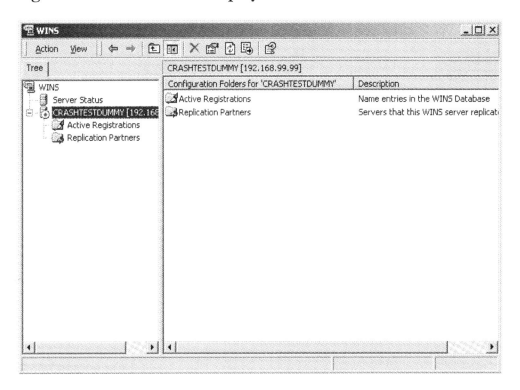

3.  Right-click **Replication Partners**, and then choose **New Replication Partner** (Figure 4.9).

## Figure 4.9 Replication Partner Selection

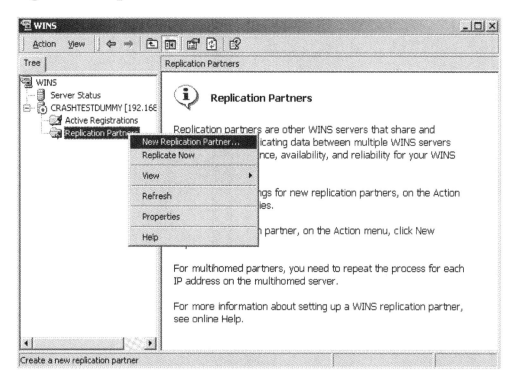

4.  Type the name of the replication partner server, and then choose **OK**.

5.  From the **Tree** pane of **WINS**, choose **Replication Partners**.

6.  From **Replication Partners**, highlight and right-click a partner server you wish to use, and then choose **Properties** (Figure 4.10).

## Figure 4.10 Replication Partner Properties

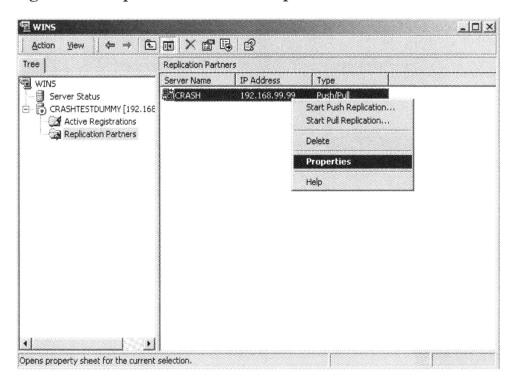

7.    From Properties, choose the Advanced property page.

8.    From the **Advanced** property page, choose **Push/Pull** in the **Replication partner type** section (Figure 4.11).

## Figure 4.11 Replication Type Selection

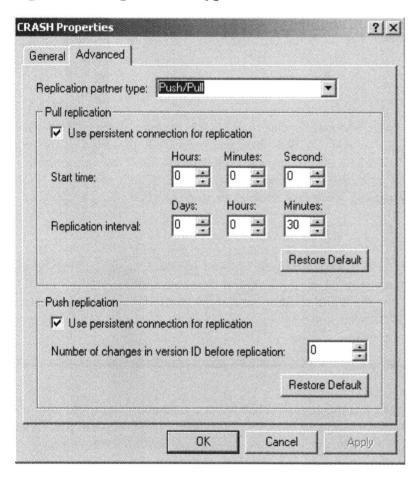

9.  Click **OK**, and then exit from **WINS**.

# Using WINS with Other Services

WINS for Windows 2000 is designed to work with two other Windows 2000 services to enhance network productivity. WINS integrates with both the Dynamic Host Configuration Protocol (DHCP) and DNS.

### *WINS-DHCP Integration*

WINS works with DHCP to provide automated updates to the WINS database. When a DHCP client initializes on the network, it first requests an IP address and other TCP/IP-related information (including the IP address of the WINS server) from a DHCP server. Once this information is received, the computer registers its NetBIOS name and newly acquired IP address with the WINS server. In this way, WINS automatically updates the database after every DHCP-issued IP change.

### *WINS-DNS integration*

Although the WINS and DNS services resolve different types of computer names to IP addresses, both services in Windows 2000 are designed to aid one another. For example, if the DNS service fails to resolve a hostname, it will query the WINS server to see if the WINS server can resolve the name as a NetBIOS name. Likewise, if WINS fails to resolve a NetBIOS name, it will query the DNS server to see if it can be resolved as a hostname.

 Note: In Windows 2000, a computer's NetBIOS name is automatically derived from the hostname. You can change a computer's hostname, but not its NetBIOS name. This allows DNS and WINS to work more closely together to resolve names.

The integration of WINS and DNS also permits the use of DNS to locate resources on older operating systems that only use NetBIOS names.

# WINS Management

When managing WINS on your network, implement a strategy that includes monitoring WINS errors and overall WINS performance. You need to ensure the availability of the WINS service to meet network demands, and persistent monitoring and testing of the WINS service will enable you to predict and meet future network demands and needs.

## Detecting WINS Errors

You implement fault tolerance and redundancy on a network so that, when a server fails, network productivity is not depreciated. However, this means that server failures may not be immediately noticed. As with any redundant or fault tolerant system, you should configure the Performance and Alerts console to monitor your WINS servers and generate an administrative alert when a server fails.

If WINS servers are failing to resolve name requests, it may mean that the WINS server is not responding, or it may mean that WINS replication is failing. If replication is not occurring, none of the WINS servers will have an up-to-date copy of the WINS database, and clients will receive errors and incorrect resolutions. In addition to monitoring individual WINS servers, you should monitor WINS replication to ensure it is occurring regularly and without error.

## Preparing for WINS Changes

Although a single WINS server can handle the network demands of a large network, changes to the network configuration (including adding a software program that requires NetBIOS name resolution) may require changes to your WINS configuration. To anticipate these changes, you should monitor the following two factors:

**WINS uptime and resolution time**—You should monitor the percent of time clients are able to successfully resolve NetBIOS names. An increasing number of failures indicate a server overload, and you should consider adding an additional server.

**WINS replication time**—If the time between WINS replications is too long, clients will receive WINS errors since not all WINS servers will have recent database information. You can reduce the errors by reducing the replication interval or adding a WINS server as part of a Windows Cluster. Clusters do not rely on replication, so both servers will always have the most up-to-date copy of the database.

## Testing WINS

When testing the WINS service, you can test the availability of the service and the security of replication. During a time of limited network use, take one WINS server offline at a time to verify that the remaining WINS servers still provide NetBIOS name resolution.

To test security, use a network analyzer (like Windows 2000 Network Monitor) to capture data during WINS replication. If you have implemented IPSec encryption, the data captured should be unreadable.

# WINS Business Goals

As with other Windows 2000 services and protocols, you should consider the use of WINS from a business perspective. Unlike many other services, the WINS service is not necessary in all networks, and so business expectations play a more important role in deciding on implementation. WINS and the four business goals (functionality, security, availability, and performance) are analyzed below.

## Meeting Business Needs

The WINS service meets business needs in the following ways:

**Functionality**—WINS provides name resolution for NetBIOS names. WINS provides the functionality needed to support networks that require the use of NetBIOS names and have older NetBIOS clients. WINS functionality is enhanced through integration with DHCP and DNS, and through support of WINS relay agents.

**Security**—Although WINS replication traffic is not a paramount security concern; the WINS service provides security by supporting data encryption using IPSec and the creation of VPNs through RRAS.

**Availability**—You can increase WINS availability by adding more WINS servers to a network. As business needs demand, you can either configure replication partners or form a WINS cluster to ensure availability.

**Performance**—As with availability, WINS performance is chiefly enhanced through the addition of WINS servers to the network. Further performance enhancement comes from enabling burst-mode name registration.

## DNS and WINS Business Scenario

Woody's Chiropractic Association (WCA) has a national network of computers. The network uses TCP/IP with the DHCP service for all communications (Figure 4.12). Originally, the full-time employees of WCA shared information among themselves and with the member doctors using a proprietary software application, ChiroLink.

## Figure 4.12 WCA Network

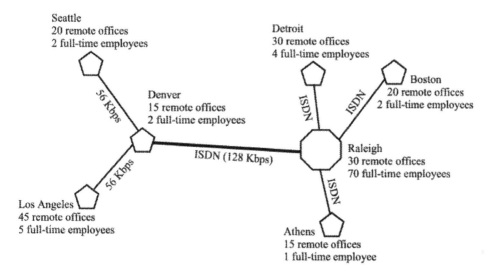

The ChiroLink programs contain many errors, and the manufacturers often issue patches and version upgrades to the software. Each of these fixes costs WCA money, but they are needed fixes. Every time a new version is installed, WCA must send representatives out to each doctor's office to retrain the office staff and the doctor on the new software.

WCA, tired of spending huge amounts of money on faulty software, has hired the CEO's daughter to design and implement both internal and external Web sites. Together, these Web sites will provide all of the services provided by ChiroLink, and will not require extensive user training.

The internal Web site will contain a chat room and online library that will be used by all full-time staff and member doctors as a place to share information. Access to a Microsoft Structured Query

Language (SQL) database will also be available. The external Web page will mainly provide information about WCA and its members to the public, but can also be used by member doctors as a portal into the WCA internal Web site.

In addition to adding the new Web sites, WCA wants to provide Internet access to all full-time employees through their Raleigh headquarters.

WCA has hired you to analyze their network and recommend needed changes to ensure that the introduction of the new internal Web site will go smoothly. According to Woody (the CEO), they want every user to be able to open a Web browser on April 1$^{st}$, enter the internal Web address, http://internal.woodychiro.com, and gain access to the new Web site.

In addition, WCA would like to restructure the existing WINS system on the network. Using the following network diagrams (Figures 4.13, 4.14, and 4.15) and list of network requirements (Table 4.1), consider implementation strategies. Then answer the questions in the Activities section found near the end of this lesson.

# Figure 4.13 Raleigh National Office

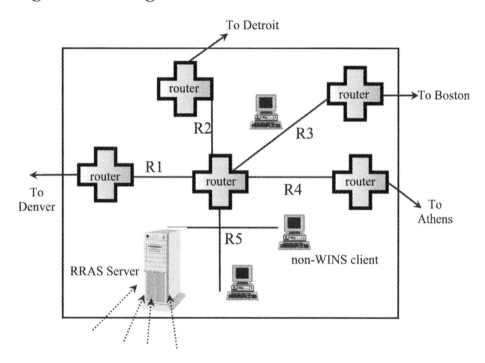

## Figure 4.14 Denver Regional Office

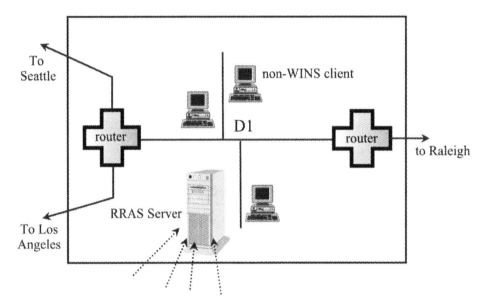

# Figure 4.15 Boston Regional Office

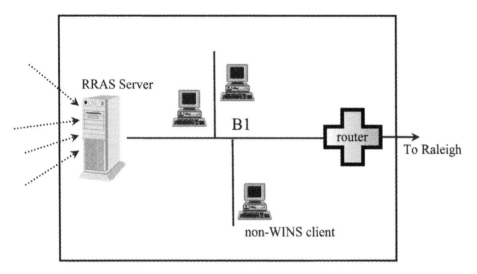

## Table 4.1 WINS Network Requirements

| Network Issue | Requirement |
|---|---|
| Physical structure | WCA does not want to change the underlying physical structure of the network. |
| Applications | In addition to the internal Web site, WCA wishes to maintain support for their old ChiroLink software, which relies on NetBIOS names for functionality. |
| Security | Since all of the doctors' offices connect to the network through dial-up connections, security is of concern, but WCA isn't particularly concerned about replication security. |
| Availability | The WINS and DNS services need to be available at all times, since ChiroLink relies upon WINS and Web page access relies upon DNS. Although the company is phasing out use of ChiroLink, they expect doctors will use it for several months to come. DNS and WINS availability must be insured even if any single point in the network fails. |
| Performance | Preliminary tests by the WCA network staff indicate that the WINS server they propose to use can handle approximately 800 clients without appreciable performance degradation. The DNS server can handle approximately the same number of clients. |

# Vocabulary

Review the following terms in preparation for the certification exam.

| Term | Description |
| --- | --- |
| Active Directory | The directory database used as a foundation of all Windows 2000 networks. |
| Active Directory-integrated DNS | DNS zone information integrated with the Active Directory database for enhanced security and easier replication. |
| broadcast messages | Messages that are sent on the network with no specified destination IP address, so that all computers on the subnet will act upon the message. |
| burst-mode name registration | When a WINS server becomes overloaded with registration requests, burst-mode name registration provides a short-term solution until the server can fully process the requests. |
| caching-only servers | DNS servers that do not contain any zone information. They only contain a list of recently resolved hostnames and IP addresses for quick retrieval. |
| client | Any computer requesting name resolution from a DNS server. |
| default name server | The first DNS server a client queries when name resolution is needed. |
| DHCP | The Dynamic Host Configuration Protocol automatically assigns TCP/IP configuration information. |
| DNS | The Domain Name System provides hostname resolution. |
| domain | The basic unit of organization in DNS, a domain is a logical collection of computers sharing a common name. |

| Term | Description |
| --- | --- |
| domain namespace | A hierarchical structure of domains that groups computers in a logical fashion. |
| Dynamic DNS | The ability of the DNS database to be updated by DHCP and DHCP clients. |
| FQDN | The Fully Qualified Domain Name is the hostname appended with the entire domain name. |
| hierarchical DNS structure | In a hierarchical domain structure, a DNS server will pass queries it cannot resolve to a higher-level name server. |
| host | Any computer on a TCP/IP network. |
| hostname | A friendly name assigned to each host on a network. |
| incremental zone transfers | The transfer of DNS zone information in which only changes are transferred, rather than the entire database. |
| IPSec | Internet Protocol Security encrypts data. |
| name resolution | Converting a NetBIOS name or hostname to an IP address. |
| name server | A DNS server. |
| NBT | NetBIOS over TCP/IP allows the functionality of NetBIOS to work with TCP/IP. |
| NetBIOS | The Network Basic Input/Output System is a Windows proprietary network protocol. |
| pull replication | During pull replication, a WINS server requests changes from other servers. |
| push/pull replication | With push/pull replication, a WINS server will notify other servers when changes occur. |
| recursive request | A request for name resolution, a recursive request expects a complete answer, not partial information. |

| Term | Description |
|------|-------------|
| redundant DNS servers | Two or more servers that provide the same DNS zone information to the network and provide load balancing and fault tolerance. |
| registration | WINS clients record their IP address and NetBIOS names with a WINS server. |
| release | WINS clients, when shutting down, notify the WINS server that their NetBIOS name and IP address are no longer being used on the network. |
| renewal | Before a WINS registration expires, a WINS client renews its registration with the WINS server. |
| replication | WINS and DNS servers copy information to other servers through replication. |
| resolution | When WINS clients request the conversion of a NetBIOS name to an IP address. |
| resolve | Convert a hostname or NetBIOS name to an IP address, or IP address to hostname or NetBIOS name. |
| root-level domain | The highest domain level, the root domain is represented by a period (.). All domains on the Internet are members of the root domain. |
| routable | A network data package that can be passed through network routers from one segment to another. |
| RRAS | The Windows 2000 Routing and Remote Access Service provides WAN connectivity and routing services. |
| second-level domain | Below top-level domains, second-level domains are usually organization-specific. |
| SID | The Security Identifier is a number assigned to each object on an Active Directory network and is used to positively identify a computer. |

| Term | Description |
|------|-------------|
| standard DNS | A DNS system that is not integrated with Active Directory but is compatible with other DNS servers. |
| subdomains | Domains below the second-level domain, subdomains are used for organization within a company. |
| top-level domain | One level below the root-level domain, top-level domains are two- or three-letter names that define the type of organization (com, net, gov, for example). |
| TTL | The Time To Live defines the lease duration for a NetBIOS name registration. |
| WAN | A Wide Area Network is a collection of two or more intranets connected by leased lines or through a Virtual Private Network. |
| Windows Clustering | A Windows 2000 service that combines two or more servers into a single logical server. |
| WINS | The Windows Internet Naming Service resolves NetBIOS names to IP addresses. |
| zone of authority | The range of hostnames for which a single DNS server is responsible. |

# In Brief

| If you want to... | Then do this... |
|---|---|
| Resolve hostnames to IP addresses | Install and configure a DNS server. |
| Resolve NetBIOS names to IP addresses | Install and configure the WINS service. |
| Support non-WINS clients on a network | Install WINS proxy agents on each network segment that contains a non-WINS client. |
| Increase DNS and WINS availability | Add additional servers and implement a server cluster. |
| Prevent rogue DNS servers on the network | Integrate DNS and Active Directory. |
| Reduce DNS management | Integrate DNS with DHCP so that IP address changes are automatically recorded. |
| Reduce WINS replication traffic | Use pull replication rather than push/pull replication. |

# Lesson 4 Activities

Complete the following activities to better prepare you for the certification exam.

1. Based on the business scenario presented, how many DNS servers and WINS servers are required to meet WCA's business needs?

2. How many WINS proxy agents are required in this scenario?

3. Which of the network segments require a WINS proxy agent?

4. Ideally, how many WINS proxy agents should you implement on the WCA network?

5. Once you have installed the WINS server(s) and proxy agent(s), what else must you do to begin using WINS on the network?

6. Considering performance and availability issues with WCA, what is an appropriate number of WINS servers and DNS servers to implement?

7. Based on the answers to Activities 4 and 6, what is the most appropriate replication method for the servers in the Raleigh location?

8. Again, based on previous answers and the network design, what is the appropriate replication method between the WINS servers in Raleigh and the other WINS servers?

9. Traffic on the link between Denver and Raleigh is too high. Short of replacing the link with a faster connection method, what changes can you make to your WINS plan to reduce this traffic? For the moment, disregard fault-tolerance and reliability requirements.

10. During WINS implementation, one of the WCA staff members in Denver configured every WINS client to also be a WINS proxy agent. What affect will this have on the network?

# Answers to Lesson 4 Activities

1.    Only one DNS server is needed, since it can handle approximately 800 clients. Likewise, a single WINS server can handle the demands of the approximately 100 WCA employees.

2.    If you use a single WINS server, at least three WINS proxy agents are needed—one for each network segment that contains a non-WINS client.

3.    You must place a WINS proxy agent on segments R5, B1, and D1.

4.    Ideally, each one of the segments mentioned in Activity 3 will have two WINS proxy agents to provide fault tolerance and load balancing. Any more than two increases network traffic and maintenance.

5.    The client computers must be configured to use WINS. If you are using DHCP, reconfigure the DHCP scope to include the IP address of the WINS server. You must also configure all WINS servers (if you have more than one) as replication partners.

6.    Given the expectation that WINS will be available, even if a single network line fails, you must place a WINS server and a DNS server at each regional office. You should also place an additional server in the Raleigh office to provide redundancy in case one WINS server fails.

7.    For the two WINS servers in Raleigh, which will be connected by a higher-speed LAN connection, push/pull replication is appropriate.

8.    Since WINS replication will occur across the slower WAN links, you should implement pull partnerships. You may also consider scheduling push/pull replication at night, when network usage is minimal.

9.    By placing a WINS server in Denver, you prevent WINS traffic from crossing between Denver and Raleigh. You can also schedule replication to only occur at night, further reducing daytime network traffic.

10.   By increasing the number of WINS proxy agents, the staff member in Denver has probably slowed the connection between Denver and Raleigh to an unusable level. Every WINS proxy agent forwards each WINS broadcast made in Denver. A single WINS broadcast generates dozens of messages across this WAN link.

# Lesson 4 Quiz

These questions test your knowledge of features, vocabulary, procedures, and syntax.

1.  What is the combination of a hostname and domain name called?
    A.   DNS
    B.   WINS
    C.   FQDN
    D.   FDQN

2.  What can you use to encrypt DNS zone transfer information?
    A.   **ENCRYPT.EXE**
    B.   **DNSENCRYPT**
    C.   The Zone Encrypter Tool
    D.   IPSec

3.  The domain name edu is most likely an example of what?
    A.   A root domain
    B.   A top-level domain
    C.   A second-level domain
    D.   A subdomain

4.  How can you install DNS on a Windows 2000 server when it will share information with existing UNIX DNS servers? (Choose all that apply).
    A.   Active Directory-integrated
    B.   Standard DNS
    C.   WINS-enabled
    D.   You cannot combine Windows 2000 DNS and UNIX DNS.

5.  Which of the following increases DNS performance? (Choose all that apply).
    A.   Using caching-only servers
    B.   Stopping all DNS zone replication
    C.   Removing the Active Directory service
    D.   Using Windows Clustering

6.  On a network segment with no non-WINS clients, how many WINS proxy agents should be installed?
    A.  0
    B.  1
    C.  2
    D.  10

7.  On a network segment with ten non-WINS clients, how many WINS proxy agents should be installed?
    A.  0
    B.  1
    C.  2
    D.  10

8.  Which of the following can resolve a hostname to an IP address? (Choose all that apply).
    A.  WINS
    B.  DNS
    C.  **RESOLVE.EXE**
    D.  Active Directory

9.  Which of the following are processes a WINS client performs with a WINS server? (Choose all that apply).
    A.  Registration
    B.  Renewal
    C.  Resolution
    D.  Release

10. What is the relationship between DNS and DHCP in Windows 2000 called?
    A.  Dynamite DNS
    B.  DHCP Update Service (DUS)
    C.  Dynamic DNS
    D.  DNS to DHCP (D2D)

# Answers to Lesson 4 Quiz

1.   Answer C is correct. The Fully Qualified Domain Name consists of a hostname and the full domain name.

     Answer A is incorrect. DNS resolves FQDNs to IP addresses.

     Answer B is incorrect. WINS resolve NetBIOS names to IP addresses.

     Answer D is incorrect. This is a fictitious term.

2.   Answer D is correct. IPSec is used to encrypt DNS information.

     Answers A, B, and C are incorrect. These are all fictitious terms.

3.   Answer B is correct. Top-level domains are typically two- or three-letter names that define the type of network organization.

     Answer A is incorrect. The root level domain is always named with a period (.).

     Answer C is incorrect. Although a second-level domain could be named EDU, most second level domains are company names.

     Answer D is incorrect. Again, a subdomain may be named EDU, but it is most commonly seen as a top-level domain.

4.   Answers A and B are correct. An Active Directory-integrated DNS server will appear as a standard DNS server to UNIX DNS, but will appear as an Active Directory-integrated server to other Windows 2000 DNS servers.

     Answer C is incorrect. WINS has nothing to do with how Windows 2000 DNS works with UNIX DNS.

     Answer D is incorrect.

5.    Answers A and D are correct. To increase DNS performance, you can add caching-only servers, building a DNS server cluster, and creating redundant zones.

      Answer B is incorrect. Stopping zone transfers does not enhance DNS, but prevents it from working properly.

      Answer C is incorrect. You cannot remove Active Directory from a Windows 2000 domain network.

6.    Answer A is correct. On a network segment without any non-WINS clients, you do not need a WINS proxy agent.

      Therefore, answers B, C, and D are incorrect.

7.    Answer C is correct. On any network segment with a non-WINS client, you should install two WINS proxy agents. The number of non-WINS clients does not matter.

      Therefore, answers A, B, and D are incorrect.

8.    Answers A and B are correct. Although the primary role of WINS is to resolve NetBIOS names, the Windows 2000 version of WINS serves as a backup to DNS if DNS fails to resolve the name to an IP address.

      Answer C is incorrect. This is not a valid command.

      Answer D is incorrect. Active Directory does not provide name resolution.

9.    Answers A, B, C, and D are all correct. A WINS client registers its NetBIOS name with WINS, renews this name, releases the name when it shuts down, and uses the WINS server to resolve names.

10.   Answer C is correct. DHCP updates the DNS database using the Dynamic DNS service.

      Answers A, B, and D are incorrect. These are fictitious terms.

# Remote Access Technologies

Windows 2000 Routing and Remote Access Service (RRAS) provides the means for extending a network beyond a single Local Area network (LAN). As a network grows, you may need to support remote users who need access to the network. In addition, you may need to connect an entire remote network to your corporate network, creating a Wide Area Network (WAN).

The two chief concerns when providing remote access are security and speed. By their very nature, remote connections typically use public lines to transmit data. These lines typically carry far less data than the cabling used for LANs. A successful remote access plan makes the most efficient use of the limited bandwidth, while ensuring that the data carried across these lines is secure from unintended (and undesired) access.

The Remote Authentication Dial-In User Service (RADIUS) works in conjunction with RRAS to centralize user authentication. The RADIUS client (which is the RRAS server) sends authentication requests to a RADIUS server. A single RADIUS server can handle requests from multiple RRAS servers.

After completing this lesson, you should have a better understanding of the following topics:

* Remote Access Technologies Overview

* Remote Access Implementation

* Remote Access Management

* Remote Access Business Goals

# Remote Access Technologies Overview

Connecting remote users and remote networks to a central network requires careful planning. Whenever data is carried across public lines, security becomes a major factor in design and implementation.

Two Windows 2000 services provide remote access connectivity. These services are Routing and Remote Access (RRAS) and Remote Authentication Dial-In User Service (RADIUS).

## Understanding Routing and Remote Access Service (RRAS)

The primary function of RRAS is to provide dial-up and Virtual Private Networking (VPN) connections to remote users. The remote access server handles user authentication for network access and data encryption to ensure security.

**Tip:** You can also use RRAS on a Windows 2000 server as an Internet Service Provider (ISP), providing dial-up access to the Internet.

RRAS supports a wide variety of network protocols, WAN technologies, and security protocols (Table 5.1), and is compatible with other remote access servers, including those running the following:

- Shiva LAN Rover

- Novell NetWare Connect

- UNIX servers using Point-to-Point Protocol (PPP) or Serial Line Internet Protocol (SLIP)

## Table 5.1 RRAS Supported Technologies

| Category | Technology or Protocol Supported |
|---|---|
| Network Protocols | Transmission Control Protocol/Internet Protocol (TCP/IP) |
| | NWLink and IPX/SPX |
| | NetBIOS Enhanced User Interface (NetBEUI) |
| | AppleTalk |
| WAN Technologies | Public Switched Telephone Network (PSTN) |
| | Integrated Services Digital Network (ISDN) |
| | Asymmetric Digital Subscriber Line (ADSL) |
| | Virtual Private Network (VPN) |
| Security Protocols | Microsoft Challenge Handshake Authentication Protocol (MS-CHAP) |
| | Microsoft Challenge Handshake Authentication Protocol, Version 2 (MS-CHAP v2) |
| | Challenge Handshake Authentication Protocol (CHAP) |
| | Extensible Authentication Protocol – Transport Level Security (EAP-TLS) |
| | Shiva Password Authentication Protocol (SPAP) |
| | Password Authentication Protocol (PAP) |

## Understanding Remote Authentication Dial-In User Service (RADIUS)

RADIUS works in conjunction with RRAS to provide a central authentication scheme. If your network supports remote users using a variety of operating systems, you need to support a variety of authentication methods and encryption protocols. By implementing RADIUS, you provide a central location from which you can authenticate remote clients.

There are two components to a RADIUS network—the RADIUS client and the RADIUS server (Figure 5.1).

### Figure 5.1 RADIUS Network

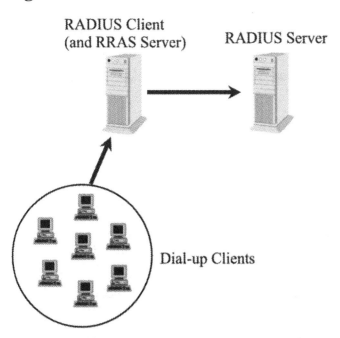

RADIUS Client
(and RRAS Server)   RADIUS Server

Dial-up Clients

---

 **Note:** RADIUS is an industry standard service that works with many different operating systems.

---

### RADIUS Client

The RADIUS client is actually an RRAS server, the computer to which users connect and gain network access. When a client dials in to the RRAS server, the RRAS server forwards the authentication requests to the RADIUS authentication server. If you implement logging with the RADIUS service, the RADIUS client will also forward logon information to the RADIUS accounting server.

### RADIUS Server

There is at least one RADIUS server in every RADIUS configuration. The RADIUS authentication server runs the Internet Authentication Service (IAS) and provides client authentication. The RADIUS accounting server (which may be the same server as the authentication server, or may be separate) maintains a log file record of remote access to the network.

**Note:** The RADIUS server must be running Internet Information Service (IIS) and Internet Authentication Service (IAS).

# Remote Access Implementation

If you need to provide remote access to users and plan to implement RRAS, you need to consider current network usage patterns, expected remote access usage, and security requirements. On a larger scale, you may consider implementing RADIUS or using the Connection Manager.

**Note:** Connection Manager is a Windows 2000 service that automates dial-up connections on the client side of the connection.

# Using Remote Access on Routed Networks

You begin the planning and implementation of RRAS by deciding whether you want to provide dial-up connections or Virtual Private Networks (VPNs). Dial-up connections are used when client computers use a modem to connect directly to modems attached to your RRAS server. VPNs are used when client computers access your RRAS server through the Internet.

## *Providing Dial-Up Connections*

Dial-up connections have several advantages over VPN connections, including the following:

- Dial-up connections may be secure

- RRAS supports caller ID and callback security features with dial-up connections that are not available with VPNs

- The hardware needed for dial-up connections (a modem and a standard telephone line) is inexpensive

If you are providing dial-up access for individual users, your RRAS implementation design must include the following considerations:

- The number of telephone lines and modems needed to handle the number of remote users

- The specific user accounts that will be granted remote access

- Any remote access restrictions you want to implement

 **Note:** By default, users are denied remote access to a network. You must enable remote access for individual user accounts in the Active Directory.

### *Providing WAN Connections*

RRAS is also used to connect to networks through a dial-up or VPN connection, creating a WAN. If you are designing a WAN connection using RRAS servers, consider the following factors in your design:

- The number of lines and the line type needed to connect the two locations

- The routing capabilities included with the RRAS service

- Whether you want to use demand-dial interfaces

- The user accounts you will assign to each RRAS server, so that each server can verify the other

- Any remote access policy restrictions you want to apply

## Using RADIUS

If you need to support remote access for clients running a variety of operating systems, add RADIUS to your network implementation plan. RADIUS provides vendor-independent authorization and authentication for dial-up and VPN connections.

The connection between the RADIUS client and the RADIUS server can be established over a LAN or WAN. Either way, the connection between the client and server must be a persistent, high-speed connection, and should have redundant routed paths to ensure connectivity.

 Note: When discussing RADIUS configuration, it is important to remember that the RADIUS client is the remote access server.

## Securing Remote Network Access

To successfully provide remote access to a network, you must consider, plan, and implement a strong security policy. Whenever data leaves the internal network, there is an increased likelihood that someone will be able to intercept and read the data.

To prevent unauthorized remote access to your network, you must choose an appropriate authentication method and data encryption protocol. Other ways to increase security include isolating the RRAS server, implementing remote access policies, and using RADIUS.

## Remote Access Authentication Protocols

RRAS supports six authentication protocols. The protocol(s) you choose to use depend on the level of security needed and the variety of clients you need to support. Table 5.2 provides a list of authentication protocols, the clients they support, and any additional benefits or disadvantages.

**Table 5.2 Authentication Protocols**

| Authentication Protocol | Clients Supported | Notes |
|---|---|---|
| MS-CHAP | Windows 95<br>Windows 98<br>Windows NT 4.0<br>Windows 2000 | Provides encrypted authentication. |
| MS-CHAP v2 | Windows 2000 only | Provides encrypted authentication. |
| EAP-TLS | Any client with a smart card reader | Uses smart card technology to provide encrypted authentication. |
| CHAP | Windows-based and non-Windows-based clients | Encrypted authentication for a wide variety of operating systems. |
| SPAP | Clients running Shiva LAN Rover software | Limited use. |
| PAP | Many client types supported | Use when remote access clients support none of the other authentication methods. |

## Remote Access Data Encryption Protocols

Encrypting the data that is carried across a remote access link ensures that, if someone taps into the line, the data will be unreadable. Only the sending and receiving computers can read the encrypted data. When implementing data encryption with RRAS, you have two choices, as follows:

**Microsoft Point-to-Point Encryption (MPPE)**—MPPE encrypts data on connections established using the Point-to-Point Protocol (PPP) or Point-to-Point Tunneling Protocol (PPTP). MPPE encryption can be used with one of the following authentication methods:

- MS-CHAP

- MS-CHAP v2

- EAP-TLS

 Note: MPPE encryption in Windows 2000 supports 40-bit, 56-bit and 128-bit encryption. Copies of Windows 2000 sold outside North America only support 40-bit encryption.

**IP Security (IPSec)**—IPSec is used to encrypt data on VPNs that use the Layer 2 Tunneling Protocol (L2TP) connection method. An advantage to IPSec over MPPE is that IPSec uses computer-based certificates of authentication, which reduces the possibility of one computer "impersonating" another. However, Windows 2000 computers only support IPSec at this time.

 Note: IPSec supports the 40-bit Data Encryption Standard (DES), 56-bit DES, and Triple DES (3DES) encryption. Copies of Windows 2000 sold outside North America support 40-bit DES and 56-bit DES only.

### Additional Remote Access Security Measures

In addition to authenticating users and encrypting data, you can increase RRAS security by isolating the RRAS server. When you do this, you make resources on the RRAS server available to dial-up users, but block access to the remainder of the intranet. In this way, an unauthorized access through a dial-up connection results in access to only one server, the RRAS server.

Furthermore, you can implement RRAS policies. Using RRAS policies, you can limit remote access to the network to specific times of day or days of the week, and can restrict access to only dial-up or VPN connections.

### RADIUS Security

Implementing RADIUS increases overall remote access security by removing user account information and authentication procedures from the remote access server.

When using RADIUS, you can increase security by encrypting the information carried between the RADIUS client (the RRAS server) and the RADIUS server. Data is encrypted using IPSec.

## Optimizing Remote Access Technologies

Both RRAS and RADIUS servers can be optimized to increase availability and performance.

### Optimizing RRAS

You can optimize RRAS by implementing the following:

**Adding Servers**—If you have placed RRAS servers in a central location, consider placing some additional servers at remote locations. By distributing the RRAS servers geographically, you prevent bottlenecks on phone lines to a central location and you decrease long-distance phone charges.

**Using RADIUS**—A final way to optimize RRAS is to implement RADIUS. By removing the authentication responsibilities from the RRAS server, overall remote access is enhanced.

### Optimizing RADIUS

You optimize RADIUS in two ways—you can optimize the RADIUS clients (which are the RRAS servers) and the RADIUS servers. Like optimizing RRAS, the number and location of RADIUS servers increases RADIUS performance. When you add additional RADIUS servers, configure the servers in a cluster or as redundant servers sharing the same account authentication database.

## Using Remote Access Technologies with Other Services

To enhance RRAS performance and availability, the RRAS service integrates with several other Windows 2000 services. The following list reviews how RRAS integrates with the Dynamic Host Configuration Protocol (DHCP), the Domain Name System (DNS), Windows Internet Naming Service (WINS), Active Directory, and RADIUS.

**DHCP integration**—RRAS obtains a block of IP addresses from the DHCP server. RRAS assigns these addresses to dial-up clients. Additionally, if the RRAS server is configured as a DHCP relay agent, dial-up clients can receive additional TCP/IP configuration information, including the DNS and WINS server IP addresses.

**DNS integration**—Through integration with DHCP, clients who connect to a network through Windows 2000 RRAS servers can update the DNS database. The DNS service must be running on Windows 2000 servers and must support dynamic DNS.

**WINS integration**—An RRAS client automatically updates the WINS database (part of the WINS registration process) after receiving an IP address.

**Active Directory integration**—Domain controllers store remote access policies on the domain controllers. RRAS uses Active Directory to retrieve and apply these policies.

**RADIUS integration**—The integration of RADIUS and RRAS permits centralized remote access authentication and administration. Integration with RADIUS also enhances logging of remote accesses to the network.

# Remote Access Management

When managing dial-up connections through RRAS servers, you should monitor the key components in the network plan and anticipate potential problems and needs before they arise. By monitoring the RRAS servers and connections, you can detect problems before they cause a loss in productivity, and can foresee the need for implementation changes.

## Detecting Remote Access Errors

If an RRAS server fails, you may not know about the failure immediately if your network has more than one dial-up server. You should implement administrative alerts on all RRAS servers so that you will be notified immediately of server failure.

Additionally, you should monitor the number of connections established at each dial-up server. Each server has a maximum number of connections, and if any one server is reaching that maximum, you need to increase the number of allowed connections before users are denied connections.

An effective monitoring scheme should also look at the number of failed dial-up connection attempts. If several failures occur from the same location in a short period of time, it may indicate an unauthorized user attempting to access the intranet. Set administrative alerts to generate a warning when several logon failures occur in close proximity.

Logon failures should be monitored at RADIUS servers, as well. Since RADIUS incorporates logging features, you should implement a strategy to check the RADIUS logs on a regular schedule.

## Preparing to Meet Remote Access Demands

By monitoring the RRAS and RADIUS servers, you can predict the need to upgrade or replace servers. Consider the following situations and solutions when monitoring RRAS and RADIUS:

**Uptime of the remote access service**—If RRAS servers are not available for all dial-up clients, you must add additional RRAS servers, additional telephone lines, and additional modems. You can also implement Connection Manager so that dial-up clients can be reconfigured with the new information automatically.

**Uptime of the RADIUS service**—If the RADIUS service is failing to meet the demands of all dial-up clients, you need to either add more RADIUS clients (RRAS servers) or additional RADIUS servers.

**Low data rates**—RRAS connections are limited by the modems used at both ends of the dial-up connection. If data rates are too slow, consider upgrading the modems attached to both the RRAS servers and the client modems. If data rates are slower than what the modems can handle, the RRAS servers may be overburdened, and should be replaced or upgraded.

**Number of simultaneous connections**—The number of simultaneous dial-up connections is a prime indicator of the need to add more RRAS servers, phone lines, and modems.

# Remote Access Business Goals

As with other Windows 2000 services and protocols, you should consider the use of remote access technologies from a business perspective. When remote access to the network is needed, consider the benefits of using RRAS and the additional functionality of RADIUS.

## Meeting Business Needs

The RRAS and RADIUS services meet business needs in the following ways:

**Functionality**—The Windows 2000 RRAS provides enhanced network functionality over other remote access technologies by supporting a variety of authentication and encryption standards not supported by other services. Included is L2TP and IPSec. Currently, only Windows 2000 RRAS servers support these protocols. The variety of supported protocols also ensures that Windows 2000 RRAS servers work with many different remote access clients.

Integrating the service with RADIUS further enhances RRAS functionality. Supporting several authentication systems enhances RADIUS functionality.

**Security**—Remote Access security is achieved through data encryption and authentication. Windows 2000 RRAS supports data encryption using MPPE and IPSec, and authentication information is encrypted using one of six possible protocols.

RADIUS adds additional security to the remote access system by centralizing user accounts and removing them from the remote access server (which is more susceptible to hacking). Information passed between RADIUS client and servers is encrypted and may be passed through a VPN.

For additional security, both RRAS and RADIUS use remote access policies stored in the Active Directory. You use these policies to restrict access times and access to resources.

**Availability and Performance**—You can increase remote access server availability by adding additional servers. Both RRAS and RADIUS support the creation of redundant servers, and RRAS also supports Windows Clustering.

Additional RRAS and RADIUS servers increase remote access performance as well.

# Business Scenario

Woody's Chiropractic Association (WCA) provides a national network through which doctors can share information about chiropractic. The national center is in Raleigh, North Carolina, and regional centers are located in Seattle, Los Angeles, Denver, Detroit, Boston, and Athens (Georgia) (Figure 5.2).

## Figure 5.2 WCA Network Structure

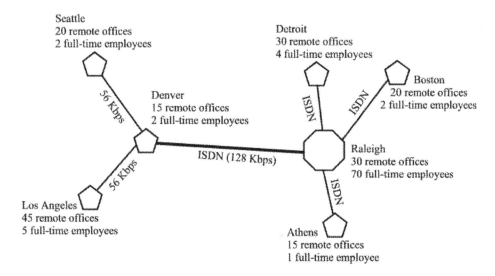

At each center, doctors connect to the network through dial-up connections. Currently, a mix of UNIX and Windows NT 4.0 servers (Figure 5.3) handles these connections. All connections use TCP/IP, as does the entire network. DHCP servers provide IP addresses to internal computers, but the remote access servers are not configured to use DHCP. Dial-up clients receive an IP address from the remote access server, but there has been little standardization. Difficulties in ensuring unique IP address assignments are common.

## Figure 5.3 Regional Center with Remote Access Server

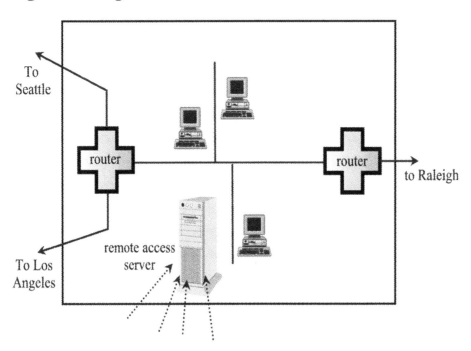

Furthermore, there has been no standardization of logon authentication. The staff at each regional center creates a dial-up username and password for each doctor. They submit these usernames and passwords to Raleigh, where they are entered into the main servers to provide access to the database servers and other resources.

WCA has hired you to standardize and simplify the remote access methods for the network. They want the following:

• Reduced administration

• Minimal cost to implement

• Enhanced security

• Network standardization

- Support for many different client operating systems, including Windows-based computers, Macintosh computers, Novell clients, and one or two Linux computers.

Using this information and your knowledge of RRAS and RADIUS, answer the questions in the Activities section near the end of this lesson.

# Vocabulary

Review the following terms in preparation for the certification exam.

| Term | Description |
|---|---|
| Active Directory | The directory database that provides the foundation of every Windows 2000 domain. |
| ADSL | Asymmetric Digital Subscriber Line is a technology that uses standard telephone lines to transmit digital data. |
| CHAP | Challenge Handshake Authentication Protocol is one of the security protocols RRAS supports. |
| data encryption | The process of applying a mathematical formula to scramble data, rendering it unreadable to everyone without the mathematical key. |
| demand-dial | A feature of Windows 2000 that allows routers to establish a connection to other routers only when the connection is needed. |
| DHCP | The Dynamic Host Configuration Protocol assigns TCP/IP configuration information to clients. |
| dial-up connections | A connection to a network established through telephone lines or ISDN lines that use a modem. |
| DNS | The Domain Name System resolves hostnames to IP addresses. |
| EAP-TLS | Extensible Authentication Protocol – Transport Level Security is one of the security protocols supported by Windows 2000 RRAS. |
| IAS | Internet Authentication Service is the Windows 2000 service that provides RADIUS server capabilities. |

| Term | Description |
| --- | --- |
| ISDN | Integrated Services Digital Network transmits data over digital telephone lines. |
| ISP | An Internet Service Provider supplies a connection to the Internet for dial-up customers. |
| L2TP | Layer 2 Tunneling Protocol is one of two tunneling protocols used by Windows 2000 to create a VPN. |
| LAN | A Local Area Network is a collection of computers in the same location, connected by a cable. |
| MPPE | Microsoft Point-to-Point Encryption is an RRAS data encryption protocol that works with PPTP and PPP. |
| MS-CHAP | Microsoft Challenge Handshake Authentication Protocol |
| PAP | Password Authentication Protocol is one of the RRAS security protocols. |
| PPP | The Point-to-Point Protocol is one of two dial-up protocols. |
| PSTN | The Public Switched Telephone Network consists of the standard telephone lines used to carry voice and analog data signals. |
| public lines | Telephone lines and other cables that provide the backbone of data transmissions. Public lines are used to carry voice, data, video, and television signals. |
| RADIUS | The Remote Authentication Dial-In User Service provides centralized account administration for remote access services. |
| RADIUS client | A remote access server that passes user authentication requests to a RADIUS server. |
| RADIUS server | A server that handles remote access user authentication. |

| Term | Description |
|---|---|
| remote access | Access to a network from a location not connected by a permanent cable. |
| RRAS | Routing and Remote Access is the Windows 2000 implementation of remote access services. |
| SLIP | Serial Line Interface Protocol is one of two dial-up protocols. |
| SPAP | Shiva Password Authentication Protocol is a security protocol supported by RAS specifically for Shiva clients. |
| user authentication | The process of verifying a username and password before granting the user access to network resources. |
| VPN | A Virtual Private Network creates a virtual tunnel in the Internet, through which data can be transmitted securely. |
| WAN | A Wide Area Network consists of two or more LANs connect by leased lines, VPNs, or other long-distance connectivity methods. |
| WINS | The Windows Internet Naming Service resolves NetBIOS names to IP addresses. |

# In Brief

| If you want to... | Then do this... |
| --- | --- |
| Provide remote access to your Windows 2000 network | Use one or more Windows 2000 servers with the RRAS service to provide remote access. |
| Start your own Internet Service Provider company using your Windows 2000 server | Purchase multiple modems and telephone lines and a fast connection to the Internet. Then configure RRAS on the server as a standard dial-up server. |
| Centralize user authentication for all remote user connections | Implement RADIUS. |
| Provide the highest level of data encryption over a dial-up connection | Require encryption using 3DES. |
| Permit a user to connect to the network through a dial-up connection | Enable remote access permission in the Active Directory. |

# Lesson 5 Activities

Complete the following activities to better prepare you for the certification exam.

1.  When considering the remote access needs of the WCA network, which concerns and requirements are important?

2.  How do you propose to handle the IP addressing problems?

3.  What protocols will you install on the RRAS servers?

4.  How do you plan to centralize administration and keep costs at a minimum?

5.  During implementation, one of the WCA staff set each RRAS server to Require data encryption, figuring the additional security can't hurt. Now, most users cannot connect to the network. Why?

6.  For enhanced security, WCA would like to verify that calls coming in from doctors' offices are really coming from those offices, and not from some other location. What can you offer to handle this?

7.  Which security protocols will you enable on the RRAS servers?

8.  Every remote access server can handle a maximum of 20 dial-up connections. How many RRAS servers do you need to install on the entire WCA network?

9.  WCA wants to ensure that a single RRAS server failure will not prevent any doctor from accessing the network. If performance is more important than cost, what would you recommend?

10. If cost is more important than performance, how would you implement remote access fault tolerance in the network?

# Answers to Lesson 5 Activities

1.  It seems as though the primary desire of the WCA staff is to simplify the entire remote access configuration for the network. You should consider the desire to have an overall standard in place for dial-up connections and IP addressing while still providing support for a variety of client operating systems. Network security is also important, and the costs involved in implementing the plan cannot be ignored.

2.  Replace the remote access servers with Windows 2000 RRAS servers, and integrate RRAS with DHCP. Each RRAS server will obtain a block of IP addresses from the DHCP scope and use these addresses for dial-up clients.

3.  The RRAS servers will need TCP/IP to support the Windows 2000 network, Windows clients and Linux clients, IPX/SPX (NWLink) to support the Novell clients, and AppleTalk to support the Macintosh computers.

4.  Although you can implement RADIUS to centralize user administration, this adds cost to the plan. Since the WCA network is Windows 2000-based, integration of the RRAS servers with Active Directory provides some centralization. All user accounts will be placed in the Active Directory, and the RRAS servers will check the Active Directory for logon verification.

5.  Unless the client computers are running Windows 2000 and are configured to use data encryption, the RRAS servers will reject every connection attempt.

6.  RRAS supports both Caller-ID and callback services for dial-up connections. Using Caller-ID, the RRAS server will refuse a connection if it does not originate from a preset phone number. Callback requires the RRAS server to call back the doctor's office at a preset phone number.

7.  Since you are supporting a variety of clients, you should enable most of the security protocols, including PAP. Because there are no Shiva clients on the network, you do not need to enable SPAP.

8.    You will need to install 11 RRAS servers on the network, as follows: 2 in Raleigh, 2 in Detroit, 1 in Boston, 1 in Athens, 1 in Denver, 3 in Los Angeles, and 1 in Seattle.

9.    Add an additional RRAS server at each regional office and in the national center. If any one RRAS server fails, this additional server can handle the load.

10.    Configure each client computer to use a secondary phone number if the primary fails. This secondary number will connect to one of the RRAS servers at another regional center. The overall number of RRAS servers can handle the extra load caused by a single server failure. The only additional cost is accrued by the doctor's office in making a long-distance phone call.

# Lesson 5 Quiz

These questions test your knowledge of features, vocabulary, procedures, and syntax.

1.  What is the default setting for Windows 2000 remote access permission?
    A.  Windows 2000 users are granted remote access permission.
    B.  Windows 2000 users are denied remote access permission.
    C.  All clients are granted remote access permission.
    D.  All clients are denied remote access permission.

2.  Which of the following is not a reason for implementing dial-up access instead of VPNs?
    A.  Dial-up connections save ISP costs.
    B.  RRAS supports callback for dial-up connections only.
    C.  RRAS supports Caller-ID for dial-up connections only.
    D.  VPNs use proprietary software that is difficult to configure.

3.  Which of the following statements about RADIUS is true?
    A.  RAIDUS is a Windows 2000-specific service.
    B.  RADIUS can run on a UNIX server.
    C.  RADIUS stands for Real Authentication for Dial-Up Servers
    D.  RADIUS places user authentication responsibility on the RRAS servers.

4.  What Windows 2000 service provides RADIUS server service?
    A.  DNS
    B.  IAS
    C.  ISA
    D.  TCP

5.  Remote access data is encrypted using which of the following protocols? (Choose all that apply).
    A.  MPPE
    B.  PPP
    C.  SLIP
    D.  IPSec

6.    Which of the following provides the highest level of data encryption?
      A.    128-bit MPPE
      B.    40-bit DES
      C.    3DES
      D     56-bit DES

7.    Which of the following provides the highest level of data encryption for an international
      network?
      A.    40-bit MPPE
      B.    40-bit DES
      C.    3DES
      D.    56-bit DES

8.    For each dial-up user, the remote access service must provide which of the following?
      (Choose all that apply).
      A.    A modem.
      B.    An RRAS server.
      C.    A user account and password.
      D.    An IP address

9.    When using RADIUS, which computers act as RADIUS clients? (Choose all that apply).
      A.    RADIUS servers
      B.    RRAS servers
      C.    RRAS clients
      D.    DNS servers

10.   Which services must be running on the RADIUS server?
      A.    IAS
      B.    IIS
      C.    TCP/IP
      D.    PPTP

# Answers to Lesson 5 Quiz

1.  Answer D is correct. By default, all users are prevented from accessing the network remotely. This permission must be enabled for each account. The choice of operating system does not change the permissions granted to user accounts.

    Therefore, answers A, B, and C are incorrect.

2.  Answer D is correct. VPNs use the same RRAS service as dial-up connections, and are easy to configure and implement.

    Answers A, B, and C are incorrect. All of these are valid reasons for considering the use of dial-up connections.

3.  Answer B is correct. RADIUS is not platform specific, and can run on many different server operating systems.

    Answer A is incorrect. The Windows 2000 implementation of RADIUS is called IAS.

    Answer C is incorrect. RADIUS stands for Remote Authentication Dial-In User Service.

    Answer D is incorrect. RRAS servers place the responsibility of user authentication on RADIUS servers.

4.  Answer B is correct. IAS is the Windows 2000 service that allows a Windows 2000 server to act as a RADIUS server.

    Answer A is incorrect. DNS provides name resolution.

    Answer C is incorrect. ISA is a hardware standard, not a service.

    Answer D is incorrect. TCP is a necessary part of the TCP/IP protocol, but does not provide RADIUS support.

5.  Answers A and D are correct. RRAS uses MPPE and IPSec to encrypt data.

    Answers B and C are incorrect. PPP and SLIP are dial-up protocols, not encryption methods.

6.    Answer C is correct. 3DES uses three 128-bit keys to encrypt data.

      Therefore, answers A, B, and D are incorrect. These are all data encryption methods, but none provide the level of encryption offered by 3DES.

7.    Answer D is correct. For international networks, the highest level of security permitted in 56-bit.

      Answers A and B are incorrect. These methods, while exportable, do not provide the level of security offered by 56-bit DES.

      Answer C is incorrect. 3DES cannot be used outside North America.

8.    Answers A, C, and D are correct. Each connection requires a separate modem. The user must have a valid username and password on the network to connect. While connecting, the RRAS server provides the client with an IP address.

      Answer B is incorrect. A single RRAS server can accommodate multiple connections.

9.    Answer B is correct. When using RADIUS, the RRAS servers are also the RADIUS clients.

      Answer A is incorrect. A RADIUS server is not also a RADIUS client.

      Answer C is incorrect. RADIUS is invisible to RRAS clients. The RRAS client does not know which computer is performing user authentication.

      Answer D is incorrect. DNS plays no role in RADIUS.

10.   Answers A, B, and C are correct. A RADIUS server requires IAS (which is the Windows 2000 version of RADIUS), Internet Information Service (IIS), and the TCP/IP protocol.

      Answer D is incorrect. PPTP is a VPN tunneling protocol that can be used on a RADIUS server, but is not required.

# Connection Manager

On large networks, where users may connect remotely from many different locations, establishment and management of an effective remote access system can be difficult. To avoid long distance telephone charges, a company may institute a series of remote access servers placed in a wide geographic range. When a user needs to connect to the network from multiple locations, the user must reconfigure the computer to dial the nearest remote access server.

The Connection Manager, a set of tools included with Windows 2000, automates the configuration of client computers, greatly simplifying remote access management. Connection Manager is also customizable.

An example of a company that can benefit from the use of Connection Manager is a national Internet Service Provider (ISP). The ISP wants to provide Internet access to customers in every major metropolitan area in the United States. For each region, the customers' computers need to be configured to dial the appropriate local access telephone number. Rather than having support staff in each region configure the computers manually, a single copy of the Connection Manager tools can be placed on each client computer. The tools configure the computer.

After completing this lesson, you should have a better understanding of the following topics:

- Connection Manager Overview
- Connection Manager Implementation
- Connection Manager Management
- Connection Manager Business Goals

# Connection Manager Overview

Connection Manager is a set of Windows 2000 services that provide dial-up connection settings to client computers. Connection Manager builds a profile and phone book files. Connection Manager stores the profile and phonebook files on each client computer, and the client computer uses these files to establish a remote access connection (Figure 6.1).

## Figure 6.1 Connection Manager Overview

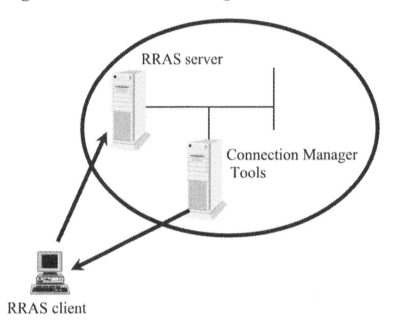

## Using Connection Manager

Connection Manager works in conjunction with the Windows 2000 Routing and Remote Access Service (RRAS) and Internet Information Service (IIS). RRAS and IIS are included on all Windows 2000 servers, and are automatically installed with the Windows 2000 software. Connection Manager provides three primary remote access services—centrally administered phone books, automatic dial-up service, and a customizable Graphical User Interface (GUI) (Figure 6.2).

## Figure 6.2 Connection Manager System

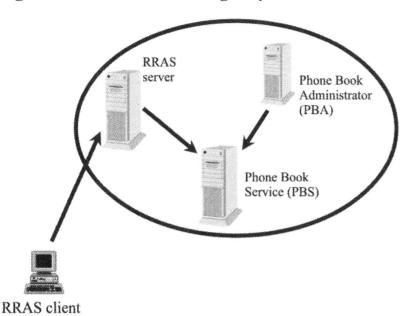

### *Centralized Phone Books*

Connection Manager creates a single central phone book database that contains the dial-up access telephone numbers. The Phone Book Service (PBS) is the service within Connection Manager that creates the phone book database. The database contains entries called Points of Presence (POP), and is linked to a central folder, stored on a PBS server. The Phone Book Administrator (PBA) service makes changes to the PBS. As changes are made to the phone book database, they are propagated to the client computers as the clients connect to the network.

### Automatic Dial-up Service

To automate dial-up client access, each remote access client is given a copy of the profile phone book. This profile contains information about local access numbers. If a local phone number changes, the phonebook is automatically updated, and the client continues to be able to connect. The phone book also provides redundancy. If one phone number is unavailable, the dial-up service will automatically dial an alternate number.

### Customizable GUI

The Connection Manager provides a user interface that is customizable, so that an ISP can place its own information and logo on the dial-up interface. The GUI can be further optimized to run custom applications when the user connects.

You use the Connection Manager Administration Kit (CMAK) to create the customized interface for each Connection Manager profile. The profile includes the phone book to use, logon scripts, and company logos.

# Connection Manager Implementation

To use Connection Manager, you install and configure the Connection Manager software on a computer, create phone books and profiles, and then distribute the files to dial-up clients.

## Implementing Connection Manager

Implementing Connection Manager involves several steps. The first step is to install the Connection Manager tools. Once installed, you do the following (Figure 6.3):

1. Create a phone book file with the Phone Book Administrator (PBA)

2. Create a Connection Manager Profile with the Connection Manager Administration Kit

3. Configure the profile to use the phone book file

4. Distribute the profile, phone book file, and Connection Manager software to remote clients

## Figure 6.3 Connection Manager Implementation

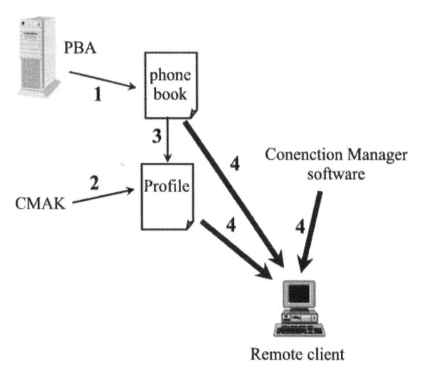

Remote client

Connection Manager is part of the Internet Explorer Administration Kit (IEAK), and is installed when IEAK is installed. Once installed, you run the CMAK to initially configure Connection Manager.

---

Tip: You can obtain the latest version of IEAK (and CMAK) directly from Microsoft's Web page, at the following address:
http://www.microsoft.com/windows/ieak/en/default.asp

---

# Distributing Connection Manager Files

Once the phone books and profiles have been created, you need to get these files and Connection Manager to the clients who will use them. Four common ways to distribute the files are as follows:

- Copy to a floppy disk or CD-ROM

- Use a software distribution system like Microsoft Systems Management Server (SMS)

- Place the files on a Web site or File Transfer Protocol (FTP) site

- Place the files on a shared network drive (for internal use)

When you need to make changes to the phone book database, you use the PBA. As changes are made to the phone book database, the PBS automatically sends the necessary updates to the clients. The steps in this automatic update are as follows:

1. Connection Manager on the client computer queries the PBS during the initial connection.

2. PBS compares the version number of the phone book used by the client with the version number in the phone book database.

3. If the phone book database is newer than the one on the client, PBS sends the phone book updates to Connection Manager on the client.

4. Connection Manager updates the phone book and changes the version number to match the number on the PBS database.

# Providing Security with Connection Manager

Each update to the phone book database requires a transmission of these changes to the remote clients. By the very nature of using Connection Manager, this data transmission occurs across public networks and telephone lines. The information stored in a phone book database may be sensitive enough to warrant concern about public transmissions.

## *Phone Book Encryption*

When encrypting phone book data, you have two choices. You can use Microsoft Point-to-Point Encryption (MPPE) or Internet Protocol Security (IPSec). IPSec uses certificates and provides better encryption. MPPE provides broader operating system compatibility.

In addition to encrypting the data, consider the following additional security measures:

**Use a firewall**—The PBS server uses Web-based access to implement changes. By placing the PBS behind a firewall, you can block all access to the PBS except for Web-based transmissions.

**Dedicate a PBS server**—By placing a PBS server separate from the corporate network, you can provide unsecured access to the PBS updates without compromising overall network security. If a hacker accesses the PBS server, he or she will not gain any important company data other than dial-up access numbers.

**Restrict Web Access**—Treat the PBS like any other Web site. Configure the PBS for read-only access and limit access to the database to a limited number of administrators. Also, disable directory listing on the PBS server.

# Increasing Availability and Performance

To increase availability of the phone book service, you should install multiple PBS servers. The servers can be configured with a redundant phone book database or as part of a Windows Cluster.

## *Redundant PBS Servers*

You can configure two PBS servers to share a common phone book database. Through replication, changes made to the database are copied to both servers. If you place the second PBS server at a remote location (across a Wide Area Network (WAN) link, for example), you provide more availability for remote users and enhance performance.

## *PBS Clustering*

Windows Clustering combines multiple servers into a single logical server. With PBS servers, this means that each server in the cluster contains an exact copy of the phone book database. A PBS cluster provides the highest level of availability for the PBS service, and provides immediate recovery from a single server failure.

**Tip:** The Windows Clustering service requires high-speed dedicated connections among all servers in the cluster. This makes a PBS cluster an inappropriate choice if you want to place a PBS server across a WAN link.

### Reduce Phone Book Sizes

To increase performance in the PBS service, consider reducing phone book sizes. In a very large company, you may have hundreds of local dial-up phone numbers (POPs). Certainly, most users in North America do not need to download updates to local access phone numbers in Mozambique. To reduce the time it takes to download updates, divide the phone book database into several smaller databases, reflecting geographic areas or some other appropriate factor.

# Connection Manager Management

The Connection Manager service running on each client computer connects to the PBS to check for updates to the phone book database. A Connection Manager management scheme must include monitoring of the PBS server to verify it is available for all connections. You should also monitor the speed of the PBS service overall. By automating the monitoring process, you can detect early signs of problems and predict the future Connection Manager needs of the company.

## Monitoring the PBS Service

Since Connection Manager provides automated connection processes for remote clients, you must ensure that the PBS servers are operating properly and that the service as a whole is keeping up with network demands.

If you have provided redundant PBS servers, either with a shared phone book database or in a cluster, users may not be aware of a single server failure. Administrative alerts should be implemented on each PBS server so that administrators know about failures immediately.

As a network grows, the PBS service you have in place may not be able to meet future demands. Typically, the speed of the service will degrade slowly with time, and so you may not be aware of the decline. By monitoring the rate at which phone book updates occur, you can make necessary changes.

If the PBS service is not providing PBS updates in a timely manner, consider adding more PBS servers to the network or reducing the size of the phone books. When considering the addition of servers, let business demands and the network structure dictate whether you will create a more expensive yet more available Windows cluster or provide redundant servers that share a database.

## Testing Connection Manager

Part of a successful management strategy includes testing the PBS service. You need to test the availability of the service and also any security measures you have implemented.

If you have redundant PBS servers, you should verify that each server is operational. During a time of lower network usage, temporarily remove PBS servers from the network and verify that the other PBS servers continue to provide service.

To test PBS security, consider the following practices:

- Capture the network data during a phone book update and verify it is encrypted

- Attempt to change information on the PBS Web site. The PBS Web site should be Read-only for all users

- Attempt to connect to the PBS Web site using an account that is not granted permission

- Attempt to browse the Web site directory listing (which should be disabled)

# Connection Manager Business Goals

As with every other Windows 2000 service, the decision to implement Connection Manager depends on the needs of the business. If business requirements suggest the need for automated dial-up connections, use the business expectations to determine the level of implementation.

## Meeting Business Goals

The four business goals are listed below. The ways these goals are met by using Connection Manager are explained as well.

**Functionality**—Connection Manager provides a way to automate the dial-up connections of thousands of remote users across a wide geographic region. For a company like an ISP, this automation greatly reduces network management and user support costs. For companies with traveling users, Connection Manager provides a simple way to change the local access phone numbers.

The functionality of Connection Manager is enhanced through integration with IIS and RRAS, interfaces many Windows 2000 network administrators are familiar with. Integration with IIS means that administration and access to phone books can be done through a Web page, an interface with which many users are comfortable.

**Security**—Network security needs are met when using Connection Manager by supporting data encryption through MPPE or IPSec. Protection of the phone book database comes from placing IIS restrictions on the PBS server. Since the PBS server runs as an IIS Web site, you can implement read-only access, deny directory listings, and specify user accounts that have access.

**Availability and Performance**—Availability and performance needs are dictated by the business. You must balance the costs of providing higher availability and performance with network expectations. Connection Manager availability is increased by adding PBS servers to the network.

## Business Scenario

Woody's Chiropractic Association (WCA) has hired you once again to work on their network. The current network configuration includes one national center and six regional centers. The regional centers provide remote access services to numerous doctors' offices. The doctors connect to RRAS servers in the regional offices, and then have access to resources throughout the network (Figure 6.4).

# Figure 6.4 WCA Network Structure

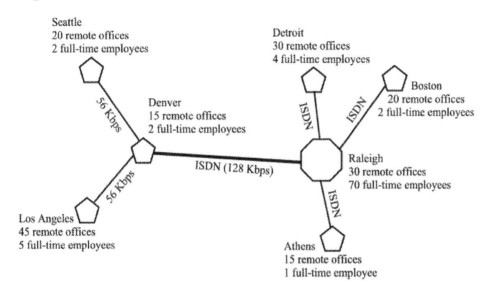

Seattle
20 remote offices
2 full-time employees

Detroit
30 remote offices
4 full-time employees

Boston
20 remote offices
2 full-time employees

Denver
15 remote offices
2 full-time employees

56 Kbps

ISDN (128 Kbps)

56 Kbps

ISDN

ISDN

Raleigh
30 remote offices
70 full-time employees

Los Angeles
45 remote offices
5 full-time employees

ISDN

Athens
15 remote offices
1 full-time employee

WCA has recently performed a hostile takeover of a national Internet Service Provider (ISP), and plans to use this infrastructure to provide dial-up access to the WCA network and to the Internet. Member doctors will connect to the RRAS servers on the WCA network, while the general public will connect to separate RRAS servers that provide Internet access.

By opening up Internet service to the general public, WCA expects to more than triple the number of network connections they have, and also expects to nearly double the number of member doctors currently subscribing to the WCA network. They currently have 175 doctors connecting to the WCA network. The ISP currently has 1,500 customers.

WCA wants you to create a strategy that meets the following criteria (Table 6.1).

## Table 6.1 WCA Network Expectations

| Network Requirement | Description |
|---|---|
| Connectivity | Doctors who are members of the WCA network should have software that automates the connection process to the nearest RRAS server.<br><br>Other users should have automated dial-up connections that provide Internet access. |
| Customization | WCA wants their logo and support information placed on the dial-up software that is sent to doctors. They want to use a different logo and different customer support phone number for Internet users. |
| Security | The connections established to the Internet do not need to be secured. However, the connections the doctors establish to the WCA network must be secure—patient information is carried over these lines. |
| Performance | Currently, the RRAS servers that provide dial-up access to the WCA network can handle approximately 50 remote connections. The RRAS servers from the acquired ISP can more than handle the expected number of dial-up Internet customers.<br><br>Internal tests suggest that a single PBS server can handle about 250 simultaneous connections and requests for phone book database updates. |
| Reliability | Connections to the WCA network and to the Internet must be available 24 hours per day, 7 days per week. |
| Flexibility | As WCA grows, it expects to gain more customers throughout the country, and will be adding local access numbers continually. They want these additions to require the least amount of network effort. |

# Vocabulary

Review the following terms in preparation for the certification exam.

| Term | Description |
|------|-------------|
| CMAK | You use the Connection Manager Administration Kit to configure Connection Manager and customize the software that clients receive. |
| Connection Manager | A collection of Windows 2000 tools that provide automated dial-up access to networks. |
| firewall | A device that prevents unauthorized access from the Internet to your network. |
| FTP | The File Transfer Protocol, part of the TCP/IP protocol suite, is the protocol used to transfer files on the Internet. |
| GUI | The Graphic User Interface is the user-friendly interface that allows people to use a mouse to select choices. |
| IEAK | Connection Manager is installed when you install the Internet Explorer Administration Kit. |
| IIS | Internet Information Service provides Web and FTP hosting on a Windows 2000 computer, and is a necessary part of Connection Manager. |
| IPSec | Internet Protocol Security provides data encryption. |
| ISP | An Internet Service Provider connects dial-up users to the internet. |
| logon scripts | A small program that executes when a user logs on to a network, and is used to automate steps that occur at every logon. |

| Term | Description |
|---|---|
| MPPE | Microsoft Point-to-Point Encryption provides data encryption. |
| PBA | The Phone Book Administrator is a service included with Connection Manager that provides a means of updating the phone book database. |
| PBS | The Phone Book Service provides access to the phone book database. |
| PBS server | A Windows 2000 server running the PBS. |
| phone book file | A database file that contains a listing of the local dial-up access numbers clients use to connect to the network. |
| POP | The Point of Presence is a local dial-up access number entry in the phone book database. |
| profile | Part of the information sent to Connection Manager clients, which defines the local access numbers. |
| remote access | The ability to connect to a network from a remote location through a dial-up connection. |
| replication | The process of copying information from one server to another. With Connection Manager, the phone book database is replicated to all PBS servers. |
| RRAS | Routing and Remote Access is a Windows 2000 service that provides remote access to the network. |
| SMS | Microsoft Systems Management Server provides overall network management solutions, including hardware inventories, computer monitoring, administrative alerts, and software distribution. |
| WAN | A Wide Area Network consists of two or more networks connected over a long distance by leased lines or though a Virtual Private Network. |
| Windows Clustering | A Windows 2000 service that combines two or more servers into a single logical server. Windows Clustering provides the highest availability for services on a network. |

# In Brief

| If you want to... | Then do this... |
| --- | --- |
| Provide automated dial-up connections | Implement Connection Manager. |
| Update the phone book database | Use the PBA |
| Increase PBS availability | Add additional PBS servers, and use replication or clustering. |
| Provide redundancy between two PBS servers on the same LAN | Use Windows Clustering. |
| Provide redundancy between two PBS servers across a WAN | Use replication. |
| Distribute Connection Manager software to customers throughout the Untied States | Place the software on a Web site that all customers can access, or place the software on a CD-ROM and ship the CD-ROM. |
| Customize the GUI for the Connection Manager software | Use CMAK. |

# Lesson 6 Activities

Complete the following activities to better prepare you for the certification exam.

1.    How will Connection Manager meet the business needs of WCA?

2.    What services must be installed on each server that will act as a PBS server?

3.    Considering only performance issues, how many PBS servers will you recommend using?

4.    Considering availability and reliability expectations, how many PBS servers will you recommend?

5.    Where do you suggest placing the PBS servers on the WCA network?

6.    Traffic across the WAN link between Denver and Raleigh must be reduced. After analyzing the network traffic, you discover a large number of phone book updates are crossing this link. What do you recommend changing?

7.    Access numbers for the WCA RRAS servers seems to change fairly often, and the time it takes to update the phone book database during every connection is unacceptable. How can you reduce this update time?

8.    Explain how Connection Manager will help with the customization expectations.

9.    Doctors must have access to the network, even if the RRAS server in the closest regional center fails. WCA is reluctant to spend the money on redundant RRAS servers at every regional office, but they have been told this is the only way to provide reliability. How do you address this problem?

10.   How does Connection Manager meet the security needs of WCA?

# Answers to Lesson 6 Activities

1.    Connection Manager will provide a way to create two customized dial-up software packages. One package can be distributed to doctors, and will provide phone numbers for the WCA RRAS servers, while the other package will provide access numbers to the ISP RRAS servers.

2.    Each PBS server must have TCP/IP, IIS, and RRAS installed.

3.    The PBS server can handle approximately 250 simultaneous connections. A single PBS server can handle the needs of all doctors who connect to the WCA network. Although the ISP has 1,500 customers, the likelihood that all 1,500 will connect at the same time is highly unlikely. To be safe, four or five PBS servers dedicated to the ISP connections should suffice.

4.    Availability of the PBS service is very important. Two PBS servers should be dedicated to meeting the needs of the WCA network. Using four or five PBS servers for the Internet clients provides fault tolerance availability.

5.    You can place both PBS servers in the Raleigh national office and configure them to share the same copy of the phone book database. For the highest availability, you can configure the servers as a cluster.

6.    WCA should consider placing a PBS server in Denver. This server could be one of the two in Raleigh or a third server. By placing a server in Denver, dial-up clients from Seattle, Los Angeles, and Denver will receive phone book updates more locally.

7.    Consider creating multiple phone book databases, based on geographic regions. Doctors who dial up from the Seattle office do not need to download changes to the access phone numbers for the Athens RRAS servers. This will significantly reduce phone book database update times.

8.    Using the Connection Manager Administration Kit (CMAK), two customized
      Connection Manager software packages can be created. One will have the WCA logo
      and a special support telephone number listed. It will contain the phone book entries for
      the WCA RRAS servers. The other software package will contain the ISP logo, a
      different customer support telephone number, and a phone book database of ISP access
      numbers.

9.    By using phone books with Connection Manager, every doctor's Connection Manager
      software will contain access numbers for every RRAS server on the WCA network. If
      their local RRAS server fails, they can connect to the network through one of the other
      RRAS servers. This requires a long-distance phone call, but at least you maintain
      connectivity to the network.

10.   You can configure the PBS servers to encrypt the phone book database updates, but this
      is not a chief concern of WCA. Their primary concern is a secure connection between
      the doctors' offices and the WCA network. Connection Manager cannot provide this
      security. The RRAS servers must be configured to require authentication and data
      encryption.

# Lesson 6 Quiz

These questions test your knowledge of features, vocabulary, procedures, and syntax.

1.  How do you install Connection Manager?
    A.  By installing PBS
    B.  By installing PBA
    C.  By installing IEAK
    D.  By installing Windows 2000

2.  What data encryption method(s) does Connection Manager support? (Choose all that apply).
    A.  IPSec
    B.  TCP/IP
    C.  MPPE
    D.  PBS

3.  What tool is used to create a Connection Manager profile?
    A.  IEAK
    B.  CMAK
    C.  EEEK
    D.  PBS

4.  How do you distribute the Connection Manager software to clients? (Choose all that apply)?
    A.  On CD-ROM
    B.  On floppy disks
    C.  By sharing a folder on a server
    D.  On an FTP site

5.  For added security, where should you place the PBS server with respect to a firewall?
    A.  The PBS server should be outside the firewall
    B.  The PBS server should be inside the firewall
    C.  The PBS server should be on a different subnet from the firewall
    D.  The PBS cannot use a firewall

6.   How does a client receive phone book updates?
     A.   E-mail notification
     B.   By querying the PBS
     C.   By querying the PBA
     D.   When an administrator forces replication

7.   How is PBS availability increased?
     A.   By reducing the number of clients
     B.   By increasing the number of clients
     C.   By reducing the number of PBS servers
     D.   By increasing the number of PBS servers

8.   If you have two PBS servers separated by a WAN link, which of the following is the
     appropriate configuration?
     A.   Create a Windows Cluster
     B.   Implement phone book sharing using replication
     C.   Pace both servers on the same side of the Wan link
     D.   Take one of the servers offline

9.   Which of the following services do you need to install in addition to Connection
     Manager?
     A.   IIS
     B.   RRAS
     C.   DHCP
     D.   DNS

10.  How should you configure IIS on the PBS server for security? (Choose all that apply).
     A.   Enable Read and Write Access
     B.   Prevent directory listings
     C.   Disable all access permissions except Read
     D.   Reduce the number of users with access permission

# Answers to Lesson 6 Quiz

1.  Answer C is correct. When you install IEAK, CMAK is also installed. IEAK can be downloaded directly from Microsoft's Web site.

    Answers A and B are incorrect. The PBS and PBA are part of the Connection Manager software.

    Answer D is incorrect. Connection Manager is not installed automatically with Windows 2000.

2.  Answers A and C are correct. Connection Manager can use both MPPE and IPSec to encrypt the phone book database.

    Answers B and D are incorrect. These are not data encryption methods.

3.  Answer B is correct. Connection Manager Administration Kit is used to create Connection Manager profiles.

    Answers A and D are incorrect. IEAK and PBS do not create Connection Manager profiles.

    Answer C is incorrect. EEEK is not a Windows 2000 utility.

4.  Answers A, B, C, and D are all correct. You can also distribute Connection Manager software on a Web site.

5.  Answer B is correct. The PBS server should be placed behind a firewall, and the firewall should be configured to block all traffic other than Web-based data.

    Answer A is incorrect. Placing the PBS outside the firewall does not provide any additional security.

    Answer C is incorrect. Placing the PBS on a different subnet does not change security.

    Answer D is incorrect. PBS should be used with a firewall.

6.    Answer B is correct. When a user connects to the network, the Connection Manager software on the client queries the PBS server for changes to the phone book database.

Answer A is incorrect. Connection Manager does not use e-mail services for any notifications.

Answer C is incorrect. The PBA server is used to make changes to the phone book database, but does not communicate with Connection Manager clients.

Answer D is incorrect. Replication does not occur between servers and clients.

7.    Answer D is correct. You increase Connection Manager availability by adding more PBS servers to the network.

Answers A and B are incorrect. The number of clients does not directly change the availability of the Connection Manager service. Reducing the number of clients may improve performance, but is not an acceptable approach.

Answer C is incorrect. Reducing the number of servers decreases availability.

8.    Answer B is correct. By implementing a shared phone book database, you reduce WAN activity and provide fault tolerance.

Answer A is incorrect. A Windows Cluster cannot be set up across a WAN link.

Answer C is incorrect. By placing both servers on the same side of the WAN link, you remove the benefits gained by having a remote PBS server.

Answer D is incorrect. Removing one of the servers from the network benefits no one.

9.    Answers A and B are correct. Connection Manager requires IIS on the same computer and RRAS servers are necessary to provide the dial-up connection services.

Answers C and D are incorrect. DHCP and DNS are not necessary parts of the Connection Manager system.

10.    Answers B, C, and D are correct. You should enable on the Read permission, prevent directory listings, and reduce the number of user accounts with access to the server.

Answer A is incorrect. Users should not have Write permission to the PBS server.

# *Lesson 7*

# Demand-Dial Routing

In a well-configured network, the amount of network traffic that must pass across a Wide Area Network (WAN) link is relatively low. Ideally, remote servers handle all network services required by the remote users. For example, the remote location may have its own domain controller and Domain Name System (DNS), Dynamic Host Configuration Protocol (DHCP), and Windows Internet Naming Service (WINS) servers. Of course, this ideal network configuration is expensive and not very realistic.

Even in this ideal situation, a reliable connection must exist between the two networks so that data is reliably delivered and functions like Active Directory replication occur without error.

Many companies opt for a permanent connection between two networks (like a dedicated leased line) to ensure a reliable connection. However, implementing demand-dial routing over an analog telephone line or an Integrated Services Digital Network (ISDN) line can significantly reduce costs. Demand-dial routing, a feature of the Routing and Remote Access Service (RRAS), establishes WAN connections when data needs to be transmitted, and then terminates the connection.

Demand-dial routing provides an inexpensive and effective backup to permanent WAN connections, as well. If a permanent connection fails, RRAS, configured to use demand-dial routing, reestablishes the connection, providing temporary connectivity until the main line can be repaired.

After completing this lesson, you should have a better understanding of the following topics:

* Demand-Dial Routing Overview
* Demand-Dial Routing Implementation
* Demand-Dial Routing Management
* Demand-Dial Routing Business Goals

# Demand-Dial Routing Overview

When two networks are linked, a router at either end of the connection connects them. Just as a router connects two network segments in a Local Area Network (LAN), routers connect WAN networks. When a Windows 2000-based router receives an IP packet that is destined for a remote network, it sends the packet to the remote router (Figure 7.1).

## Figure 7.1 Basic WAN Configuration

With demand-dial routing, a Windows 2000-based router will automatically establish a connection to the remote location, transmit the data, and then disconnect after a specified time. As far as the user is concerned, a permanent connection exists between the two networks (Figure 7.2).

## Figure 7.2 Demand-Dial Routing Connection

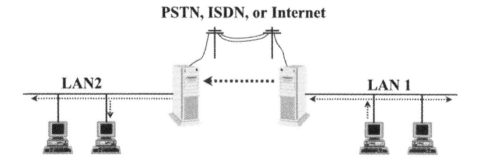

## Using Demand-Dial Routing

Demand-dial routing works over the Public Switched Telephone Network (PSTN), ISDN, and through the Internet as a Virtual Private network (VPN). With any of these methods, security is achieved by implementing data encryption and router authentication. You can configure demand-dial routing to require mutual router authentication, in which each router must provide credentials before data transmission occurs.

**Note:** Asymmetric Digital Subscriber Line (ADSL) uses the PSTN, and so is also supported by demand-dial routing.

When using the Internet to establish demand-dial routing connections, the routers use a VPN. The VPN creates a tunnel by using either the Point-to-Point Tunneling Protocol (PPTP) or Layer 2 Tunneling Protocol (L2TP).

For WAN links that must be available at all times, demand-dial routing provides a relatively inexpensive way to provide fault tolerance in case the permanent WAN connection fails. Although the demand-dial routing may not provide the same bandwidth as a permanent connection, network operations can continue during the failure. Like a temporary spare tire on a car, a demand-dial routing connection allows data to get to its destination, albeit a bit more slowly.

Note: There is a delay in remote network communication when using demand-dial routing each time the router establishes the remote connection. Some applications may time-out before the connection is established, and may register a network failure.

# Demand-Dial Routing Implementation

Demand-dial routing is part of the RRAS service in Windows 2000. Before implementing a demand-dial routing strategy, RRAS is installed. Once installed, you configure demand-dial routing through the RRAS console.

## Installing Demand-Dial Routing

Installation of demand-dial routing requires installing RRAS and a modem (or ISDN adapter), and then configuring RRAS and the modem to use demand-dial routing.

### Installing and Configuring RRAS

To install demand-dial routing, begin by installing and starting the Routing and Remote Access Service. RRAS is automatically installed when you install Windows 2000. To start the service, follow these steps:

1.  From the **Start** menu, choose **Programs**, **Administrative Tools**, and then select **Routing and Remote Access**.

2.  From the **Tree** pane of **Routing and Remote Access**, right-click the server name, and then choose **Configure and Enable Routing and Remote Access** (Figure 7.3).

# Figure 7.3 Enabling RRAS

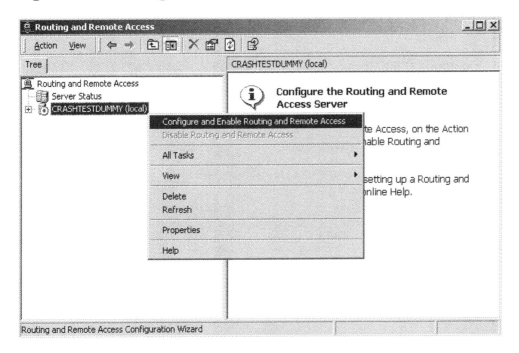

3.  From the Routing and Remote Access Configuration wizard, choose Next.

4.  Choose **Network Router**, and then select **Next**.

5.  Verify the protocols you wish to use are listed, and then choose **Next**.

6.  Choose **Yes** to the question about using demand-dial connections, and then select **Next**.

7.  If you are using the Dynamic Host Configuration Protocol for RRAS connections, choose **Automatically**, and then select **Next**.

8.  Choose **Finish** to save your changes and enable RRAS.

### Configuring the Modem for Demand-Dial Routing

Once RRAS is installed, you enable the modem or ISDN adapter for use with demand-dial routing. To do this, follow these steps:

1. From the **Tree** pane of **Routing and Remote Access**, expand the server, right-click **Ports**, and then choose **Properties** (Figure 7.4).

## Figure 7.4 RRAS Ports Configuration

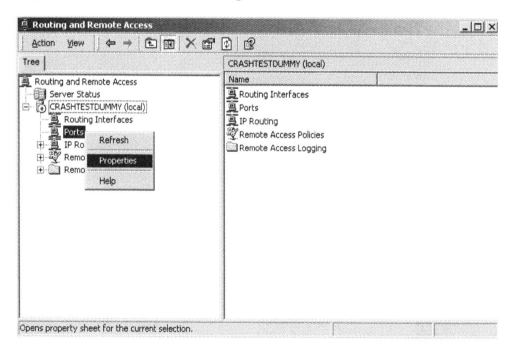

2. From Ports Properties, choose the modem, and then select Configure.

3. From **Configure Device**, place a check mark in the box next to **Demand-dial routing connections (inbound and outbound)** (Figure 7.5).

## Figure 7.5 Modem Configuration

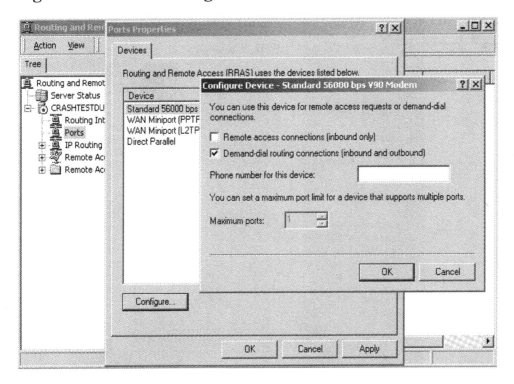

4.   Click **OK** in each open window to save your changes.

### *Creating a New Demand-Dial Interface*

To create a new demand-dial interface, follow these steps:

1.   From the **Tree** pane of **Routing and Remote Access**, expand the server, right-click **Routing Interfaces**, and then choose **New Demand Dial Interface**.

2.   Choose **Next** to begin the **Demand-Dial Interface** wizard.

3.   Type a name for the connection, and then choose **Next**.

4.   Choose a demand-dial connection type (PSTN, ISDN or a VPN), and then select **Next** (Figure 7.6).

## Figure 7.6 Demand-Dial Routing Connection Type

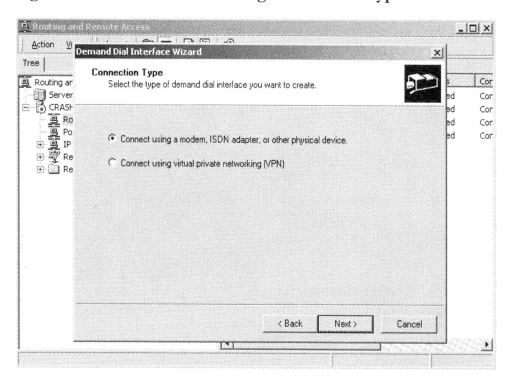

5.   Choose a connection method (modem, ISDN or VPN), and then select Next.

6.   Type the phone number (or IP address if using a VPN) of the remote router, and then choose **Next**.

7.   Choose the security options you wish to implement, and then select **Next**.

8.   Type a user name, the domain in which the user name exists, and a password the router will use to log on to the remote router, and then choose **Next** (Figure 7.7).

## Figure 7.7 Router Authentication Information

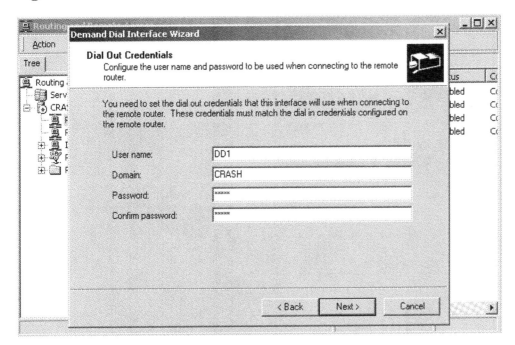

9.  Choose **Finish** to end the wizard and create the new demand-dial interface.

# Configuring Demand-Dial Routing

Several configuration parameters for the demand-dial routing interface occur through RRAS, while other configuration choices are set through the demand-dial property page options.

## *Configuring Demand-Dial Interface Properties*

To configure demand-dial interface properties, follow these steps:

1.  From the **Start** menu, choose **Programs, Administrative Tools**, and then select **Routing and Remote Access**.

2.  From the **Tree** pane of **Routing and Remote Access**, expand the server, and then choose **Routing Interfaces**.

3.  In the **Detail** pane, right-click **Demand-Dial Interface** and choose **Properties** (Figure 7.8).

## Figure 7.8 Demand-Dial Interface Properties

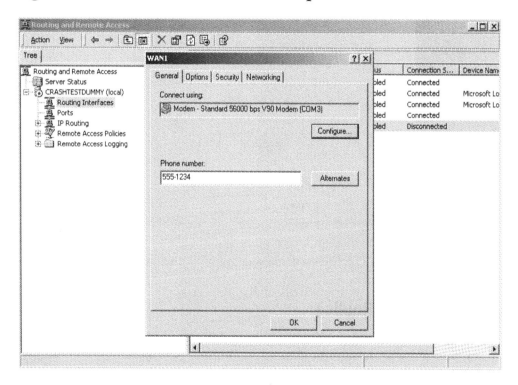

4.  From **Demand-Dial** properties, you can choose several options (Table 7.1).

## Table 7.1 Demand-Dial Interface Properties Options

| Property Page | Option | Description |
|---|---|---|
| General | Configure | Configure the modem, ISDN adapter, or VPN Server. |
| | Phone Number | Defines the primary phone number to use to establish the connection. |
| | Alternates | Allows you to enter alternate phone numbers if the primary number does not work. |
| Options | Connection Type | Allows you to change the connection to a persistent connection and to specify the connection duration before disconnecting. |
| | Dialing policy | Allows you to define the number of re-dial attempts to make if the connection fails or the line is busy. |
| | Callback | Requires a callback connection, which increases security and may save long distances charges for one end of the connection. |
| | X.25 | Configure a connection based on the X.25 protocol. |

| Property Page | Option | Description |
|---|---|---|
| Security | Security Options | Includes the type of authentication to require and whether to require data encryption. |
| | Interactive logon and scripting | Allows you to automate the authentication procedure and run code during the connection process. |
| Networking | Type of dial-up server I am calling | Defines settings for the type of connection server. |
| | Components checked are used by this connection | Defines the protocols and services used during the connection. |

 Note: The default demand-dial connection duration is 5 minutes.

## Configuring Other Demand-Dial Settings

Three other demand-dial settings are made from the RRAS console. When you right-click the demand-dial interface, the following three options appear in the menu (Figure 7.9):

# Figure 7.9 Demand-Dial Interface Menu

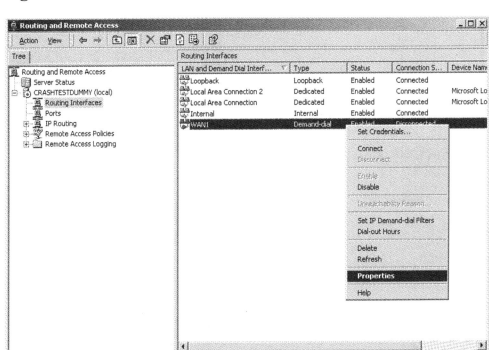

**Set Credentials**—Allows you to change the username and password used to log on to the remote router.

**Set IP Demand-Dial Filters**—From this option, you can filter all network traffic that does not meet specific IP information, including the source or destination IP address, and the TCP or UDP port number.

**Dial-Out Hours**—Defines the hours during which the demand-dial interface is enabled. By defualt, a demand-dial interface is available at all times of the day, every day of the year.

**Note:** If an active demand-dial conenction extends into a restricted time, the connection is not terminated until the time-out period is reached.

# Implementing Security with Demand-Dial Routing

Depending on the needs of the business, you implement different security measures in demand-dial routing. You configure demand-dial routing security by adjusting the settings regarding router authentication and data encryption.

## *Router Authentication*

Router authentication is an important part of any demand-dial connection, and Windows 2000 requires some form of authentication for every connection. The less secure and simplest form of router authentication uses the Password Authentication Protocol (PAP). PAP transmits the logon information in clear text, increasing the possibility that someone could obtain this information. However, it is the most compatible authentication method, and is most likely to work with non-Windows 2000 servers.

A more secure authentication method uses the Challenge Handshake Authentication Protocol (CHAP), Microsoft CHAP (MS-CHAP) version 1, or MS-CHAP version 2 (MS-CHAP v2). Using one of the CHAP-based protocols, the logon information is encrypted, so that it cannot be obtained by capturing network data.

## *Mutual Authentication*

Using one of the CHAP-based protocols, one router authenticates the other. In networks requiring the highest level of security, implement mutual authentication. Using mutual authentication, each router verifies the identity of the other before any data is transmitted. To implement mutual authentication, use one of the following protocols:

**Extensible Authentication Protocol-Transport Layer Security (EAP-TLS)**—EAP-TLS uses public keys to identify each router. EAP-TLS uses a user key to identify the calling router and a computer-based certificate to identify the called router.

---

**Tip:** You cannot use EAP-TLS unless you have a public key infrastructure implemented on the network.

---

**MS-CHAP v2**—MS-CHAP v2 is the only CHAP-based protocol that incorporates mutual authentication. Although MS-CHAP v2 uses encryption keys, it does not require the presence of a public key infrastructure.

## Data Encryption

You can implement one of four data encryption settings for each demand-dial interface. The four options are as follows:

**No encryption allowed**—The connection does not use data encryption. If the called router requires encryption, the session is disconnected.

**Optional encryption**—The calling router negotiates encryption with the remote router. If both support encryption, the data is encrypted. If the remote router does not support encryption, the data is sent unencrypted.

**Require Encryption**—Both routers must support encryption. If the remote router does not support encryption, the session is terminated.

**Maximum strength encryption**—Both servers must support the highest level of encryption, or the session is terminated.

### Using Remote Access Policies

Because demand-dial routing is part of RRAS, you can use remote access policies to increase demand-dial routing security. You can use a remote access policy to do the following:

• Restrict network access by the time of day, the protocol used, or to certain user accounts

• Enforce an authentication and encryption method

# Updating Routing Tables

Routers know how to route IP packets by checking their routing tables. These tables are continuously updated as changes are made to the network. However, routing tables cannot be sent over inactive network connections, like the type of connection created using demand-dial routing. To overcome this limitation, demand-dial routing supports manually updating the routing tables.

To enable a router to accept manual updates to the routing table, configure the Routing Information Protocol (RIP) for auto-static mode. Then schedule the updates using the command **NETSH**.

### Updating Routing Information

Using the **NETSH** utility, you create scripts that update the routing tables across a demand-dial routing connection. Once the scripts are created, you schedule their execution using the Windows 2000 Task Scheduler.

 **Note:** By default, auto-static mode is enabled for RIP.

You can also manually update the routing tables from the Routing and Remote Access configuration interface. When you initiate a routing table update from within the Routing and Remote Access configuration interface, the demand-dial connection is automatically started.

# Demand-Dial Routing Management

Once demand-dial routing is implemented, you need to monitor the connection to ensure it is meeting the needs of the business. Management includes monitoring the network and generating administrative alerts, anticipating needed changes to the demand-dial routing configuration, and testing the connections periodically.

## Detecting Demand-Dial Routing Errors

When managing a network with demand-dial routing connections, you should monitor the following features to ensure the demand-dial routing connection is functioning properly:

**High utilization**—If the demand-dial routing link shows a high usage, you may need to consider replacing the link with a permanent connection or a faster medium (like changing from PSTN to ISDN).

**Segment failure**—If the demand-dial routing is used as a backup to a permanent connection, you may not know that the demand-dial routing connection has failed until it is needed. The time when the demand-dial routing connection is most needed is not the time to discover it has failed.

**Router failure**—Like the demand-dial routing connection itself, if a router is used only for fault tolerance, you may not know it has failed until it is needed. Monitor the routers for any errors.

**Router saturation**—If too many network demands are placed on the demand-dial router, it may become saturated and incapable of handling the network demands. If your monitoring indicates saturation, replace the router with one that can handle more traffic, or add a redundant router.

## Preparing for Demand-Dial Routing Changes

You can anticipate the need for changes in a demand-dial routing connection by monitoring several conditions of the connection. These conditions include the following:

**Uptime and utilization of the network segment**—Uptime defines the availability of the link. If the connection is not as available as needed for a productive network, consider replacing the link with a higher-bandwidth connection or adding a second router.

**Router saturation**—As mentioned above, router saturation indicates the need for a faster router or the addition of a second router to handle some of the network demands.

## Testing Demand-Dial Routing

When testing your demand-dial routing connection, you should test both the availability of the connection and the security offered. If your demand-dial routing connection provides the only link between two networks, it is tested every time the network is used. However, if the demand-dial routing connection is used as a redundant path, you should regularly test it.

To test a redundant demand-dial routing connection, find a time of low network usage. Disconnect the main connection between the two networks, and then attempt to send information in both directions. The routers should establish a demand-dial routing connection and the information should be successfully transmitted.

 **Note:** It is normal to see a decrease in network performance because the demand-dial routing connection usually uses lower-bandwidth media. There is also a delay associated with the time required to establish the connection.

When testing security, you can do several things. Consider the following suggestions as ways you can test the demand-dial routing connection:

- Use a network analyzer to capture data on the demand-dial routing connection and verify this data is encrypted and unreadable

- Change the security requirements of one router so that it does not require encryption, but maintain an encryption requirement on the other; the connection should fail

# Demand-Dial Routing Business Goals

As with each of the protocols and services in this book, you must consider the implementation of demand-dial routing with respect to the four business goals: functionality, security, availability, and performance. The section that follows analyzes the relationship between demand-dial routing and the four goals. You are then presented with a business scenario to help you apply some of the concepts and to prepare for the Microsoft exam.

## Meeting Business Needs

Demand-dial routing meets the four business goals as follows:

**Functionality**—Demand-dial routing provides an inexpensive way to connect two networks over a WAN. Functionality of Windows 2000 demand-dial routing is increased by support for both dial-up and VPN connections and by adhering to the Internet Engineering Task Force (IETF) specifications. In any situation where a WAN link connection is charged by the time used, demand-dial routing provides a method for exchanging information at a reduced cost.

**Security**—You can increase security measures with demand-dial routing by requiring mutual authentication of routers and data encryption. Furthermore, you can establish a demand-dial routing connection across a VPN.

**Availability**—The availability of demand-dial routing will depend, in part, on the expectations of the network users. If information across the WAN connection must arrive in a timely fashion, consider adding a second link, a faster connection media, or a permanent connection. If expectations are less demanding, the availability offered by a single link may be sufficient.

**Performance**—Like availability, the performance of a demand-dial routing connection depends on the type of medium used to transmit the information. If performance is more of an issue than cost, use demand-dial routing over an ISDN or fast line rather than a PSTN connection. Additional redundant WAN links will also provide greater bandwidth and higher performance.

## Business Scenario

Woody's Chiropractic Association (WCA) provides a national system for chiropractors to share information and resources (Figure 7.10). WCA has one national center in Raleigh, and six regional centers. Each center provides dial-up access for the doctors' offices. Full-time WCA employees have Internet access through a T1 connection to the Internet.

## Figure 7.10 WCA Network

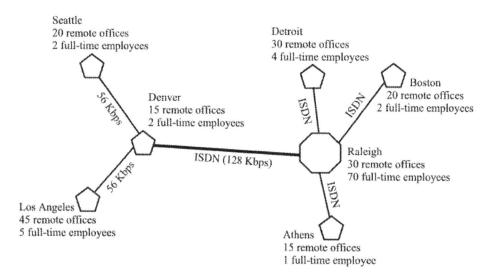

WCA has asked you to provide a redundant link between each regional center and the national center. Cost is a concern, so they do not want to lease permanent connections. Security is also a concern—the information that passes between regional centers is often confidential medical information. WCA also wants to ensure that the Internet connection is fail-safe.

You offer the following solution to upgrade the WCA network (Table 7.2). Use this table and your knowledge of the network to answer the questions in the Activities section near the end of this lesson.

## Table 7.2 Proposed WCA Network Changes

| Objective | Proposed Solution |
|---|---|
| Provide redundant links | Install a RRAS demand-dial router in each regional office.<br><br>Install four demand-dial routers in the Raleigh office. |
| Secure Data Transmissions | Use CHAP for mutual RRAS authentication. |
| Performance | Configure the demand-dial routers to use ISDN modems and lines. |
| Internet Access | Add an additional RRAS-based demand-dial router in Raleigh that uses an ADSL phone connection to the Internet. |

# Vocabulary

Review the following terms in preparation for the certification exam.

| Term | Description |
| --- | --- |
| auto-static mode | A RIP setting that enables a router to receive manual updates to the routing information tables across demand-dial connections. |
| bandwidth | The amount of data that can be transmitted across a network connection. |
| CHAP | Challenge Handshake Authentication Protocol is one of the router authentication protocols. |
| data encryption | Data is encrypted to make it unreadable by all computers except the sending computer and the intended recipient. |
| demand-dial routing | Demand-dial routing is a Windows 2000 service that provides an inexpensive way to connect to networks and to provide a backup WAN connection. |
| EAP-TLS | Extensible Authentication Protocol-Transport Layer Security (EAP-TLS) uses public keys for mutual router authentication. |
| filter | A TCP/IP filter prevents data from transmitting unless it meets specific TCP/IP characteristics. |
| ISDN | Integrated Service Digital Network is a networking and communications standard for transmitting information across digital phone lines. |
| L2TP | Layer 2 Tunneling Protocol is one of the tunneling protocols used with VPNs. |
| LAN | A Local Area Network is a collection of computers in a single area, connected by cables. |

| Term | Description |
|---|---|
| MS-CHAP | Microsoft Challenge Handshake Authentication Protocol version 1 is one of the router authentication protocols. |
| MS-CHAP v2 | Microsoft Challenge Handshake Authentication Protocol version 2 is one of the router authentication protocols, and the only CHAP-based protocol that supports mutual authentication. |
| mutual authentication | The ability of both routers in a connection to authenticate the other simultaneously. |
| PAP | Password Authentication Protocol is the least secure of the router authentication protocols, sending authentication information in an unencrypted state. |
| PPTP | Point-to-Point Tunneling Protocol is one of the tunneling protocols used with VPNs. |
| PSTN | Public Switched Telephone Network consists of the standard telephone lines used to carry voice information and data when used with a modem. |
| RIP | The Routing Information Protocol is a dynamic routing protocol that enables routers to automatically update the routing information tables. |
| router authentication | The ability of one router to verify the router to which it is connected, before transmitting network data. |
| RRAS | The Routing and Remote Access Service in Windows 2000 provides remote connectivity and routing functions for the network. |
| VPN | Virtual Private Networks use tunneling protocols to create a secure channel for data transmission across the Internet. |
| WAN | A Wide Area Network connects two or more LANs across a wide geographic area. |

# In Brief

| If you want to... | Then do this... |
| --- | --- |
| Provide an inexpensive WAN connection | Implement demand-dial routing. |
| Provide a backup link for a permanent WAN connection | Use demand-dial routing. |
| Provide the highest level of security across a demand-dial routing link | Require the highest-level data encryption and mutual server authentication. |
| Update demand-dial routing tables manually | Install RIP in auto-static mode. |
| Increase availability of the demand-dial routing servers | Add additional servers and connections across the WAN link. |

# Lesson 7 Activities

Complete the following activities to better prepare you for the certification exam.

1.  In the proposed solution for the WCA network, are the criteria for redundant links between regional offices met?

2.  Does the proposed solution meet the security needs of WCA?

3.  What would you propose to increase security across the demand-dial connections?

4.  The CEO of WCA has heard a lot about VPNs lately, and has decided they would be a good idea on the network. How can you modify the proposed solution to implement VPNs?

5.  How are the cost issues addressed in the proposed solution?

6.  How can you reduce the costs of implementing the demand-dial solution?

7.  Is redundancy to the Internet properly handled in the proposed solution?

8.  If a fire strikes the Raleigh office and shuts down the entire office for a time, will regional offices continue to operate effectively? Why or why not?

9.  Propose a solution that provides connectivity for all other offices if a single regional center is disconnected.

10.  How will you configure the routing protocols on the demand-dial routers?

# Answers to Lesson 7 Activities

1.    No. Connections between Raleigh and Denver, Detroit, Boston, and Athens are taken care of, but there is no redundancy for the connections between Denver and Seattle and Los Angeles.

2.    No. CHAP does not provide mutual server authentication, and also does not encrypt the data.

3.    Since all demand-dial routers will run on Windows 2000 RRAS servers, you can implement MS-CHAP v2 and require data encryption for all connections. MS-CHAP v2 provides mutual server authentication.

4.    Establish VPN connections between all RRAS-based demand-dial routers. Security is not sacrificed by this plan, nor is overall cost of implementation or management.

5.    Cost considerations are not addressed in the proposed solution. ISDN lines are expensive and are typically charged on a per-use basis.

6.    Instead of configuring the demand-dial routers to use ISDN, configure them to use PSTN and modems. The modems will provide very slow connections. As a possible compromise between speed and cost, suggest using ADSL lines.

7.    Yes. A demand-dial connection to the Internet will provide a backup for the T1 connection, but it will be very slow. Since speed is not mentioned as an important aspect, and cost is, this is an appropriate solution.

8.    No. All regional offices connect to the Raleigh center, and there are no connections between regional offices. Furthermore, all Internet access is through the Raleigh office.

9.    In order to provide total fault tolerance, a mesh network must be created using demand-dial routers. Each regional center must connect to the Raleigh office and at least one other regional center. These connections include demand-dial connections from Seattle and Los Angeles to Raleigh and to other regional centers. Since you are using demand-dial routing, the costs do not extend beyond those of installing and configuring additional Windows 2000 servers.

10.   The demand-dial routers must first be configured with static routing until connections are established. You can then implement RIP or OSPF.

# Lesson 7 Quiz

These questions test your knowledge of features, vocabulary, procedures, and syntax.

1.  By default, how long is a demand-dial routing connection kept open?
    A.  5 minutes
    B.  30 minutes
    C.  1 hour
    D.  5 hours

2.  Which protocols support mutual router authentication? (Choose all that apply).
    A.  EAP-TLS
    B.  MS-CHAP
    C.  MS-CHAP v2
    D.  PAP

3.  What line types does demand-dial routing support? (Choose all that apply).
    A.  PSTN
    B.  ISDN
    C.  T1
    D.  ADSL

4.  What services or protocols must be installed on the demand-dial router? (Choose all that apply).
    A.  Connection Manager
    B.  RRAS
    C.  Internet Information Service (IIS)
    D.  TCP/IP

5.  What routing protocols must be installed on a demand-dial routing server?
    A.  Static routing table
    B.  OSPF
    C.  RIP
    D.  IGMP

6.    Which of the following statements is true?
      A.    Demand-dial routing costs more than a leased line connection.
      B.    Demand-dial routing can authenticate servers but not encrypt data.
      C.    Demand-dial routing can encrypt data but not authenticate users.
      D.    Demand-dial routing uses T1 connections.

7.    How do you manually update a demand-dial router's routing tables?
      A.    Implement OSPF
      B.    Use RIP for IPX
      C.    Use auto-static RIP
      D.    With a table updater

8.    Which authentication protocol requires the presence of a certificate authority on the network?
      A.    PAP
      B.    CHAP
      C.    MS-CHAP v2
      D.    EAP-TLS

9.    How do you test a redundant demand-dial routing connection?
      A.    Run the **DDRTEST** command from a command prompt.
      B.    Break the permanent connection.
      C.    Use a packet analyzer.
      D.    Redundant connections cannot be tested.

10.   A demand-dial router configured with Optional Encryption connects to a demand-dial routing server with the Required Encryption setting. What happens?
      A.    The connection is terminated.
      B.    The connection is established with encryption.
      C.    The connection is established with one-way encryption.
      D.    The connection is established without encryption.

# Answers to Lesson 7 Quiz

1.  Answer A is correct. A demand-dial routing connection remains open for 5 minutes by default.

    Therefore, answers B, C, and D are incorrect.

2.  Answers A and C are correct. EAP-TLS and MS-CHAP v2 provide mutual server authentication.

    Answers B and D are incorrect. PAP and MS-CHAP do not support mutual authentication.

3.  Answers A, B, and D are correct. Demand-dial routing uses standard phone lines (PSTN) and ISDN. ADSL uses standard phone lines, and so is also supported.

    Answer C is incorrect. T1 lines do not support dial-up connections.

4.  Answers B and D are correct. Demand-dial routing is part of RRAS, and requires the TCP/IP protocol.

    Answer A is incorrect. Connection Manager is not used with demand-dial routing.

    Answer C is incorrect. Although IIS can be installed on a demand-dial router, it is not a necessary component of demand-dial routing.

5.  Answer A is correct. A static routing table is required at first, so that the demand-dial router knows when to establish a connection.

    Answers B, C, and D are incorrect. All three answers can be installed on a demand-dial router, and at least one of them likely will be. However, none are required protocols, as the question asks.

6.    Answer C is correct. Demand-dial routing provides data encryption and computer authentication, but not user authentication.

Answer A is incorrect. Although the initial cost of installing demand-dial routing servers may exceed the cost of installing a leased line, the demand-dial routing solution provides a lower overall cost.

Answer B is incorrect. Demand-dial routing provides server authentication as well as data encryption.

Answer D is incorrect. Demand-dial routing supports only dial-up connections.

7.    Answer C is correct. Manually configuration of the demand-dial routing tables is accomplished by installing RIP and configuring it in auto-static mode.

Answer A is incorrect. OSPF does not support manual updates.

Answer B is incorrect. RIP for IPX is an implementation of RIP for networks using the IPX/SPX protocol.

Answer D is incorrect. This is a fictitious term.

8.    Answer D is correct. The only authentication protocol that uses certificates is EAP-TLC.

Answers A and B are incorrect. PAP and CHAP do not use certificates for authentication, and so a certificate authority is not required on the network.

Answer C is incorrect. Although MS-CHAP v2 uses encryption keys, it does not use public keys, and so a certificate authority is not needed.

9.    Answer B is correct. To test a redundant connection, you must temporarily disconnect the permanent connection and verify the demand-dial routing connection is then established and working properly.

Answer A is incorrect. This is a fictitious term.

Answer C is incorrect. A packet analyzer will not tell you if a redundant connection is working properly.

Answer D is incorrect. As a network administrator, you need to find ways to test all services.

10.    Answer B is correct. When a server that can optionally use encryption connects to a server that requires encryption, then the connection is established and both computers send encrypted data.

Answer A is incorrect. Since both servers can use encryption, they negotiate an encryption level. If the first server were set to No Encryption Allowed, then the connection would be terminated.

Answer C is incorrect. You cannot have one-way encryption.

Answer D is incorrect. Since the second server requires encryption, it will only establish a connection that uses encryption.

# IP Routing and Multicasting

For any Transmission Control Protocol/Internet Protocol (TCP/IP)-based network larger than a single segment, data must be routed (directed) from its source to its destination. The data, in the form of Internet Protocol (IP) packets, travels from the originating computer to one or more routers, which are responsible for placing the IP packet on the appropriate segments to reach its intended destination. Windows 2000-based routers support two dynamic routing protocols: the Routing Information Protocol (RIP) and Open Shortest Path First (OSPF).

Generally, information sent on a segmented network must be directed—it must have a specific destination. General messages sent to every computer (called broadcasts) are not passed on to other segments by routers. Routers prevent broadcasts on the network to reduce overall traffic. If you wish to send a single copy of data to multiple computers on an IP-based network, you must use multicasting.

Windows 2000 supports multicasting on single-router networks, and also provides minimal support for connecting to multi-router networks that use multicasting (like the Internet).

After completing this lesson, you should have a better understanding of the following topics:

- IP Routing Overview

- IP Routing Implementation

- Multicasting Implementation

- IP Routing and Multicasting Management

- IP Routing and Multicasting Business Goals

# IP Routing Overview

As networks grow and the number of computers attached to a single segment increases, so does the amount of network traffic. Eventually, a decrease in network response time leads network administrators to break the network into smaller pieces. If planned and segmented correctly, these segments (or subnets) contain computers that most often share information, thus reducing the amount of traffic that travels between segments.

## Understanding IP Routing

Each subnet is connected to the other subnets by a router. A router can be a stand-alone device or a computer with two or more Network Interface Cards (NICs) installed.

Note: A computer with several NICs installed is said to be multihomed—at home on more than one network segment.

When a router receives an IP packet, it checks a routing table for information on the location of the destination. Based on the information in the routing table, the router forwards the IP packet to the appropriate subnet. Routing tables can be manually updated (called a static table) or automatically using a dynamic routing protocol.

Tip: Windows 2000-based routers also work on networks using the Internetwork Packet Exchange (IPX) protocol. Routing tables use RIP for IPX and the Service Advertising Protocol (SAP) for IPX.

### Static IP Routing

In small networks, or ones in which the routing information changes rarely, you can implement static routing tables. There is little reason to use static tables, since every change must be updated manually on each router. However, using static routing slightly reduces overall network traffic.

### Dynamic IP Routing

When you implement a dynamic routing protocol on your network, each router shares its routing table information with the other routers. This ensures that, without manual intervention, all routers know of changes to the routing information. The two dynamic routing protocols supported by Windows 2000 are RIP and OSPF.

**RIP**—RIP-based routers use a distance vector algorithm to calculate the direction and distance a packet must travel from one segment to another. RIP routers share their routing table with the other routers, and each router calculates its own distance vectors. RIP requires very little preliminary configuration.

 **Note:** By default, RIP-based routers share their routing table information every 30 seconds. This can generate a significant amount of network traffic, especially on larger networks.

There are two versions of RIP. RIP version 1 (RIP v1) is defined in the Request For Comments (RFC) 1058. RIP version 2 (RIP v2) is defined in RFC 2353. RIP v2 supports several newer features, including password protection to authenticate routing table update messages. RIP v2 also uses multicasting announcements, which reduces overall network traffic generated during routing table updates.

**OSPF**—With OSPF, each router shares exchange information with neighboring routers, so that an overall tree of network paths is created. The router then uses this map of network paths to direct an IP packet to the shortest path. Unlike RIP, OSPF does not send its routing table to all routers on the network, making it more suitable for larger networks.

**Note:** RIP considers both distance and bandwidth when directing a packet. OSPF calculates only the shortest distance.

# IP Routing Implementation

Planning the network structure before implementing an IP routing scheme is important. If you are using static routers, every change in the network requires an update of the routing table on each router. However, by the very nature of dynamic routing protocols, significant changes to the network can occur without increasing management of routers.

IP routing implementation begins with configuring the Routing and Remote Access Service (RRAS).

## Installing IP Routing

IP routing is part of the Routing and Remote Access Service (RRAS). When you install Windows 2000 Server or Windows 2000 Advanced Server, RRAS is partially installed, but not enabled or configured.

### Enabling RRAS

If you have not yet done so, run **Routing and Remote Access** (from the **Start** menu, choose **Programs**, **Administrative Tools**, and then select **Routing and Remote Access**. Right-click the server and choose **Configure and Enable Routing and Remote Access**).

## Installing Dynamic Protocols

Once RRAS is installed and enabled, you must install the dynamic routing protocols. To install the protocols, follow these steps:

1.  From the **Tree** (left) pane of **RRAS**, expand the server, expand **IP Routing,** right-click **General**, and then choose **New Routing Protocol** (Figure 8.1).

# Figure 8.1 RRAS Display

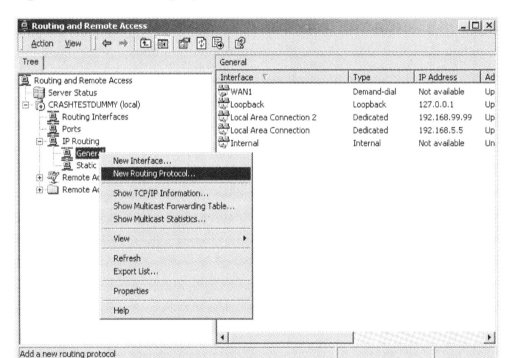

2.  Choose the protocol you wish to install (either **Open Shortest Path First (OSPF)** or **RIP Version 2 for Internet Protocol**), and then select **OK.**

3.  The newly installed protocols display in the **Tree** pane beneath **IP Routing** (Figure 8.2).

# Figure 8.2 Newly Installed Protocols

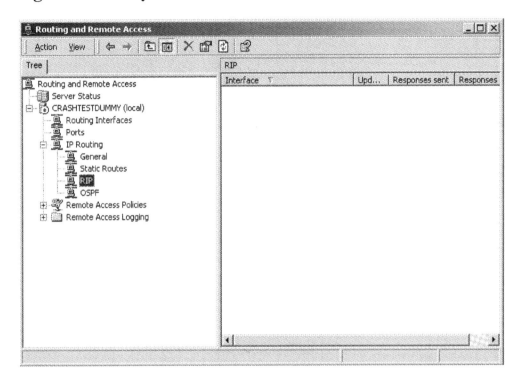

## *Enabling the Protocols*

Once you have installed the protocols, you must enable them for each network interface. To do so, follow these steps:

1.  From the **Tree** pane of **RRAS**, expand the server, expand **IP Routing**, right-click the protocol (**RIP** or **OSPF**), and then choose **New Interface** (Figure 8.3).

## Figure 8.3 New Interface

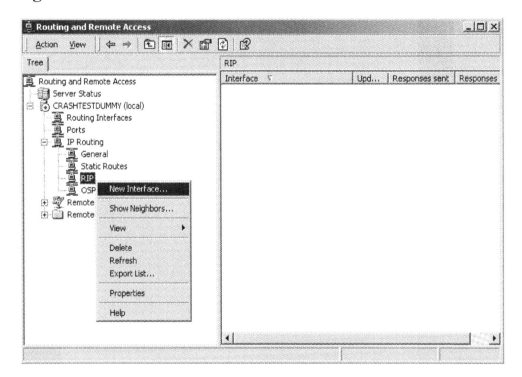

2.  Choose the interface that will use the protocol, and then select **OK.**
    The **RIP** properties for the specific interface displays. These settings are discussed in detail below.
    Close the window.

## Creating Static Routes

Although this lesson and the Microsoft exam are primarily concerned with configuring the dynamic routing protocols, you should be familiar with updating routing tables. Updates to static routing tables are made from either the RRAS interface or from a command prompt.

## *Using RRAS to Update a Table*

To update or create a routing table from within the RRAS interface, follow these steps:

1. From the **Start** menu, choose **Programs**, **Administrative Tools**, and then select **Routing and Remote Access**.

2. From the **Tree** pane of **RRAS**, expand the server, expand **IP Routing**, right-click **Static Routes**, and then choose **New Static Route**.

3. From **Static Route** (Figure 8.4), type the information, using Table 8.1 as a guide. Click **OK** when finished.

# Figure 8.4 Static Route

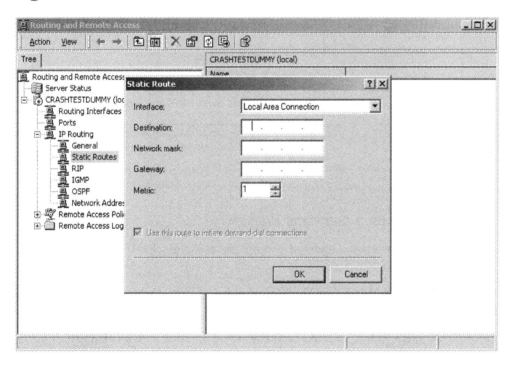

## Table 8.1 Static Route Options

| Option | Description |
|---|---|
| Interface | Select the interface used to send packets on this route. |
| Destination | Type the IP address of the destination network. This can be a network ID, an IP address for a host, or 0.0.0.0 to create a default route. |
| Network Mask | Type the subnet mask to use with the destination ID above. For any host route, set the network mask to 255.255.255.255. For a default route, set the mask to 0.0.0.0. |
| Gateway | Enter the IP address of the router used to send packets to this destination. |
| Metric | Adjust the value to represent the cost of this connection, whether it is the number of hops (routers through which the packet must travel) or some other measurement of preference. |
| Use this route to initiate demand dial connections | If you chose a demand-dial interface, select this option to allow demand-dial routing. |

### *Updating a Routing Table from a Command Prompt*

You update static route tables from a command prompt by using the **ROUTE** command. The **ROUTE** command takes the following form:

**ROUTE ADD** *DESTINATION* **MASK** *NETWORK_MASK* *GATEWAY* **METRIC** *METRIC* **IF** *INTERFACE*

Where *DESTINATION*, *NETWORK_MASK*, *GATEWAY*, *METRIC*, and *INTERFACE* correspond with the settings described in Table 8.1. To make the route persistent (so that it remains after rebooting the router, add the **-p** switch after the route command. For example, to add the persistent route 192.168.2.32 with a subnet mask of 255.255.255.254, a gateway of 10.25.3.77, and metric of 3, use the following command:

**ROUTE–P ADD 192.168.2.32 MASK 255.255.255.254 10.25.3.77 METRIC 3**

 Tip: Routes can be viewed using the **ROUTE PRINT** command, and persistent routes are deleted using the **ROUTE DELETE** command.

# Configuring Dynamic IP Routing

Configuration of the two dynamic routing protocols differs significantly. Of the two, RIP requires less configuring because the routers communicate with one another to build routing table s. However, the simplicity of RIP configuration results in more network traffic.

## Configuring Routing Information Protocol (RIP)

When implementing RIP, you first set the general parameters to which all routers on the network will adhere, and then you configure the individual interfaces. To configure the global RIP properties, follow these steps:

1.  From the **Start** menu, choose **Programs, Administrative Tools**, and then select **Routing and Remote Access**.

2.  From the **Tree** pane of **RRAS**, expand the server, expand **IP Routing,** right-click **RIP,** and then choose **Properties**.

3.  From **RIP Properties**, configure the global settings, including the timing of RIP triggered updates and the level of event logging. You can also choose which routers will participate in RIP announcements (Figure 8.5).

## Figure 8.5 RIP Properties

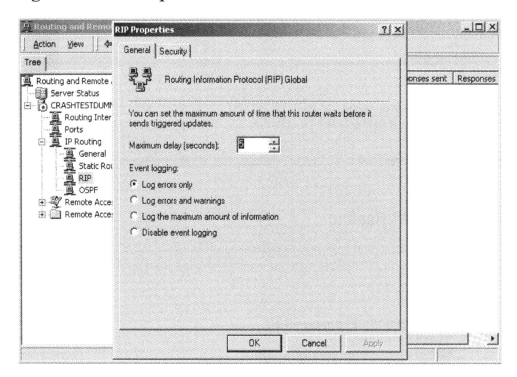

To configure individual interfaces, follow these steps:

1.  From the **Tree** pane of **RRAS**, expand the server, expand **IP Routing,** and then choose **RIP**.

2.  In the **Details** pane, right-click the interface, and then choose **Properties**.

**Tip:** If no interfaces are listed in the Details pane, you have not mapped any interfaces to the RIP protocol. Follow the steps earlier in this lesson for assigning an interface to RIP.

3.  From **RIP Properties—Interface Properties**, adjust the RIP settings that are specific to this interface.

---

 Note: The detailed configuration of the RIP and OSPF protocols is beyond the scope of this book. Windows 2000 Help provides more detailed information on configuring both RIP and OSPF.

---

### Configuring Open Shortest Path First (OSPF)

Much like installation of RIP, when you configure OSPF, you first configure the global settings, and then make specific settings for each interface. To access the global OSPF settings, follow these steps:

1.  From the **Start** menu, choose **Programs**, **Administrative Tools**, and then select **Routing and Remote Access**.

2.  From the **Tree** pane of **RRAS**, expand the server, expand **IP Routing**, right-click **OSPF**, and then choose **Properties**.

3.  From **OSPF Properties**, configure the global settings.

To configure individual interfaces for OSPF, follow these steps:

1.  From the **Tree** pane of **RRAS**, expand the server, expand **IP Routing**, and then choose **OSPF**.

2.  In the **Details** pane, right-click the interface, and then choose **Properties**.

3.  From **OSPF Properties—Interface Properties**, adjust the OSPF settings that are specific to this interface.

## Using OSPF on Larger Networks

The discussion of RIP and OSPF so far has assumed a relatively small network, one with fewer than about 50 routers. If a network grows beyond this approximate limit, RIP generates too much network traffic to be of much use, and routers using OSPF begin to experience problems maintaining a routing table list.

**Note:** The maximum number of hops in a Windows 2000-based RIP network is 14 routers. RIP is limited to networks of 40 to 50 routers and fewer than 100 populated network segments.

For larger networks on which you want to use the OSPF protocol, you must split the network into separate management zones. These zones are called Autonomous Systems (AS), and each AS contains numerous areas (Figure 8.6). Each area is a set of contiguous networks.

## Figure 8.6 Dividing an OSPF Network

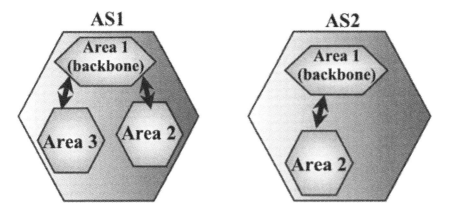

Within each AS, there is one area defined as the backbone area. The backbone area is always defined with the IP address 0.0.0.0. All routing traffic passes through this backbone area, so you must ensure that it matches the physical backbone of your network.

**Note:** By default, each router using OSPF is a member of the network 0.0.0.0 (the backbone area).

Routers within an AS share routing information, but this routing information is not shared between autonomous systems. If your network contains more than one AS, certain routers may be configured as boundary routers, which are capable of sharing routing table information across the AS boundaries (Figure 8.7).

## Figure 8.7 Boundary Routers

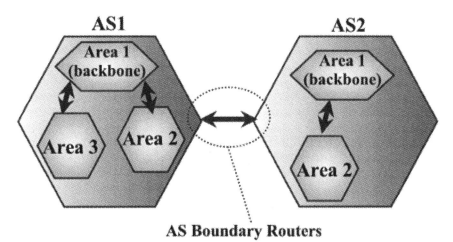

You can configure the boundary routers to share this inter-AS information with the remaining routers in the AS, although this is not always necessary. The connection between autonomous systems uses an Exterior Gateway Protocol (EGP), like Border Gateway Protocol version 4 (BGP v4). Windows 2000 does not support BGP v4, so hardware routers are needed to connect ASs.

**Tip:** For more information about AS configurations, refer to RFC 2328. RFC documents can be found at several Web sites, including *http://www.rfc-editor.org.*

## Combining Hardware and Software Routers

Many networks are built using hardware routers—devices specifically designed to route network traffic and do little else. If you are responsible for managing such a network and wish to add Windows 2000-based routers, you should consider the benefits of both hardware and software routers, and then consider some integration issues.

Advantages to using a hardware router include the following:

**Fast**—hardware routers are faster than software routers, because they have little overhead. The hardware is designed for one task (routing), and so it does not have to support and run a full server operating system (like Windows 2000).

**Standard**—One or two companies (for example, Cisco Systems) build many of the hardware routers, and they are well known and well supported by many network administrators.

**Stable**—Without the overhead of a complete operating system, hardware routers are very stable. Most major router manufactures have very strong reputations for building reliable products.

Software-based routing solutions also have their benefits. Consider the following two benefits:

**Overall lower cost**—Although a hardware router is less expensive than a new server running Windows 2000, the server running Windows 2000 can act as a router, remote access server, Dynamic Host Configuration Protocol (DHCP) server, Domain Name System (DNS) server, and more. Software routers are particularly useful when connecting remote locations over a WAN link, where a single computer can serve as the remote access server and router.

**Manageability**—If you are familiar with Windows 2000 and its tools, maintaining a Windows 2000-based router is relatively simple. The tools are all centrally located in the RRAS interface.

### Integrating Windows 2000 with Hardware Routers

If you decide to integrate Windows 2000-based routers in an existing hardware-based network, consider the following requirements:

•  Ensure that Windows 2000 supports the routing protocols in use, including the version and specific features of the protocol

•  Ensure the routers are compatible with Windows 2000. Some of the OSPF features (including cryptography) are not supported by Windows 2000

•  If possible, test the integration on a test network before full implementation

# Multicasting Implementation

IP routers are used to segment a network and reduce the network traffic on each segment. One way in which routers reduce network traffic is by preventing the

re-transmission of broadcast messages. A broadcast message is a single copy of data that has no specific IP address destination, so all computers that receive the message act upon it.

On a segmented network, where the routers do not permit broadcasting, multicasting provides a means for sending a single copy of data simultaneously to multiple computers.

## Understanding Multicasting

Multicasting provides a way to send information to many computers without

re-transmitting the data for each computer. Standard network communication (called a unicast transmission) is inefficient use of network bandwidth. If a RIP router, for example, is sharing its routing table with the other routers on a network, it must send the table individually to each of the other routers. If the router supports multicasting (and is using RIP v2, which also supports multicasting), the router can send a single copy of the routing table to all of the routers. Each router receives the table at (more or less) the same time (Figure 8.8).

## Figure 8.8 Multicast Transmission

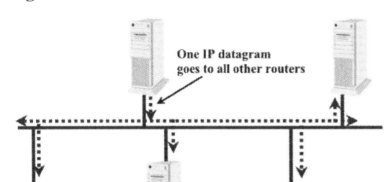

## Installing the Internet Group Management Protocol (IGMP)

The heart of multicasting lies in the Internet Group Management Protocol (IGMP). IGMP is part of the Transmission Control Protocol/Internet Protocol (TCP/IP) suite, and is installed when TCP/IP is installed. The IGMP routing protocol—used to support multicast forwarding by servers—is installed through the RRAS interface.

The process of installing the IGMP routing protocol is the same as adding RIP or OSPF. You first install and configure RRAS. From within the RRAS interface, you install IGMP and then associate the protocol with specific interfaces. This association enables the interface to use the protocol.

## Configuring IGMP

Once IGMP is installed and assigned to the interfaces, you configure the global IGMP settings, and then the specific settings for each interface. There is a single global setting you can change for IGMP—the amount of diagnostic logging you wish to implement.

To configure interface-specific IGMP settings, follow these steps:

1.  From the **Start** menu, choose **Programs**, **Administrative Tools**, and then select **Routing and Remote Access**.

2.  From the **Tree** pane of **RRAS**, expand the server, expand **IP Routing**, and then choose **IGMP.**

3.  In the **Details** pane, right-click the interface, and then select **Properties** (Figure 8.9).

## Figure 8.9 IGMP Interface Properties

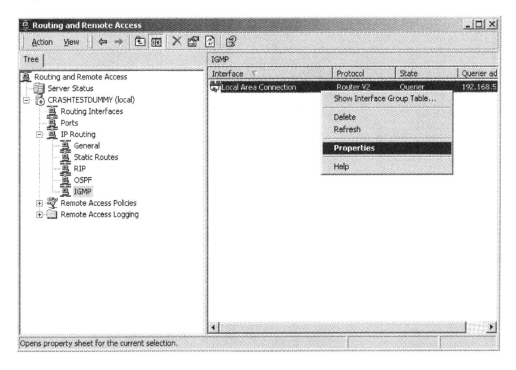

4.  From IGMP Properties, choose the General property page.

5.  From the **General** property page, you can enable or disable IGMP, choose the version of IGMP to use (**Version 1 or 2**), and select the IGMP mode (**IGMP router** or **IGMP proxy**) (Figure 8.10).

## Figure 8.10 IGMP General Property Page

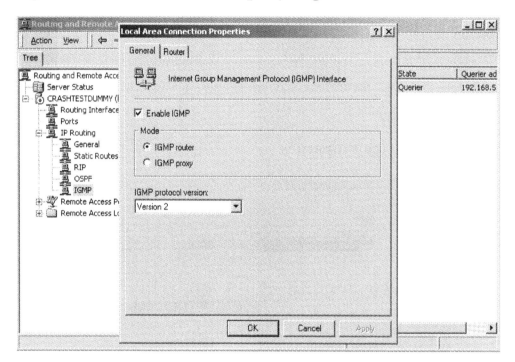

6.  The **Router** property page allows you to customize the behavior of multicast routing. These settings are beyond the scope of this book, but details about each setting are contained in the Windows 2000 Help file.

### Configuring Multicast Forwarding and IGMP Proxy Services

Using multicast forwarding, a router can pass multicast information from one network segment to anther. IGMP is used to update the multicast forwarding table. IGMP also allows a Windows 2000 server to act as a multicast proxy. Although the server is not actually a multicast server, it appears as one to computers on a private network.

To use a Windows 2000 server as a multicast proxy, or to implement multicast forwarding, the server must have at least two NICs. The NIC connected to your private network is configured as an IGMP router, and the NIC connected to a public network is configured as an IGMP proxy (Figure 8.11).

# Figure 8.11 IGMP Server Configuration

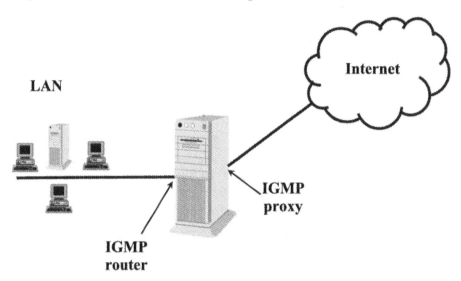

On each network segment, the multicast router acts as a querier. The querier queries the network segment for all multicast hosts. If a computer wants to receive multicast information, it responds to the query issued by the IGMP router. On any network segment, only one IGMP router can be the querier, and by default, every IGMP router acts as a querier. If an IGMP router discovers another querier on the network, the IGMP router with the lower IP address will be the querier.

## *Defining Multicast Boundaries*

When using multicasting, you must ensure that the multicast information only travels to the intended computers. Confinement of the multicast is important in reducing network traffic and increasing security. For example, if you are multicasting a videoconference within a corporation, you want to ensure that this multicast does not reach the Internet. Likewise, you may have network segments with users who do not need to receive such a multicast. To reduce the traffic on those segments, you confine the multicast transmission to only the necessary segments.

Multicast boundaries can be defined in the following ways:

**IP addresses**—You can define a multicast boundary based on a range of IP addresses.

**Time to Live (TTL) boundaries**—A multicast router will route or forward a multicast packet based on the TTL value.

**Rate limiting**—You can specify the maximum rate (in kilobits per second) of multicast traffic to pass through a multicast router.

### Multicast Heartbeat

The multicast heartbeat is a feature of Windows 2000 that allows a router to verify that multicasting is working properly. The router listens for a multicast notification that occurs at a regular interval. If the router does not detect a heartbeat within the allotted time, it generates an error message.

 Note: The multicast heartbeat feature requires implementation of the Simple Network Monitor Protocol (SNMP) on the network. The router must be an SNMP agent. If a heartbeat is not detected, the router issues an SNMP trap to its management station.

# IP Routing and Multicasting Management

Error detection and monitoring are important parts of overall network management. With IP Routing and multicasting, you will concentrate on monitoring network traffic patterns and the routers. This monitoring and testing will aid in predicting future network needs, as well.

## Detecting Routing and Multicasting Errors

When analyzing IP Routing, look for failures and saturations in both the routers and the network segments. Use the following guidelines for monitoring IP Routing:

**Segment saturation**—Saturation indicates too much traffic on a segment. Although data may arrive at its destination, saturation leads to many network failures, retransmissions, and further network slowdowns.

**Segment failure**—If you have provided redundant network segments, you may not be aware of a segment failure. More than likely, though, a segment failure will become immediately apparent.

**Router saturation**—if a router becomes saturated, it is unable to handle the number of routing requests demanded by the network. You should carefully monitor routers and detect the signs of saturation before they cause a router failure.

**Router failure**—Unless the router provides redundancy, you will know about router failures because one or more network segments can no longer communicate with the remainder of the network. Carefully monitor routers to detect early signs of failure.

Multicast errors typically match those of IP routers. Monitor each network segment for saturation and failure, and monitor the multicast routers for indications of saturation and failure.

## Making Changes to IP Routing and Multicasting Designs

As you monitor the network segments and routers, you can predict needed changes in the network configuration. If you notice an increase in demands on one particular router, for example, you should consider replacing the router with one that can handle the higher demands, or add a redundant router. Likewise, if a Wide Area Network (WAN) link is experiencing saturation, you must replace the link with a faster connection medium or add additional network paths.

## Testing IP Routing

There are two aspects of IP routing and multicasting that you must test on occasion. If you have implemented redundant paths on your network, you may not know that a path is inoperable until the main link fails. To test redundancy, find a time of low network usage, and disconnect redundant routers, one at a time. Ensure that network connectivity remains intact.

To test IP routing security, use a network analyzer to capture routing table information as it is shared between routers. Verify that routers running Internet Protocol Security (IPSec) are mutually authenticating one another. Also verify that the data transferred is encrypted using IPSec or Microsoft Point-to-Point Encryption (MPPE).

# IP Routing and Multicasting Business Goals

As with other Windows 2000 services and protocols, you should consider the use of IP routing and multicasting from a business perspective. The four business goals (functionality, security, availability, and performance) are analyzed below, and you are presented with a business scenario using the IP routing and multicasting capabilities of Windows 2000.

## Meeting Business Needs

Using IP routing and multicasting with Windows 2000, you can meet the four business goals as follows:

**Functionality**—IP routing provides functionality in a business network by supporting both RIP and OSPF protocols. A Windows 2000 router running either protocol can be integrated into an existing network that uses hardware routers. Further functionality is achieved by using a single Windows 2000 router as the router for a WAN connection and as the remote access server for the same connection.

The multicasting routing and forwarding capabilities of Windows 2000 allow RIP v2 to send multicast routing table updates and also allow a company to use multicasting tools across the internal network.

**Security**—Both IP routing and multicasting support data encryption using IPSec and MPPE. Routers are authenticated to ensure proper delivery of routing table and multicast information, and mutual authentication is achieved with IPSec.

**Availability**—To make WAN links more available for network use, IP routing supports the creation of redundant links and the use of redundant routers. Of course, redundancy costs money, and so the need for availability must be weighed against the costs involved.

**Performance**—Multicasting improves network performance by decreasing the number of transmissions caused by unicasting. RIP v2 supports multicasting as a means of updating routing table s.

## Business Scenario

Woody's Chiropractic Association (WCA) has decided to implement multicasting on their national network (Figures 8.12, 8.13, and 8.14). They have installed a multicast server in the Raleigh regional office, and want you to use existing Windows 2000 RRAS servers to ensure the multicast traffic is forwarded and routed properly.

# Figure 8.12 WCA Network

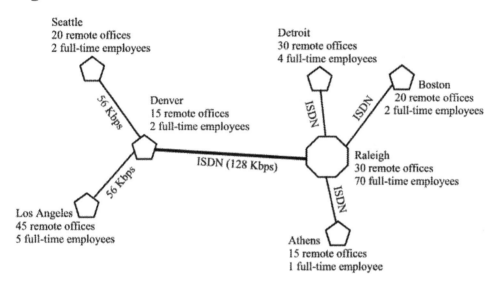

## Figure 8.13 Raleigh National Office Network

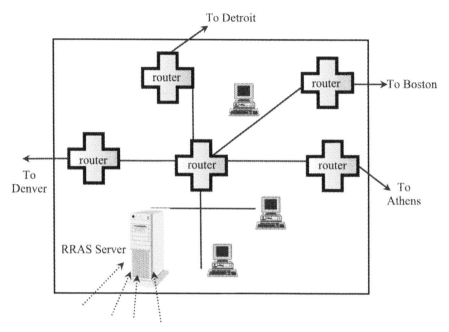

## Figure 8.14 Typical Regional Office Network

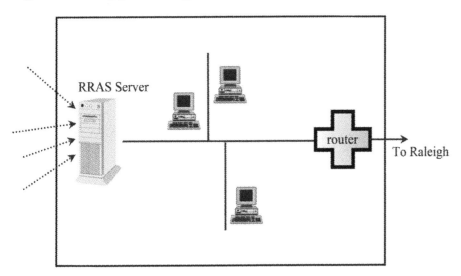

In addition to the standard configuration, WCA would like to hold monthly video broadcasts, in which data is sent across the Internet to subscribing doctors' offices. These monthly events will be multicast to reduce overall network traffic.

Using this information and your knowledge of IP routing and multicasting, answer the questions in the Activities section near the end of this lesson.

# Vocabulary

Review the following terms in preparation for the certification exam.

| Term | Description |
| --- | --- |
| area | One part of an AS, areas define small zones of a large routed network. |
| AS | An Autonomous System is a management zone within a large routed network, and consists of one or more areas. |
| backbone area | Within each AS, the zone identified with the IP address 0.0.0.0. |
| BGP | Boundary routers use the Border Gateway Protocol to transmit information between autonomous systems. |
| boundary routers | Routers that transfer information between ASs. |
| broadcasts | IP packets sent to every computer on a network. |
| cryptography | The method of encrypting data, rendering it unreadable to all but the intended recipient. |
| distance vector algorithm | The mathematical function used by RIP to determine the best route on which to send an IP packet. |
| hardware routers | Hardware devices that are specifically designed for routing data and typically serve no other function on the network. |
| IGMP | The Internet Group Management Protocol is part of the TCP/IP protocol suite and provides the foundation of Windows 2000 multicasting. |
| IP packets | Data is segmented in packets before transmission on a TCP/IP network. |
| IPX | Internet Protocol Exchange is part of the Novell's proprietary IPX/SPX network protocol. |

| Term | Description |
|------|-------------|
| multicast forwarding | The ability of a Windows 2000 computer to pass multicast information from one network to another. |
| multicast heartbeat | A method used by Windows 2000 routers to verify that multicasting is working properly. |
| multicast proxy | A Windows 2000 server that acts as a multicast server on a private network by receiving multicast information from the Internet and passing it to local multicast clients. |
| multicasting | Sending a single copy of data to multiple computers simultaneously. |
| multihomed | A computer with two or more NICs installed. |
| NIC | The Network Interface Card connects a computer to the network medium. |
| OSPF | Open Shortest Path First is one of two dynamic routing protocols supported by Windows 2000. |
| querier | The computer responsible for identifying the multicast hosts on a network segment. |
| RIP | The Routing Information Protocol is one of two dynamic routing protocols supported by Windows 2000. |
| route | The path an IP packet travels from its source to destination. |
| router | A device that routes (directs) traffic across network segments. |
| routing table | The list of network segments a router uses to determine the best path on which to send an IP packet. |
| SAP | The Service Advertising Protocol is a routing protocol used with IPX. |

| Term | Description |
|------|-------------|
| software routers | Computers that also serve as routers on a network, the computer must be multihomed and must run the Windows 2000 RRAS service. |
| static table | A routing table that only changes when manually updated. |
| subnet | A single network segment. |
| TTL | The Time To Live indicates the number of routers through which a message will pass before it is stopped by a router. |
| unicast | The traditional way to send a message, unicast messages travel from a single source to a single destination. |

# In Brief

| If you want to... | Then do this... |
| --- | --- |
| Build a routed network using Windows 2000 servers | Install and configure the Routing and Remote Access Service (RRAS). |
| Configure the routing protocol on a specific NIC | Select the interface from within RRAS, and then associate the routing protocol with the interface. |
| Enhance multicasting on your Windows 2000 network | Configure Windows 2000 servers as multicast proxies and enable multicast forwarding. |
| Use Windows 2000 routers on a large network | Configure RRAS to use OSPF instead of RIP. |
| Combine hardware and software routers | Ensure that Windows 2000 supports the protocols used by the hardware routers (and vice versa). |

# Lesson 8 Activities

Complete the following activities to better prepare you for the certification exam.

1. Which Windows 2000 services and protocols must be installed on the network before you can use multicasting?

2. On which routers in the network should you implement multicast routing?

3. What can you do to increase multicasting availability?

4. How do you provide security for RRAS-based multicasting?

5. How will you configure the multicast routers that are responsible for sending the multicast data across the Internet to the doctors' offices?

6. The CEO of WCA is concerned that "all of this multicasting stuff" will just slow the network down even more. How would you respond to this concern?

7. What must you do to the Windows 2000 client computers on the network to prepare them to receive multicasting data?

8. While analyzing the network for multicasting, you look at the overall IP routing configuration. You notice that all of the routers are configured with static routing tables. Would you recommend any changes? Why?

9. Which dynamic routing protocol would you recommend?

10. What is a good reason NOT to use dynamic routing and stay with static routing on the WCA network?

# Answers to Lesson 8 Activities

1.    You need to make sure RRAS is configured properly and that the network uses TCP/IP. You must also install IGMP from within RRAS.

2.    Each router in the regional offices should be configured to route multicast traffic. In the Raleigh national center, only the internal router (the one that does not connect to any regional offices) should be configured. The remaining routers, that connect Raleigh to the other locations, cannot serve as intermediary multicast routers.

3.    There are two things you can do to increase availability: install an additional link between each of the regional offices and the national center, and install additional RRAS servers at each regional center.

4.    IGMP does not support password exchanges, so security must come in the form of IPSec machine authorizations and through Virtual Private Networking (VPN) technologies.

5.    Since the corporate information will be sent across the Internet, data encryption is important. You can configure the routers to use IPSec or you can create VPNs from the routers to the doctors' offices.

6.    Multicasting actually enhances network performance, since a single copy of data can be sent to multiple computers. By implementing a multicasting strategy, network speed is increased.

7.    No client configuration is necessary. Windows 2000 clients are configured to receive multicasting data.

8.    Because of the size of the network, WCA may want to switch over to a dynamic routing protocol. The dynamic routing protocol will reduce administrative efforts required to maintain the routers. However, if the network configuration rarely changes, the use of static routing protocols is not unreasonable.

9.    Since all routers on the network are Windows 2000 RRAS-based computers, you can use either RIP or OSPF. The size of the network does not preclude the use of either. However, RIP generates more network traffic, so perhaps OSPF would be a better choice.

10.   Static routers do not generate network traffic through routing table updates. On a network composed of several WAN links, reducing network traffic is very important.

# Lesson 8 Quiz

These questions test your knowledge of features, vocabulary, procedures, and syntax.

1.  What does it mean for a computer to be multihomed?
    A.    It is running Windows 2000.
    B.    It has RRAS installed.
    C.    It has two NICs
    D.    It can't be used as a router.

2.  What command can you use to view the routing table on a Windows 2000-based router?
    A.    **ROUTE VIEW**
    B.    **ROUTE PRINT**
    C.    **RTABLE VIEW**
    D.    **RTABLE PRINT**

3.  Which of the following must be installed on a Windows 2000 server before it can serve as a router? (Choose all that apply).
    A.    RRAS
    B.    TCP/IP
    C.    DNS
    D.    IGMP

4.  Which of the following must be installed on a Windows 2000 server before it can serve as a multicast router? (Choose all that apply).
    A.    RRAS
    B.    TCP/IP
    C.    DNS
    D.    IGMP

5.  What is the backbone area's address?
    A.    255.255.255.255
    B.    255.255.0.0
    C.    255.0.0.0
    D.    0.0.0.0

6.   Which routing protocol is best used on large (enterprise-scale) networks?
     A.   RIP v2
     B.   OSPF
     C.   Static routing tables
     D.   NBT

7.   Windows 2000 can act in what capacity on a multicasting network? (Choose all that apply).
     A.   multicast proxy
     B.   multicast router
     C.   multicast server
     D.   multicast client

8.   Which routing protocol determines the best route based only on the distance?
     A.   RIP
     B.   DNS
     C.   DHCP
     D.   OSPF

9.   How do you install RIP?
     A.   From the Add/Remove Programs Control Panel, under Add/Remove Windows Components.
     B.   From the properties page for the NIC, under Network Properties.
     C.   From the RRAS interface.
     D.   You do not need to install RIP—it is installed when Windows 2000 is installed.

10.  Why would you consider using static routing?
     A.   Dynamic routing is too complicated.
     B.   Dynamic routing uses more bandwidth.
     C.   Not all Windows 2000 servers support dynamic routing.
     D.   Static routing is cool.

# Answers to Lesson 8 Quiz

1.    Answer C is correct. A multihomed computer is one in which two or more network cards (NICs) are installed.

    Therefore, answers A, B, and D are incorrect.

2.    Answer B is correct. The **ROUTE PRINT** command displays the current entries in the routing table .

    Answers A, C, and D are incorrect. These are not valid commands.

3.    Answers A and B are correct. A Windows 2000 server must have the TCP/IP protocol and the RRAS service installed and configured before it can act as a router .

    Answer C is incorrect. DNS is not used in routing.

    Answer D is incorrect. The IGMP protocol is not a necessary part of routing.

4.    Answers A, B, and D are correct. In addition to TCP/IP and RRAS, a router that will forward multicast messages also requires the IGMP protocol.

    Answer C is incorrect. DNS is not used with multicasting servers.

5.    Answer D is correct. In multicasting, the backbone area has an address of 0.0.0.0.

    Therefore, answers A, B, and C are incorrect.

6.    Answer B is correct. OSPF is best suited for larger networks.

    Answer A is incorrect. RIP cannot handle the demands of a network larger than about 50 routers.

    Answer C is incorrect. Static routing tables are the least suitable option for large networks.

    Answer D is incorrect. NetBIOS over TCP/IP (NBT) is not a routing protocol.

7.    Answers A, B, and D are correct. Windows 2000 computers can provide multicast forwarding and proxy services, and can receive multicast data as clients.

Answer C is incorrect. A Windows 2000 server cannot be a multicast server.

8.    Answer D is correct. OSPF uses only the distance a packet must travel as the factor in determining the best route.

Answer A is incorrect. RIP uses both the distance and the bandwidth to determine the best route.

Answers B and C are incorrect. DNS and DHCP are not routing protocols.

9.    Answer C is correct. RIP is installed from within the RRAS interface.

Answer A is incorrect. Although many services and protocols are installed from the Add/Remove Programs Control Panel, RIP is not one of them.

Answer B is incorrect. Although many protocols are configured here, RIP is not.

Answer D is incorrect. The RIP files are loaded when Windows 2000 is installed, but RIP is not installed until you install it from within RRAS.

10.    Answer B is correct. Dynamic routing generates network traffic, while static routing does not.

Answers A, C, and D are all incorrect.

# Secure Data Transmission

Virtual Private Networking (VPN) provides a means of securely transmitting information across the Internet. Many corporations are using VPNs to connect both remote networks and remote users to the main corporate inter-network. While Wide Area Network (WAN) technologies are used for the same purpose, VPNs provide a means of connecting networks for far less money. No expensive leased lines or long-distance telephone charges are incurred when using a VPN, and the data travels as securely as it does across private lines.

While many people are concerned with protecting data that travels across public lines (like the Internet), the security of data within a corporate intranet is often overlooked. However, physical access to the intranet can mean the capture of sensitive data. In networks that require the highest levels of security, Windows 2000 supports Internet Protocol Security (IPSec). IPSec provides data encryption and computer authorization.

After completing this lesson, you should have a better understanding of the following topics:

*   Virtual Private Networking (VPN) and IPSec Overview

*   VPN Implementation

*   IP Security (IPSec) Implementation

*   VPN and IPSec Management

*   VPN and IPSec Business Goals

# Virtual Private Networking (VPN) and IPSec Overview

Network security is quite possibly the primary concern of every corporation with an Internet connection. Whether the data travels across the Internet from remote networks and users, or whether the data stays "in-house," you must ensure that it remains private to all but the intended recipient.

## Understanding Virtual Private Networking (VPN)

Many networks support remote users and many companies have remote locations. Connectivity between these remote locations and users and the main network is as important as connecting users within the main network. These Wide Area Networks (WANs) present a new set of security concerns and network costs.

Typical WAN connections involve the purchase or lease of a connection medium like an Integrated Services Digital Network (ISDN) or T1 line. These lines are expensive, and companies may be charged on a usage basis as well as a flat fee. The alternative, using the Public Switched Telephone System (PSTN) is less expensive but the company still incurs long-distance telephone charges.

VPNs provide a secure tunnel on the Internet through which data travels in an encrypted state. There are typically no long-distance charges, since each end of the connection establishes only a local connection to the Internet, and there are no leased lines involved (Figure 9.1).

**Figure 9.1 A VPN WAN**

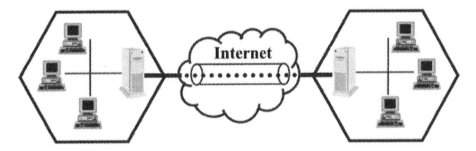

A VPN is also used to connect individual remote users to a network, in the same fashion that a dial-up server provides access. In many instances, dial-up connections are being replaced with VPN connections because of the reduced costs and lower administrative overhead (Figure 9.2).

## Figure 9.2 A VPN Remote Access Connection

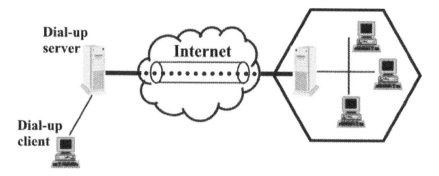

Windows 2000 VPNs support two tunneling protocols: Point-to-Point Tunneling Protocol (PPTP) and Layer 2 Tunneling Protocol (L2TP). PPTP is an industry standard tunneling protocol, ensuring compatibility with other VPN servers and clients. L2TP uses IPSec to provide additional security.

 Note: Windows 2000 is currently the only operating system that supports L2TP.

## Understanding IP Security (IPSec)

When used in conjunction with L2TP, IPSec provides additional authentication and encryption services for VPNs. But the usefulness of IPSec is not limited to VPNs. IPSec provides computer authentication and data encryption, providing additional security to private networks. The computer authentication and data encryption are transparent to network users.

Although every Windows 2000 network requires a username and password to access the network, mischievous individuals may be able to capture data traveling across the network lines, whether they are public or private. IPSec does not prevent people from capturing the data, but it renders the data unreadable to all but the intended recipient.

IPSec supports three authentication methods, as follows:

- Kerberos version 5

- Exchange of certificate authority

- Exchange of pre-configured private keys

IPSec also provides three levels of data encryption, as follows:

- Data Encryption Standard (DES)

- Triple DES (3DES)

- 40-bit DES

IPSec uses standard IP packets to transmit information; so IPSec-encrypted data is fully routable and behaves exactly as any other IP-based data.

 **Note:** Currently, Windows 2000 is the only operating system that uses IPSec. IPSec has been proposed to the Internet Engineering Task Force (IETF) as a standard, but it has yet to be approved.

# VPN Implementation

If your business network needs include the need to connect remote users or networks to your corporate intranet, consider implementing VPN. Even if the current network infrastructure includes remote access connections and WANs, switching these connections to VPNs may save the company considerable costs.

## Providing Remote Access

The Windows 2000 Routing and Remote Access Service (RRAS) provides dial-up and VPN connections for remote users of the network. A single RRAS server can support hundreds of simultaneous connections. One of the strengths of using Windows 2000 RRAS for VPN connectivity is its ease of administration. Configuring a VPN connection is no more difficult than configuring a dial-up connection (Figure 9.3).

## Figure 9.3 Remote Access Through a VPN

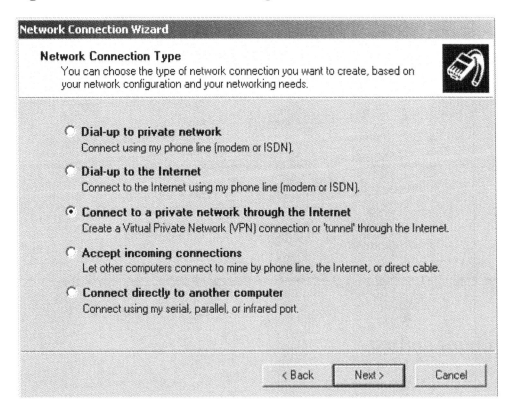

When designing a remote access VPN network plan, consider the maximum number of simultaneous connections that you need to support, the user accounts that will be granted remote access, and any policy restrictions you wish to implement.

## Providing WAN Connectivity

RRAS is also used to connect two networks with a VPN. An RRAS server acts as an IP router, repackaging the IP packets and sending them across the VPN to a receiving RRAS server at the other end of the link (Figure 9.4).

## Figure 9.4 Using VPN for a WAN

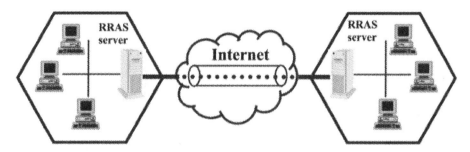

## Using a Firewall with a VPN

The purpose of establishing a VPN is to enable secure communication across the Internet. Any time you add a connection to the Internet, you increase the possibility of unauthorized access to your intranet. While firewalls provide security, the placement of the VPN server with respect to the firewall is crucial. You can place the VPN outside the firewall (between the firewall and the Internet) or inside the firewall (as part of the intranet).

### External VPN Server

Placing the VPN server outside the firewall means that the VPN server is more susceptible to attack from outside sources (Figure 9.5). However, there are several benefits to placing the VPN server externally.

## Figure 9.5 External VPN Server

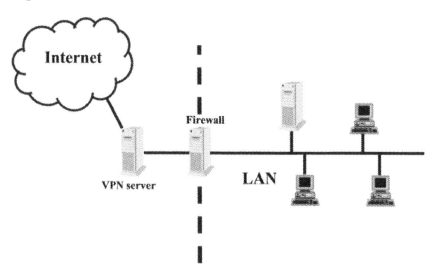

As long as the VPN server does not contain any network information, it is of little consequence if someone gains unauthorized access to the server. Furthermore, by placing the VPN server outside the firewall, the firewall can still block most of the incoming IP data.

To maximize security when placing a VPN externally, follow these guidelines:

*   Make the VPN server a member server (not a domain controller) so that no Active Directory information is stored on it

*   Encrypt all data between the VPN and the internal RRAS server

*   Create an IPSec tunnel between the RRAS server and the VPN server, and configure the firewall to allow communication through this tunnel; this reduces the number of firewall filters needed and reduces administration on the firewall

### *Internal VPN Server*

Placing the VPN server internally (behind the firewall) protects the VPN server from external attacks (Figure 9.6).

## Figure 9.6 Internal VPN Server

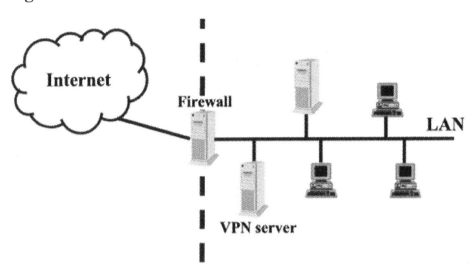

Although this configuration seems more secure (and it may be), you must enable all PPTP-and L2TP-based traffic to pass through the firewall (for the valid range of IP addresses). By placing the VPN internally, you reduce the effectiveness of the firewall.

## Using a VPN with a Proxy Server

Proxy servers and Network Address Translation (NAT) servers provide connectivity to the Internet. By using a proxy server and a single connection to the Internet, all clients on the network can share Internet access. The proxy server or NAT server translates the private IP addresses used on the intranet to public IP addresses used on the Internet.

When you place a VPN server behind a proxy server or NAT server, the encrypted IP packets must first pass through this server. NAT servers can accept IP packets that are encrypted with either of the tunneling protocols, but some applications require an indication of the IP address of the originating computer. When using PPTP, NAT servers can add this information to the header. When using L2TP, the IP header is encrypted, and so these applications will not work properly.

Tip: If certain applications are not functioning properly over an L2TP-based VPN with a NAT server, try changing the tunneling protocol to PPTP.

## Using Authentication Protocols

Windows 2000 VPN servers support several authentication protocols. When a user initiates a VPN connection, the user needs to be authenticated by the VPN server. The authentication protocol you use will depend on the level of security and the variety of clients you need to support. Table 9.1 outlines the authentication protocols supported by Windows 2000 VPNs and the clients supported by each protocol.

### Table 9.1 Authentication Protocols

| Protocol | Supported Clients |
|---|---|
| MS-CHAP | Windows 95, Windows 98, Windows NT 4.0, and Windows 2000. |
| MS-CHAP v2 | Windows 2000 only. |
| EAP-TLS | Clients with smart card support. Can only be used when the VPN server is a member of a Windows 2000 domain. |
| CHAP | Microsoft and many non-Microsoft operating systems. |
| SPAP | Shiva LAN Rover clients only. |
| PAP | Many clients. The only authentication protocol that does not send encrypted authentication information. Use this only as a last resort for compatibility. |

# Using Data Encryption

Once a VPN connection is established, Windows 2000 VPNs support two types of data encryption, Microsoft Point-to-Point Encryption (MPPE) and IPSec.

MPPE uses user-based authentication, which is less secure than computer-based authentication, to encrypt data on PPTP connections. Because it does not use computer-based authentication, the presence of a certificate server is not needed. MPPE works with MS-CHAP, MS-CHAP v2, and EAP-TLS authentication methods.

L2TP connections use IPSec to fulfill data encryption needs.

# Optimizing the VPN Server

On networks where a large number of simultaneous VPN connections are likely, you need to optimize the VPN servers. There are many things you can do to optimize VPNs.

## Dedicating and Upgrading the Server

The first thing to do to optimize VPN connections is to remove all networking services from the VPN server except for those needed to provide the VPN connection. If your VPN server also acts as a Domain Name System (DNS) server, domain controller, and Dynamic Host Configuration Protocol (DHCP) server, the processing capabilities and memory capacity are not optimized for VPNs. Security concerns also dictate removing these services from the VPN server.

If you are using a dedicated VPN server and it is still not meeting network expectations, upgrading the processor and Random Access Memory (RAM) in the server will increase performance.

## Adding VPN Servers

You can add VPN servers to a network to increase the number of connections supported. The VPN server can be added as part of a Windows server cluster. In a server cluster, each VPN server acts as part of a whole system, with each member sharing network demands and providing fault tolerance in case one or more servers in the cluster fail.

You can also add VPN servers with Domain Name System (DNS) round-robin entries. The DNS service uses round-robin entries to pass network demands to a series of servers, alternating the demands according to the number of entries in the list. For example, if a request is made for the server vpn.lightpointlearning.net, the DNS server may have 6 servers in its round-robin list that correspond to that hostname. The IP address of the first server on the list is returned to the requesting client, and then that server is placed at the bottom of the list. The next request for the same hostname will receive the IP address of the second server, and so on (Figure 9.7).

## Figure 9.7 DNS Round Robin

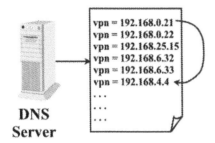

vpn = 192.168.0.21
vpn = 192.168.0.22
vpn = 192.168.25.15
vpn = 192.168.6.32
vpn = 192.168.6.33
vpn = 192.168.4.4
. . .
. . .
. . .

**DNS Server**

### *Integrating Remote Authentication Dial-in User Service  (RADIUS)*

The RADIUS service provides centralized administration of remote access user accounts. Since VPN connections are treated the same as dial-up connections, you can increase overall VPN functionality by placing the authentication demands on the RADIUS server, freeing up the VPN servers to handle networking and routing of information. Integrating VPNs with RADIUS also increases overall network security.

## Integrating VPN with Other Services

Windows 2000 VPN service is designed to take advantage of several other Windows 2000 networking services. Of course, VPN is part of RRAS, and RRAS is integrated with many of these services, as follows:

**DHCP**—VPN servers use DHCP to provide temporary IP addresses and other TCP/IP-related information to VPN clients. When the VPN first initializes, it reserves 11 IP addresses from the DHCP server. If more IP addresses are needed later, the VPN server reserves them in blocks of 10 addresses.

**WINS and DNS**—VPN clients, upon receiving an IP address, automatically update the Windows Internet Naming Service (WINS) and DNS servers on the network. The DNS servers must support dynamic DNS.

**RADIUS**—A VPN server can act as a RADIUS client, passing all user authentication requirements to the RADIUS server.

**Active Directory**—A VPN server will use remote access policies stored in the Active Directory to restrict remote connections.

# IP Security (IPSec) Implementation

Before you use IPSec on a network, you need to consider the expectations and needs of the business. Implementing IPSec is not difficult, but it can be time-consuming and adds a level of complexity to the network. If your company does not need to provide extra data protection for the internal network, only implement IPSec on the VPN connections. Likewise, if network security is a top concern, you need to implement IPSec network-wide, and decide on the level of security.

## Enabling IPSec

When implementing and enabling IPSec on the network, you decide the level of security and the authentication method you want to use.

### IPSec Security Policies

The default installation of Windows 2000 includes three IPSec policies. These policies are useful for most IPSec implementations, but can be modified if needed. Table 9.2 describes the three default policies.

## Table 9.2 IPSec Security Policies

| IPSec Security Policy | Description |
| --- | --- |
| Client (Respond Only) | The client will send requests to transmit in an unsecured form, but will negotiate a security method with a requesting server. Clients using this policy cannot communicate with secure servers. |
| Server (Request Security) | Servers with this policy accept unsecured requests from clients, but will negotiate a secure form of communication with the client. If, after 40 seconds, the negotiation fails, data is sent unsecured. |
| Secure Server (Require Security) | A server with this policy rejects all unsecured requests, and data sent from the server is always secured with IPSec. |

## *IPSec Authentication Methods*

IPSec supports three computer authentication methods. Each of these methods transparently authenticates the sending and receiving computers, ensuring proper delivery of data. The three methods are as follows:

**Kerberos v5**—Kerberos v5 is a standard authentication method supported by Windows 2000 and UNIX clients.

 **Note:** Windows 2000 Active Directory uses Kerberos v5 for computer authentication in the domain.

**Certificate Authority (CA)**—CAs provide X.509 certificates that are used for authentication on the Internet and intranets. Any client that supports X.509-compatible certificates will work with the IPSec implementation.

 **Note:** To use Certificate Authority authentication, your Windows 2000 network must have at least one trusted CA.

**Text-based key**—Used to authenticate clients that do not support Kerberos or X.509, text-based keys are not as secure and do not provide data encryption.

## Configuring and Customizing IPSec

IPSec can be configured in two modes—transport mode and tunnel mode. Transport mode is useful when establishing peer-to-peer communications on a Local Area Network (LAN). The default mode with IPSec, transport mode provides a secure connection between two clients running Windows 2000 (Figure 9.8).

## Figure 9.8 IPSec Transport Mode

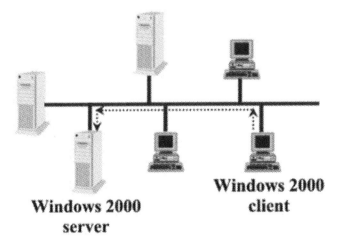

**Windows 2000 server**

**Windows 2000 client**

In tunnel mode, IPSec works with L2TP to create a secure tunnel across the Internet, useful for linking two networks. You establish the tunnel between two RRAS servers (Figure 9.9).

## Figure 9.9 IPSec Tunnel Mode

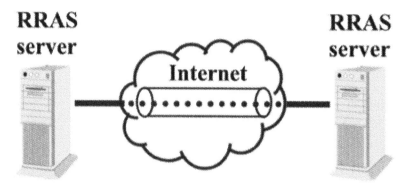

When you configure tunnel mode, you provide IPSec on each RRAS server with the hostname or IP address of the Windows 2000 RRAS server at the other end of the tunnel. Although an RRAS server may support several different tunnels, each IPSec tunnel requires a separate IPSec policy.

### Creating Security Policies

You will often find that one of the three default IPSec policies will meet your networking needs. However, if they do not, you can create your own custom IPSec policies.

An IPSec policy contains rules, and each rule contains a list of filters (Figure 9.10). The rules dictate how communication is established. The filters within a rule are associated with actions. When the criteria in a filter are matched, the associated action is performed.

## Figure 9.10 IPSec Policies, Rules, and Filters

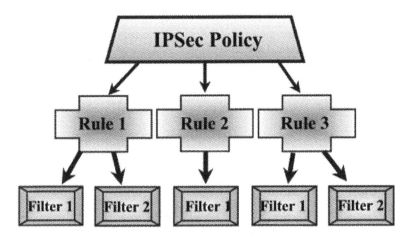

Each policy rule contains the following information:

- IP filter list that identifies the IP addresses of hosts that use this policy

- Negotiation policy that governs the security negotiation

- Authentication method

- Tunnel settings

- Connection types that use this rule

A single IPSec policy may apply to many computers on the network. Using the filters, you can specify how certain computers will use the policy. Filters are used to restrict access based on the following criteria:

- IP address (individual or a range of addresses)

- TCP or UDP port number

- The authentication method used

- IPSec negotiation method

### *Choosing an Encryption Method*

IPSec encrypts both data and the authentication information. When two computers are authenticated using IPSec, the information may be encrypted with one of the following two methods:

**Secure Hash Algorithm (SHA)**—A very high-security method, SHA uses a 160-bit security key.

**Message Digest 5 (MD5)**—Most commonly used in commercial applications. MD5 provides strong security (128-bit) with less overhead than SHA.

IPSec supports three levels of the Data Encryption Standard (DES), as follows:

**56-bit DES**—Relatively low security, but suitable for export outside North America.

**40-bit DES**—Less secure than 56-bit DES, used for export to France.

**3DES (Triple DES)**—This is by far the most secure data encryption, but uses two-and-a-half times more processing time than 56-bit DES. 3DES uses three **128-bit keys to encrypt data.**

## Optimizing IPSec

You optimize IPSec by reducing the overhead generated by IPSec as much as possible. If a network does not require the strongest level of encryption, especially for internal data, reduce the level of data encryption. Furthermore, if only some of the network data is highly sensitive, consider implementing IPSec only on those computers that need access to the sensitive information. Since all other computers will not need access, they do not need to run IPSec. Finally, consider reducing the number of filters used with IPSec.

Tip: IPSec filters support the use of wildcards, which helps in reducing the number of filters needed.

# VPN and IPSec Management

When managing network security over VPNs, you should monitor the key components in the network plan and anticipate potential problems and needs before they arise. By monitoring the RRAS servers and connections, you can detect problems before they cause a loss in productivity and can foresee the need for implementation changes.

## Detecting Errors

If an RRAS server providing VPN support fails, you may not know about the failure immediately if your network has more than one VPN server. You should implement administrative alerts on all VPN servers so that you will be notified immediately of server failure.

Additionally, you should monitor the number of connections established at each VPN server. Each server has a maximum number of connections, and if any one server is reaching that maximum, you need to increase the number of allowed connections before users are denied access.

### Detecting Unauthorized Accesses

If you monitor RRAS servers for failed logon attempts, you may discover a series of several failures in a row. These failures may indicate someone trying to gain unauthorized access to your network, or may be an indication of a remote user in need of technical support.

### IPSec Errors

With IPSec, you need to monitor the IPSec servers for failures, and should also monitor the number of failed security associations. A failed security association may indicate a user trying to access resources over an IPSec connection. This user may be unauthorized, or you may have incorrectly configured a filter to exclude the user or computer.

## Planning to Meet VPN Demands

The VPN needs of the company are dictated by the number of remote users or remote networks that need connectivity to the main network. As you monitor the RRAS servers for errors, pay close attention to the number of simultaneous connections. As this number increases, the capacity of the server to handle the connections will decrease.

### VPN Data Rates

The data rate for all VPN connections should never drop below the maximum rate handled by the connecting computer's modem. That is, the slowest link in the VPN connection should always be the modem, not the VPN server. If users are connecting to your VPN server using 56-Kbps (Kilobits per second) modems, monitor the connections to ensure that data is flowing at an appropriate rate.

 **Note:** Due to limitations in the telephone lines, 56-Kbps modems never achieve data rates of 56 Kbps. You can only use the speed of the modem as a general guideline for the connection speed users can achieve.

If VPN connections are slower than what the modems can handle, the VPN server needs to be upgraded, or you need to add additional servers to handle the demands.

## Testing the VPN Service and IPSec

Since IPSec and VPN connections, above all else, exist to provide secure means of connecting to a network, when testing either service, you test its security. To test the security offered by a VPN service, test the following:

**Unauthorized access**—Attempt to gain unauthorized access. Make sure the attempts fail and are recorded in a log file. Also make sure that, after a certain number of failures, an administrative alert is generated.

**Encryption**—Capture data sent through the VPN to ensure it is encrypted and unreadable.

**Restricted access**—Connect to the VPN, and then attempt to reach resources beyond the VPN. Ensure that access only exists for the VPN server or specific resources within the intranet.

Similar tests are appropriate for testing IPSec. Ensure that unauthorized accounts are rejected and that the failures are logged. Also verify that data is encrypted, and that access to non-IPSec based computers is restricted.

# VPN and IPSec Business Goals

As with other Windows 2000 services and protocols, you should consider the use of Virtual Private Networking and IPSec from a business perspective. The four business goals (functionality, security, availability, and performance) are analyzed below, and you are presented with a business scenario using VPNs and IPSec.

## Meeting Business Needs

Using VPNs with Windows 2000, you can meet the four business goals as follows:

**Functionality**—VPNs provide a secure and inexpensive means of connecting networks and remote users across the Internet. The Windows 2000 implementation of VPN services provides additional functionality by supporting a variety of tunneling protocols and support for numerous connection media (PSTN, ISDN, and Asymmetric Digital Subscriber Line (ADSL)).

**Security**—For increased security support, Windows 2000 VPN service supports numerous authentication protocols and data encryption methods.

**Availability**—Availability of Windows 2000 VPN servers is enhanced by adding additional servers. RRAS supports redundant servers sharing the same authentication methods, protocols, and remote access policy.

**Performance**—Like availability, performance with Windows 2000 VPN servers is enhanced by adding additional VPN servers sharing the same remote access policies and connection settings.

IPSec meets the four business goals as follows:

**Functionality**—IPSec provides data encryption and computer authentication over VPN connections and over standard intranet connections. IPSec meets functionality designs by supporting a wide variety of authentication methods, certificate authorities, and data encryption methods. IPSec supports connections from many different clients.

**Security**—The purpose of IPSec is to provide secure data transmissions on the network. To this end, IPSec provides computer authentication and data encryption up to 3DES, which uses three 128-bit encryption keys.

**Availability and Performance**—You can increase the availability and performance of IPSec by adding additional domain controllers (which provide the Kerberos v5 authentication), certificate authorities (for X.509 certificates), and use Windows Clustering for authentication servers.

## Business Scenario

Network security has become more of an issue on the national network supporting Woody's Chiropractic Association (WCA). Furthermore, the expense and unreliable nature of the WAN connections has lead Woody (the CEO) to consider alternative methods for connecting the six regional offices to the national center in Raleigh.

Currently, the regional centers are connected to the Raleigh center by ISDN lines (Figure 9.11). Through several network measures already taken, the amount of traffic across these lines has been reduced. Furthermore, WCA is facing financial setbacks and needs to reduce overall network costs. However, they absolutely do not want to reduce network security. The information passing between offices typically contains confidential patient medical information.

## Figure 9.11 WCA Network Structure

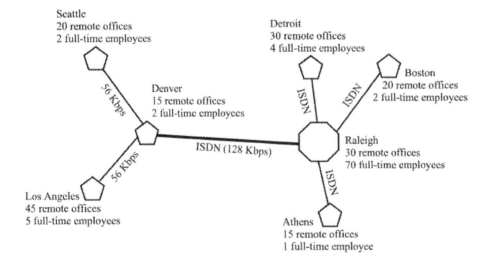

From previous work with WCA, you have installed Windows 2000 servers at each regional office and in the national center. These servers are currently acting as routers between networks, and are also providing dial-up access to the doctors' offices (Figure 9.12).

WCA wants to provide access to the network for those doctors who travel extensively. The RRAS servers in Raleigh must be enabled to support VPN connections to the network. WCA is concerned about unauthorized access to the network from the Internet, and wants you to "use a firewall."

## Figure 9.12 Typical Regional Office Network

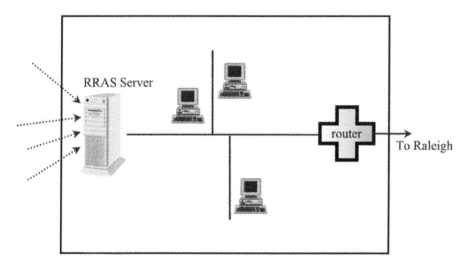

The doctors use a wide variety of client computers. WCA has always held the belief that the doctors should be able to use any computer to connect to the WCA network, and they do not want that to change. Some of the doctors still need access to the proprietary ChiroLink software, although most are now using the corporate intranet Web page.

WCA also believes that the information traveling within each regional center (and the national center) should be encrypted. The medical information should be protected internally as well as when passing between centers.

Using this information and your knowledge of data security, answer the questions in the Activities section near the end of this lesson.

# Vocabulary

Review the following terms in preparation for the certification exam.

| Term | Description |
|---|---|
| 3DES | Triple Data Encryption Standard uses three 128-bit keys for data encryption and is the highest level of encryption supported by Windows 2000. |
| 40-bit DES | A Data Encryption Standard that uses one 40-bit encryption key. |
| 56-bit DES | A Data Encryption standard that uses a single 56-bit key. |
| authentication protocol | A protocol used to authenticate users connecting through a VPN. |
| CA | A Certificate Authority provides X.509 certificates for IPSec authorization. |
| data encryption | Applying a mathematical formula to data, rendering it unreadable by anyone other than the intended recipient. |
| DHCP | The Dynamic Host Configuration Protocol automatically assigns TCP/IP configuration information to clients. |
| DNS | The Domain Name System resolves hostnames to IP addresses. |
| filter | A filter is used to block certain network traffic based on IP-related information. |
| firewall | A firewall connects an intranet to the Internet, and provides security by preventing certain traffic from flowing in either direction. |
| intranet | An internal network of computers. |

| Term | Description |
|------|-------------|
| IPSec | Internet Protocol Security provides data encryption and computer authentication for VPNs and intranets. |
| IPSec policies | IPSec policies define how a computer uses IPSec. There are three default IPSec policies in Windows 2000. |
| ISDN | The Integrated Services Digital Network defines a method of transmitting voice and data over digital telephone lines. |
| Kerberos | An authentication method used by Windows 2000 Active Directory and IPSec. |
| L2TP | Layer 2 Tunneling Protocol is one of two tunneling protocols used for VPNs in Windows 2000. Only Windows 2000 computers support L2TP. |
| MD5 | Message Digest 5 provides 128-bit data encryption. |
| MPPE | Microsoft Point-to-Point Encryption provides user-based authentication for PPTP connections. |
| NAT | Net Address Translators, like proxy servers, allow multiple computers to share a single Internet connection. |
| PPTP | Point-to-Point Tunneling Protocol is one of two tunneling protocols used by Windows 2000 VPNs. |
| proxy server | A proxy server allows multiple computers to share a single Internet connection. |
| PSTN | The Public Switched Telephone System is the system of standard telephone lines used with a modem to carry data. |
| RADIUS | Remote Authentication Dial-In User Service centralizes remote user authentication and removes this work from the RRAS server. |
| RAM | Random Access Memory is the memory in a computer that programs use to run. |

| Term | Description |
|---|---|
| round-robin DNS | A configuration of Windows 2000 DNS that allows multiple computers with different IP addresses to share a single common hostname. |
| server cluster | Connecting several servers so that they act as a single logical server. |
| SHA | The Secure Hash Algorithm provides 160-bit data encryption for IPSec. |
| transport mode | One of two IPSec modes, transport mode is useful on intranets. |
| tunnel mode | One of two IPSec modes, tunnel mode uses L2TP to create a tunnel for VPNs. |
| VPN | A Virtual Private Network allows the sharing of private information across public networks. |
| WAN | A Wide Area Network consists of two or more Local Area Networks connected across a long distance by leased lines or VPNs. |
| WINS | The Windows Internet Naming Service resolves NetBIOS names to IP addresses. |

# In Brief

| If you want to... | Then do this... |
| --- | --- |
| Provide an inexpensive and secure method of connecting remote users to your network | Install and configure RRAS servers, implement VPN connections, and then configure the client computers to use the VPNs. |
| Connect two networks without the expense of a leased line | Configure RRAS servers at each network to use a VPN connection between them. |
| Increase VPN security | Use the highest level of user authentication supported by the VPN clients and require the highest level of data encryption supported by the clients. |
| Encrypt data on your internal network | Implement an IPSec strategy. |
| Use the highest level of IPSec security | Implement 3DES data encryption, which uses three 128-bit encryption keys. |
| Use IPSec on an international network | Use 56-bit DES, which provides the highest level of security that can be legally exported outside North America. |

# Lesson 9 Activities

Complete the following activities to better prepare you for the certification exam.

1.    To meet the needs of WCA, you suggest removing all ISDN connections between the regional offices and Raleigh and implementing VPNs. The regional offices will establish the VPN by connecting to local Internet Service Providers (ISPs) through a single dial-up connection, and then connecting to the Raleigh servers through the VPN tunnel. What immediate effects will this have on overall network performance?

2.    More specifically, you have decided to use L2TP with IPSec for each VPN connection between the regional offices and Raleigh. Will this work?

3.    What added benefit do you gain by using L2TP with IPSec. Think about other network requirements.

4.    In Raleigh, you add a firewall and place the VPN server outside the firewall. How does this affect network security?

5.    The WCA staff does not like the idea of placing any computer outside the firewall, and asks you to place the VPN behind the firewall. Explain what affect this will have on network security.

6.    After implementing the VPN using L2TP and IPSec, those doctors who still use ChiroLink are complaining about dropped connections and "weird errors" when using the program. What do you think is happening, and what do you recommend?

7.    WCA likes the money they are saving by not leasing ISDN lines from the telephone company, but the decrease in network performance has upset many of the doctors. What do you recommend as a possible solution?

8. After adding an additional Windows 2000 RRAS server to act as a VPN server between Raleigh and Denver, you monitor network and server performance. It appears as though network performance did not increase as expected. Closer evaluation indicates that for the pair of RRAS servers in Denver and in Raleigh, one server is handling 80% of the VPN connections, while the other is handling only about 20%. What can you do about this?

9. Given WCA's cost and security issues, what level of data encryption will you recommend to use with IPSec?

10. Encryption of IPSec authentication information is necessary on the network as well as encryption of data. Given the security needs and the bandwidth of VPN connections, how will you encrypt the IPSec authentication information?

# Answers to Lesson 9 Activities

1.  Since the connections were using 128 Kbps ISDN connections previously, users will notice a sharp decrease in overall network performance. You must clearly explain this to the WCA staff before implementation.

2.  This proposal should work, since every VPN server on the network is running Windows 2000.

3.  By implementing IPSec on the VPN connections, you have established a system for encrypting the data within the network, as well. IPSec can be used to encrypt all data on the network.

4.  By placing the VPN server outside the firewall, you make it more susceptible to hackers. However, if you do not store any information on the VPN server, then a successful hacker will not be able to gain any information.

5.  By placing the VPN behind the firewall, you protect it from hackers. However, you must loosen restrictions provided by the firewall to enable legitimate VPN connections. Although this can be done relatively safely, it may be a less secure configuration overall.

6.  Some applications do not work well with L2TP, since the IP address header information is encrypted. ChiroLink is probably one such application. Unless WCA wants to finally stop using the proprietary software, you can change the VPNs to use PPTP. PPTP does not encrypt the IP header information.

7.  You can increase the availability and performance of the VPN servers by adding additional servers for each connection.

8.  You should implement DNS round-robin entries for the VPN servers, so that the network load is more equally balanced. Alternately, you can combine the two VPN servers into a server cluster. However, Windows Clustering requires Windows 2000 Advanced Server, which adds to network costs.

9.  You should consider implementing 3DES. 3DES provides the highest level of data encryption and does not cost any more than any other encryption method. 3DES does not require the addition of Certificate Authorities, and since the entire WCA network is within North America, 3DES may be legally used.

10. You have two choices for encrypting IPSec authentication information: SHA and MD5. Although SHA provides a slightly higher level of authentication encryption, MD5 produces less overhead and increases performance. Given the complaints about slow connections, increasing performance is perhaps more important than adding a small amount of extra encryption security.

# Lesson 9 Quiz

These questions test your knowledge of features, vocabulary, procedures, and syntax.

1.  Which of the following tunneling protocols supports VPN connection between a Windows 2000 server and a Windows 98 client? (Choose all that apply).
    A.   PPTP
    B.   L2TP
    C.   DHCP
    D.   IPSec

2.  Which authentication method does Active Directory use?
    A.   Text-based
    B.   Kerberos v5
    C.   3DES
    D.   L2TP

3.  Where can you place a VPN server with respect to a firewall?
    A.   Behind a firewall.
    B.   Outside the firewall.
    C.   On the same computer as a firewall.
    D.   You cannot have a firewall on the same segment as the VPN server.

4.  Which authentication protocol supported by Windows 2000 VPNs is the best choice when supporting a wide variety of clients?
    A.   MS-CHAP
    B.   PAP
    C.   SPAP
    D.   EAP-TLS

5.  The Windows 2000 VPN service integrates with which other Windows 2000 services? (Choose all that apply).
    A.   DHCP
    B.   DNS
    C.   WINS
    D.   RADIUS

6.   Which of the following is required to use X.509 authentication?
     A.   DHCP
     B.   DNS
     C.   WINS
     D.   CA

7.   Which of the following is NOT an advantage to using a VPN WAN connection instead of a leased-line WAN connection?
     A.   VPN is faster.
     B.   VPN is less expensive.
     C.   VPN is more secure.
     D.   VPN is more reliable.

8.   When using L2TP, how is data encrypted?
     A.   With IPSec
     B.   With PPTP
     C.   Using Kerberos
     D.   Using MS-CHAP

9.   Which of the following is a disadvantage to using IPSec?
     A.   Lack of security.
     B.   It does not work with L2TP.
     C.   Non-Windows 2000 computers do not support it.
     D.   It is slow.

10.  The ability of several VPN servers to share a single fully qualified domain name is called what?
     A.   Dynamic DHCP
     B.   Dynamic DNS
     C.   Round-robin DHCP
     D.   Round-robin DNS

# Answers to Lesson 9 Quiz

1.  Answer A is correct. Both Windows 2000 and Windows 98 support PPTP.

    Answer B is incorrect. L2TP only works with Windows 2000.

    Answers C and D are incorrect. DHCP and IPSec are not tunneling protocols.

2.  Answer B is correct. Active Directory uses Kerberos v 5 for user authentication in Windows 2000 domains.

    Answer A is incorrect. Text-based authentication is less secure than Kerberos, and is not used by Active Directory.

    Answers C and D are incorrect. 3DES and L2TP are not authentication protocols.

3.  Answers A, B, and C are correct. A VPN server can be placed internally or externally on the network. Although it may not be the best network solution, the Windows 2000 server that acts as a firewall can also host the VPN service.

    Answer D is incorrect.

4.  Answer B is correct. When supporting many different operating systems, you need to use an authentication method that is widely supported. PAP is the most widely supported.

    Answer A is incorrect. MS-CHAP only works with Microsoft operating systems.

    Answer C is incorrect. SPAP only works with Shiva clients.

    Answer D is incorrect. Only clients with smart cards support EAP-TLS.

5.  Answers A, B, C, and D are all correct. VPN uses DHCP to assign IP addresses to VPN clients, the clients then update both the WINS and DNS servers with the new information (if the DNS server supports dynamic updates), and the VPN server can be configured as a RADIUS client, using the RADIUS server to authenticate users.

6.  Answer D is correct. The generation of X.509 certificates happens at a Certificate Authority. You must have a CA on the network before implementing X.509 authentication.

    Answers A, B, and C are incorrect. None of these services play a role in X.509 authentication.

7.  Answer A is correct. VPNs are not faster than leased-line connections, and may be a bit slower because of the additional overhead.

    Answer B and C are incorrect. Both of these statements are good reasons to implement a VPN.

    Answer D is incorrect. VPNs tend to be more reliable, since they do not depend upon a single connection from one network to another, but rely on the infrastructure of the Internet.

8.  Answer A is correct. L2TP uses IPSec for data encryption.

    Answer B is incorrect. PPTP is a tunneling protocol that relies on other protocols for data encryption.

    Answers C and D are incorrect. Kerberos and MS-CHAP are authentication protocols, not data encryption protocols.

9.  Answer C is correct. Windows 2000 is currently the only Microsoft Operating System (OS) which supports IPSec.

    Answers A, B, and D are incorrect. IPSec is very secure, works with L2TP, and is not slow.

10. Answer D is correct. Using round-robin DNS, a DNS server will send each network message to one of several computers all sharing the same hostname.

    Answers A and C are incorrect. These are fictitious terms.

    Answer B is incorrect. Dynamic DNS is the ability of DHCP servers and clients to update Windows 2000 DNS servers.

# Internet Connectivity

Most companies are connected to the Internet. A connection to the Internet provides employees with access to global resources, and provides the public with access to a company Web site. An Internet connection also serves as a means for establishing a Virtual Private Network (VPN) between two intranets.

To connect directly to the Internet, a computer must have a valid public IP address. These addresses are not easily obtained (due to a shortage) and are expensive. In all but the smallest companies and organizations, it is not reasonable to provide a direct Internet connection for each computer. Instead, these computers must share an Internet connection.

Windows 2000 provides two ways to share Internet connectivity. The first,  included with every copy of Windows 2000, is called Connection Sharing. The second, Microsoft Proxy Server, is an add-on that runs on Windows NT 4.0 and Windows 2000 servers.

After completing this lesson, you should have a better understanding of the following topics:

- Internet Connection Sharing (ICS) and Proxy Servers Overview

- Internet Connection Sharing (ICS) Implementation

- Proxy Server Implementation

- Internet Connection Management

- Internet Connectivity Business Goals

# ICS and Proxy Server Overview

When you build a Transmission Control Protocol/Internet Protocol (TCP/IP)-based network, you typically use private IP addresses. Private IP addresses are those addresses reserved for use on intranets and cannot be used for hosts on the Internet. Private IP addresses are free, and—unlike public IP addresses—you do not need to register them.

When a network that uses private IP addresses is connected to the Internet, at least one computer must have two interfaces—one that connects to the intranet, using a private IP address, and one that connects to the Internet using a public IP address. One of these interfaces is a Network Interface Card (NIC). The other establishes the connection to the Internet, and may be a modem, an Integrated Services Digital network (ISDN) adapter, or another NIC that connects to an external device (Figure 10.1).

### Figure 10.1 Computer With Two Interfaces

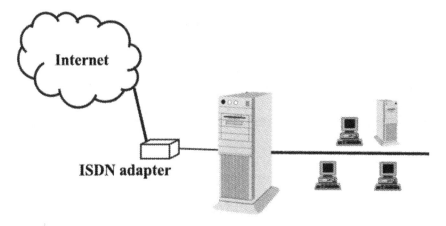

You run software on this computer that allows it to share its Internet connection with the rest of the computers on the intranet. The software is either the ICS service or Microsoft Proxy Server.

**Note:** When capitalized, Proxy Server refers specifically to the Microsoft product. Not capitalized, proxy server refers to the general technology. There are many different proxy server products on the market.

## Understanding Connection Sharing

The ICS server receives IP data packets from computers on the intranet. If these packets are intended for a computer on the Internet, the ICS server converts the private IP address to its own public IP address, and then sends the packet on to its destination.

**Tip:** ICS is the Windows 2000 implementation of a standard called Network Address Translator (NAT). NAT is defined in the Request For Comments (RFC) 1631.

For every address translation it performs, the ICS server records the initiating computer's private IP address. When the requested data from the Internet arrives, the ICS server repackages the data with the proper private IP address (Figure 10.2).

## Figure 10.2 ICS Server

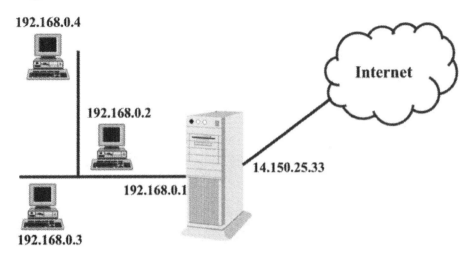

**Note:** The entire ICS process is transparent to both the internal computer and the Internet host. Only the ICS server knows that address translation is occurring.

ICS provides additional services in Windows 2000. Beyond performing address translations, ICS provides automatic TCP/IP configuration and name resolution services. On larger networks, the Dynamic Host Configuration Protocol (DHCP) service provides automatic TCP/IP configuration and the Domain Name System (DNS) and Windows Internet Naming Service (WINS) provide name resolution. On smaller networks, where the costs of installing and implementing DHCP, DNS, and WINS are prohibitive, ICS provides an inexpensive and easily configured solution.

## Understanding Microsoft Proxy Server

Proxy Server is a program that provides fundamentally the same service as Connection Sharing. A proxy server shares its Internet connection with the other computers on the intranet. However, Proxy

Server is a much more powerful program than Connection Sharing. Benefits of Proxy Server include the following:

**Added security**—You can configure Proxy Server to block IP traffic in either direction, based on the source or intended destination of the data.

**Enhanced caching**—Proxy Server provides extensive caching of File Transfer Protocol (FTP) and Web requests. When a computer requests a file or Web page that has been recently retrieved from the Internet, the proxy server can serve the file without going to the Internet a second time.

**Array support**—As a network grows, multiple servers can be combined in a Proxy Server array, each server sharing the network load.

# ICS Implementation

If you need to provide shared Internet connectivity for a network, you should consider the size of the network and the security needs of the company. When creating a shared connection, you have three choices. You can purchase and install Proxy Server, you can load and configure Connection Sharing, or you can install Shared Access. Shared Access is similar to Connection Sharing, but contains fewer features.

 Note: Shared Access does not provide Network Basic Input/Output System (NetBIOS) name resolution (the WINS service) and does not support the use of multiple public Internet connections.

# Using Shared Access

For the smallest networks, Shared Access provides a shared Internet connection. It has fewer features than Connection Sharing, and configuration is less flexible. As with other shared Internet connection methods, the computer on which you install Shared Access must have two interfaces—one to the private network, and one to the Internet. The connection to the Internet is usually a dial-up connection using a Public Switched Telephone Network (PSTN) or Integrated Services Digital Network (ISDN) modem.

## Enabling Shared Access

To use Shared Access on a dial-up interface, follow these steps:

1. From the desktop of a Windows 2000 Professional computer, right-click **My Network Places**, and then choose **Properties**.

2. From **Network and Dial-up Connections**, right-click the icon that represents your dial-up connection, and then choose **Properties** (Figure 10.3).

## Figure 10.3 Dial-up Properties

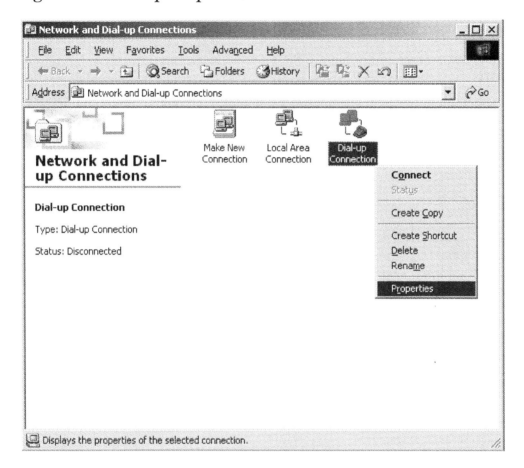

3.  From Dial-up Connection Properties, choose the Sharing property page.

4.  Choose **Enable Internet Connection Sharing for this connection**, and then select **Enable on-demand dialing** (Figure 10.4).

## Figure 10.4 Enable Shared Access

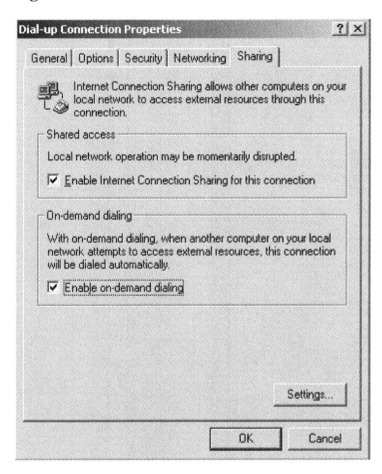

5. Click OK to save your changes.

6. A dialog box displays, providing information about enabling shared access. Choose **Yes** to confirm the installation.

The following changes are made to your Shared Access computer:

- The IP address of the (LAN) interface is changed to 192.168.0.1

- The subnet mask is changed to 255.255.255.0

- A DHCP-like service is started

You must configure all other computers on the Local Area Network (LAN) to receive their TCP/IP information automatically. When you do so, they will receive configuration information from the Shared Access computer.

If you enable ICS on a NIC (rather than a dial-up modem connection), you cannot select **Enable on-demand dialing** (Figure 10.5). Otherwise, configuration is the same.

## Figure 10.5 ICS on a NIC

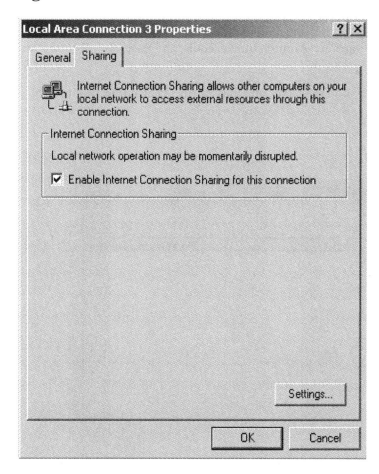

## Installing Connection Sharing

You install Connection Sharing, the Windows 2000 implementation of NAT, from the Routing and Remote Access (RRAS) console. You first install the NAT protocol, then assign NAT to an interface (the Internet connection), and then configure the interface properties.

## Installing NAT

To load NAT (Connection Sharing), follow these steps:

1.  From the **Start** menu, choose **Programs**, **Administrative Tools**, and then select **Routing and Remote Access**.

2.  From the **Tree** pane of **RRAS**, expand the server, and then expand **IP Routing** (Figure 10.6).

# Figure 10.6 RRAS Console

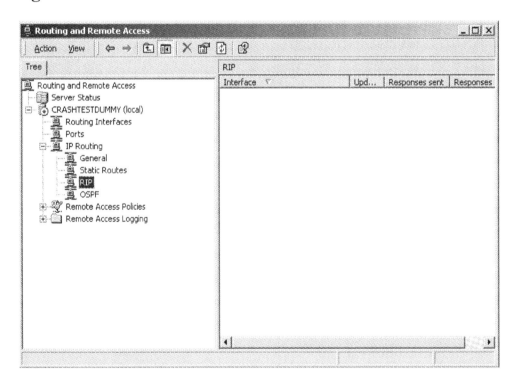

**Tip:** If the RRAS interface is not yet configured, you must run the RRAS Configuration Wizard. For detailed instructions on the initial configuration of RRAS, refer to the lesson in this book on Demand-Dial Routing and the Windows 2000 Help.

3. Right-click **General** and choose **New Routing Protocol** (Figure 10.7).

## Figure 10.7 New Routing Protocol

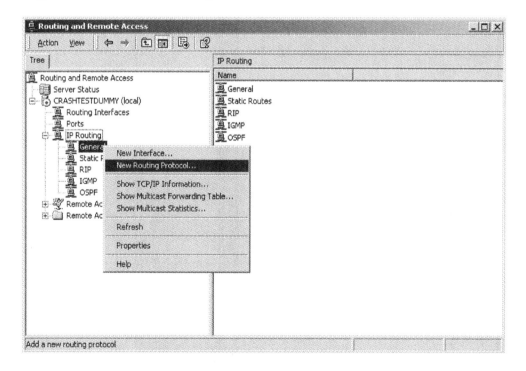

4. Choose **Network Address Translation (NAT)**, and then select **OK**.

### *Assigning NAT to an Interface*

NAT is now installed. Before configuring NAT, you need to assign NAT to the interface that connects to the Internet. To do so, follow these steps:

1. In the **Tree** pane, choose **IP Routing**.

2. In the **Details** pane, right-click **Network Address Translation (NAT)**, and then choose **New Interface** (Figure 10.8).

## Figure 10.8 New Interface

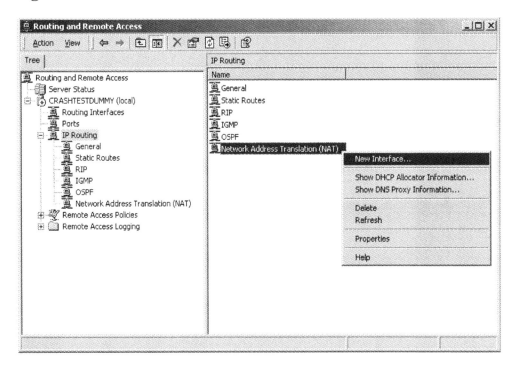

3. Choose the **ICS** interface you will use, and then select **OK**.

4. **Network Address Translation–Interface Properties** displays. Choose **OK**.

# Configuring Connection Sharing

To configure Connection Sharing, you need to configure both the NAT protocol and the specific interface used with NAT. You access both from within the RRAS console.

## *Configuring NAT Properties*

To configure NAT, follow these steps:

1. From the **Start** menu, choose **Programs**, **Administrative Tools**, and then select **Routing and Remote Access**.

2. From the **Tree** pane of **RRAS**, expand the server, and then expand **IP Routing**.

3. From the **Tree** pane, choose **Network Address Translation (NAT)**, and then select **Properties** (Figure 10.9).

## Figure 10.9 NAT Properties

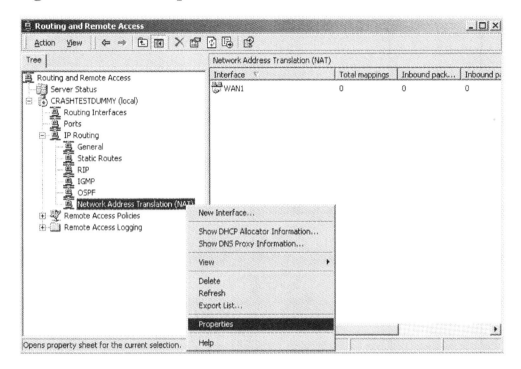

4.  From **Network Address Translation (NAT) Properties**, choose the **General** property page (Figure 10.10).

## Figure 10.10 General Property Page

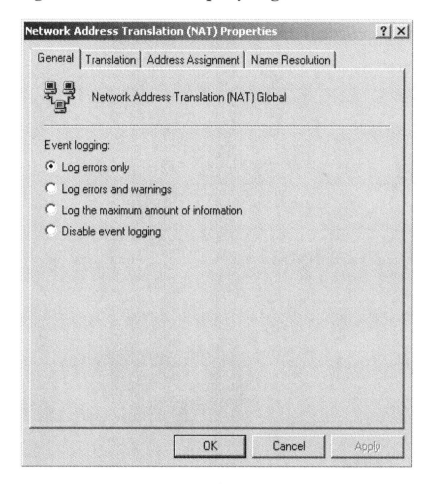

5. From the **General** property page, select the level of logging you wish to enable. Your choices are described in Table 10.1

## Table 10.1 NAT Logging Options

| NAT Logging Option | Description |
| --- | --- |
| Log errors only | Only problems with the ICS connection will be recorded. |
| Log errors and warnings | Provides more detail about the NAT connection. |
| Log the maximum amount of information | This setting is useful for troubleshooting, but requires significantly more processing time and disk space on the ICS server. |
| Disable event-logging | Does not generate any log files about the NAT connection. |

6.  From **Network Address Translation (NAT) Properties**, choose the **Translation** property page (Figure 10.11).

## Figure 10.11 Translation Property Page

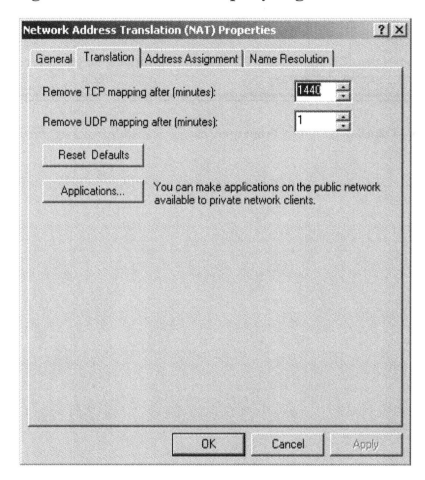

7.  From the **Translation** property page, you can set the amount of time ICS will maintain Transmission Control Protocol (TCP) and User Datagram Protocol (UDP) mappings. When internal traffic passes through the ICS server, the server keeps track of the private IP address so that it can direct the traffic from the Internet to the appropriate internal host.

**Note:** The default times that ICS will maintain TCP and UDP mappings are 1440 minutes (24 hours) and 1 minute, respectively.

8. From **Network Address Translation (NAT) Properties**, choose the **Address Assignment** page (Figure 10.12).

## Figure 10.12 Address Assignment Page

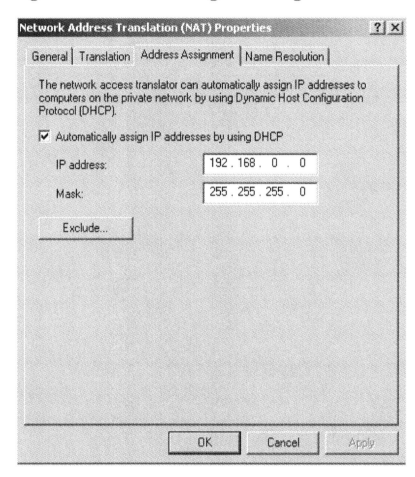

9. Choose **Automatically assign IP addresses by using DHCP**, and then enter the IP address and subnet mask to use for the first address in the scope. The combination of the address and subnet mask define the entire scope of available addresses.

**Tip:** By default, ICS does not provide automatic IP addressing. You must enable this feature.

10. From **Network Address Translation (NAT) Properties**, choose the **Name Resolution** property page (Figure 10.13).

## Figure 10.13 Name Resolution Property Page

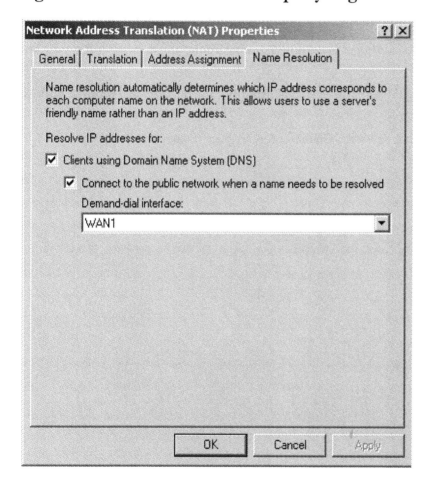

11. From **Name Resolution**, choose **Resolve IP address for** to provide DNS name resolution to internal clients. If the ICS server receives a DNS query it cannot resolve, you can enable it to connect to the Internet to resolve the request.

12. When you have configured the **NAT** protocol properly, click **OK** to save changes.

## Configuring the Interface

To configure the ICS interface, follow these steps:

1. From the **Start** menu, choose **Programs**, **Administrative Tools**, and then select **Routing and Remote Access**.

2. From the **Tree** pane, expand the server, expand **IP Routing**, and then choose **Network Address Translation (NAT)**.

3. Choose **Properties** and then select the **General** property page (Figure 10.14).

# Figure 10.14 Interface General Property Page

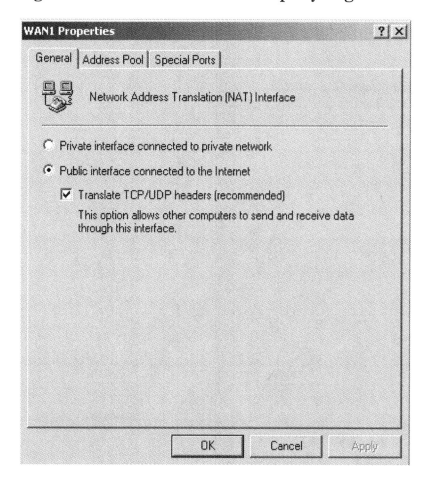

4.  Choose Public interface connected to the Internet, and then select Translate TCP/UPD headers (recommended).

5.  Choose the **Address Pool** property page (Figure 10.15) to configure the range of assigned public addresses.

## Figure 10.15 Address Pool Property Page

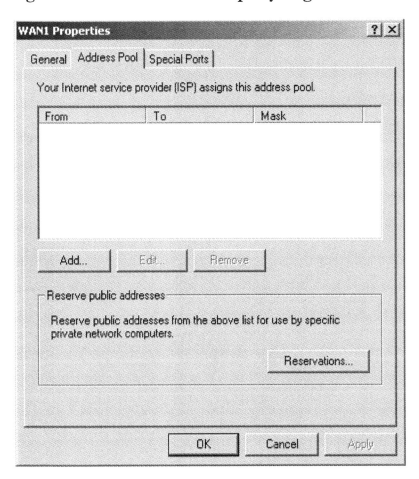

6.   Choose the **Special Ports** property page (Figure 10.16) to select a TCP/IP or UDP port.

## Figure 10.16 Special Ports Property Page

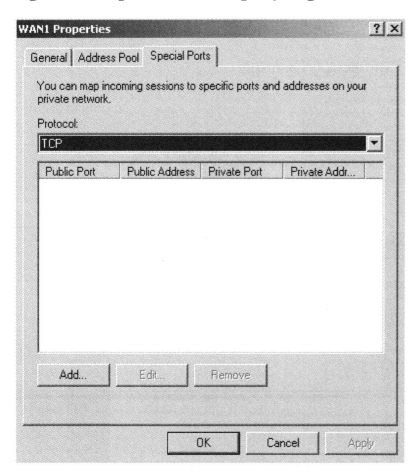

7.  Click **OK**.

### *Restricting Inbound Connections*

Using the Special Ports property page within the Interface Properties, you can enable Internet users to access certain resources on the intranet. For example, you may wish to host a company Web site on an internal computer running Internet Information Services (IIS). The IIS computer has an IP address of 192.168.122.1. After creating the Web site, you assign the TCP port 8080 on the ICS server to map to this internal Web page (Figure 10.17).

## Figure 10.17 Inbound Connection Example

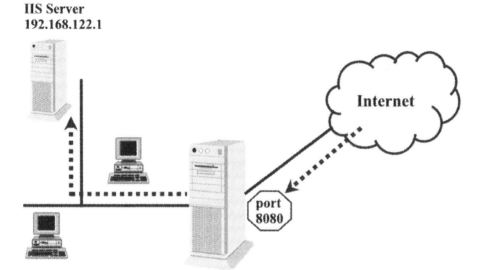

Tip: Each computer on the private network that will provide resources to the Internet must have a static (unchanging) IP address.

## Understanding ICS Limitations

ICS works by converting the IP packet header information from a private IP address to a public IP address. However, some protocols that use IP do not allow the header information to be altered. Applications that use these protocols will not work with a ICS server. Applications based on the following protocols will not work with a shared Internet connection using Connection Sharing:

- Internet Protocol Security (IPSec)

- Lightweight Directory Access Protocol (LDAP)

- Simple Network Management Protocol (SNMP)

- Microsoft Component Object Model (COM)

- Remote Procedure Call (RPC)

If your network needs to use these protocols, you must consider an alternate connection sharing method. In this case, an appropriate choice is Microsoft Proxy Server.

# Proxy Server Implementation

Like the ICS service and Shared Access, Microsoft Proxy Server provides Internet connection sharing, but also provides numerous enhancements over these other services. Proxy Server can handle IP packets sent with certain protocols and includes caching and filtering features.

Proxy Server is not included with Windows 2000 or Windows NT 4.0. It is a separate program, sold individually or as part of the Microsoft BackOffice suite of programs. Like most other tools in Windows 2000, Proxy Server uses the Microsoft Management Console (MMC) to provide a common interface for configuration.

 **Note:** Entire Microsoft courses are dedicated to Proxy Server. The installation and configuration of this product is beyond the scope of this book and the Microsoft exam. However, you need to know what Proxy Server is capable of doing.

# Filtering Internet Access

Proxy Server acts as a firewall, filtering IP traffic that flows between the private network and the Internet. If the proxy server is the only computer on the network with a public IP address, all traffic must pass through that computer. By implementing filters, you can prevent Internet users from gaining access to resources on the network and prevent internal users from accessing particular Web sites.

When a packet arrives at the server, Proxy Server examines the source and destination IP addresses and ports, compares this information to its list of filters, and then forwards the packet based on the filtering information.

You can configure Proxy Server filters to do one of the following:

• Forward IP packets that meet the filter criteria, and reject all others

• Reject IP packets that meet the filter criteria, and forward all others

Filters are based on one or more TCP/IP settings. The settings you can use are described in Table 10.2.

**Table 10.2 Proxy Server Filter Variables**

| TCP/IP Setting | Description |
| --- | --- |
| Domain name | You can filter information based on the domain or subdomain name of the source or destination computer. For example, block all Internet data from www.virusesRUs.com. |
| IP address | Filter information based on the IP address of the source or destination computer. |
| IP protocol type | Filter the traffic based on whether it is TCP- or UDP-based. |
| TCP or UDP port | Filter certain types of information. For example, by filtering TCP port 21, you prevent File Transfer Protocol (FTP) traffic from passing through the Proxy Server. |

# Providing Reverse Proxies

You use a reverse proxy when you have an IIS Web page within the intranet. When Proxy Server receives Universal Resource Locator (URL) requests for the Web page, it analyses the request, and then forwards the request to the internal Web server.

This service is not unlike that provided by ICS servers, but is more secure.

# Optimizing Proxy Servers

An additional benefit of using Proxy Server over ICS is the scalability of Proxy Server. Computers running Proxy Server can be optimized by increasing cache settings, creating a proxy array or Windows cluster, and using DNS round-robin.

## Increasing Cache

By increasing the Random Access Memory (RAM) in the proxy server and adjusting the cache settings in Proxy Server, you can increase the overall performance of the server. When the server receives a request for an Internet resource, it first checks the cache. The larger the cache, the more likely the resource will be found locally. This results in less Internet traffic, significantly reducing the time to retrieve Web pages and files.

 Tip: Cached files are stored not only in RAM, but also on the local hard disk. The files must be stored on a drive formatted with the New Technology File System (NTFS) file system.

There are two caching methods supported by Proxy Server. These methods are described in Table 10.3.

**Table 10.3 Proxy Server Caching Methods**

| Caching Method | Description |
| --- | --- |
| Active | Content is cached based on the age of the file, the Web page header information, and URL. Active caching requires more processing power, but reduces overall Internet traffic and hard disk space used. |
| Passive | The server replaces the oldest cached material with new material when the cache is full. Passive caching uses more hard disk space than active, but requires less processing power. |

## Proxy Server Arrays

In a proxy server array, multiple proxy servers provide connectivity to the Internet. They may share a single Internet connection, but each contains its own cache of Web files. Proxy Server utilizes Cache Array Routing Protocol (CARP), which places different cached Web pages on each server in the array.

Proxy server arrays not only provide enhanced performance, but also immediate fault-tolerance, If a single proxy server fails in the array, the other proxy server continues to provide connectivity to the Internet. Only the cached files on the failed server are lost. When the server is restored, those cached files must be retrieved from the Internet again.

## Using Windows Clustering

Windows Clustering combines two or more servers into a single logical server. When used with Proxy Server, clustering provides fault tolerance and increased performance for the Internet connections. Unlike a proxy array, the servers in a cluster do not use CARP, and therefore do not contain unique cached files.

Clustering provides higher availability of the proxy service, but requires more processing power from the servers and does not use the cache as effectively. If a member of the cluster fails, and is then restored, it does not need to rebuild its cache from the Internet. It simply obtains a copy from the other members of the cluster.

### *Using DNS Round-Robin*

DNS round-robin allows multiple servers to share a single hostname, even though they each have a unique IP address. When a client requests name resolution for that particular hostname, DNS returns the IP address of the server at the top of its round-robin list. It then places this server at the bottom of the list, so that the next server is at the top. In this way, network demands for a service are evenly distributed to multiple servers.

Proxy Server supports integration with DNS round-robin entries, enhancing Proxy Server availability and performance.

# Internet Connection Management

After implementing either ICS or Proxy Servers on the network, management includes monitoring the connection to ensure it is meeting the needs of the network users, detecting errors, and preparing for changes in the implementation.

## Detecting Errors

The most obvious problem caused by a failure in ICS or with proxy servers is the inability to provide Internet access. If this occurs, you should check the following:

- Verify the proxy server (or ICS server) can access the Internet

- Verify the other computers can contact the proxy server

If the proxy server has a good connection to the Internet and other computers can contact the proxy server, than the connection problem must be with the software configuration on the proxy server, or the server is overburdened.

If a proxy server or ICS server receives too many network requests, it becomes saturated. A saturated server drops requests and fails to route information in a timely fashion.

On servers running Proxy Server, you should also monitor the number of cache hits. A cache hit represents a time when a requested Web page or file was found in the proxy cache. The more hits, the more efficient the proxy service. If, while monitoring and logging cache hits, you notice a decline in the ratio of hits to total requests, consider upgrading the server and increasing the cache.

## Planning to Meet Internet Connectivity Demands

As with other services, you should implement a management plan that includes monitoring the proxy server for saturation. Saturation occurs when a server can no longer handle the connection sharing demands of the internal computers. By detecting the problem early, you can add additional servers to alleviate the problem before users lose Internet connectivity.

## Testing the Internet Connections

There is little you can do to test the Internet connection beyond what the network users do daily. However, if you have proxy servers in an array or Windows cluster, you need to ensure that all redundant servers are operational.

In a proxy array or cluster, verify that all servers are connected to the Internet and are maintaining a cache of files. One way to test them is to intentionally disconnect all servers but one, and ensure that server is still providing connectivity. Repeat this for each server in the array or cluster.

 Tip: If you shut down a member of a proxy array, that server loses its cached files, and must rebuild its cache by fetching information from the Internet.

# Internet Connectivity Business Goals

As with other Windows 2000 services and protocols, you should consider the use of ICS or Proxy Server from a business perspective. If the business is small and does not have a great deal of money to spend on connectivity and support, ICS is a viable option. For larger companies, or those that need to run applications across the shared connection, Proxy Server may be more appropriate. ICS and Proxy Server are analyzed with respect to the four business goals (functionality, security, availability, and performance) below.

# Using ICS to Meet Business Needs

ICS meets business needs in the following ways:

**Functionality**—For smaller networks, ICS provides the functionality needed to connect computers to the Internet. In addition to saving money by sharing a single Internet connection, ICS provides lower network management costs through automatic IP addressing implementation and name resolution.

**Security**—ICS acts as a firewall, hiding the private IP addresses of the network from users on the Internet. It should not be used as a total firewall solution, but it provides a level of security sufficient for many networks. Furthermore, ICS supports the passing of data encrypted with the Point-to-Point Tunneling Protocol (PPTP), and secure Web page transactions using Secure Socket Layer (SSL).

**Availability and Performance**—ICS supports multiple connections to the Internet. These multiple connections provide fault tolerance if one connection fails (thus enhancing availability) and greatly increase the network bandwidth, improving performance.

# Using Proxy Server to Meet Business Needs

Microsoft Proxy Server meets business needs as follows:

**Functionality**—Proxy Server provides a very functional Internet connectivity solution for larger businesses. By providing enhanced caching, array configurations, and clustering, the scalability of Proxy Server makes it a strong choice for very large networks. Further functionality is provided through support for reverse proxies, which allow you to place Internet Web pages behind the proxy, where they are more secure but still accessible to Internet users.

**Security**—Proxy Server acts as a full-featured firewall on the network. Extensive filtering features allow you to closely control the information that passes through the proxy server, and extensive logging features allow you to track usage.

**Availability**—Proxy Servers have more availability than ICS servers because they support arrays and Windows clustering.

**Performance**—Proxy arrays greatly enhance Internet connection performance by spreading the cache and processing demands across two or more servers.

## Internet Connectivity Business Scenario

Woody's Chiropractic Association (WCA) has hired you once again to help meet their network needs. WCA has a national network that consists of 6 regional offices, a national center, and numerous doctors' offices (Figure 10.18).

## Figure 10.18 WCA Network

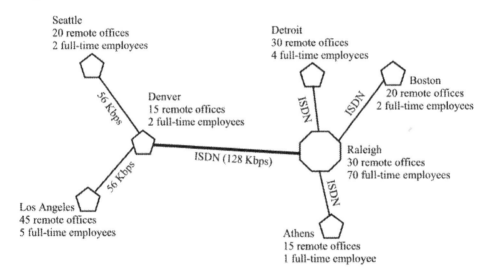

Currently, all full-time employees have Internet access through a Linux server in the Raleigh national center. The Linux server has a single public IP address and provides proxy services to the Internet through a T1 line. Originally, the connection was through an ISDN line, but when employees complained about slow connections, WCA's Internet Service Provider suggested upgrading to a T1. This upgrade has helped some, but employees are still complaining that Internet access is much slower than it should be.

WCA wants to rectify this problem once and for all. They have upgraded most of their network to Windows 2000. Installed services include DHCP, DNS, and WINS. All of the routers on the network are Windows 2000 servers running RRAS.

Table 10.4 outlines the current state of the WCA network. It is followed by two proposed solutions.

## Table 10.4 WCA Network Statistics

| Business Component | Comments |
|---|---|
| Number of users | Approximately 85 full-time employees; 70 in the national center and the rest at various regional centers. |
| Expected growth | 10% per year is expected. |
| Functionality | The solution must provide fast Internet connectivity for all full-time employees. |
| Cost | The CEO does not want to allocate funds for an additional T1 line or other connection, because the previous line upgrade did not meet expectations or justify the cost. |
| Current hardware | WCA will consider the purchase of a few new servers, but wants to use the existing infrastructure as much as possible. |
| Security | Security is crucial. The Linux server has been very effective as a firewall, and WCA absolutely does not want to reduce security levels. |
| Web servers | Currently, WCA has two Web servers. One provides information to internal users. The other provides an Internet presence for WCA. This external Web server is currently located offsite, but WCA wants to move it internally, where they have better control over the server and content. |

| Business Component | Comments |
|---|---|
| Performance | Performance is the main issue. Internet connection speeds must be increased. Your own tests indicate that a single Windows 2000 Proxy Server can handle the needs of 50 simultaneous connections. A single computer running ICS can handle approximately 20 simultaneous connections. |
| Availability | Internet access is not currently a fundamental part of the WCA network. If the connection fails, employees can still be productive. However, once the Web server is moved to the WCA network, there must be a fail-safe connection to the Internet. |
| Employee productivity | Although the CEO acknowledges the usefulness of an Internet connection, he believes that the Internet may distract his employees. He is concerned that employees are not as productive because of the Internet connection. |

## Proposed Solution 1

You propose the following network configuration:

- Replace the Linux server with two Windows 2000 Proxy Servers

- Configure the Proxy Servers in an array

- Enable IP filtering, preventing access to all internal computers from the Internet

- Use IP filtering to prevent internal access to "questionable" Internet sites

- Implement a logging scheme on the Proxy Servers to monitor all Internet access

## *Proposed Solution 2*

To provide an alternative, you also offer this solution:

- Delegate an existing Windows 2000 server at each regional center as the ICS server

- Dedicate two Windows 2000 servers at the national center to running Connection Sharing

- Use the existing ISDN lines at each regional center to connect to the Internet, and then create VPNs to connect the regional centers to Raleigh

# Vocabulary

Review the following terms in preparation for the certification exam.

| Term | Description |
|---|---|
| array | A collection of two or more proxy servers sharing Internet connectivity responsibilities. |
| cache hit | When a cached file fulfills a request for an internet resource. |
| caching | Storing recently accessed Web pages and files on the proxy server. |
| CARP | The Cache Array Routing Protocol distributes cached files among all members of a proxy array. |
| DHCP | The Dynamic Host Configuration Protocol provides automatic TCP/IP configuration to clients. |
| dial-up connection | A connection between two computers that involves dialing the connection using a modem or ISDN adapter. |
| DNS | The Domain Name System resolves hostnames to IP addresses. |
| DNS round-robin | A feature of DNS that allows multiple computers to share a single hostname. |
| domain name | The name assigned to a logical collection of computers, the domain name can be used as an IP filter criterion. |
| fault tolerance | The ability of a system to recover from a single point of failure. |
| firewall | A device that prevents unauthorized access to a network. Proxy Server and ICS provide firewall capabilities. |

| Term | Description |
| --- | --- |
| FTP | File Transfer Protocol is a TCP/IP protocol used to transfer files on the Internet. |
| ICS | Internet Connection Sharing is a Windows 2000 service that provides shared Internet connectivity. |
| ICS server | Any Windows 2000 computer with a shared Internet connection using ICS. |
| IIS | Internet Information Services is a service that provides Web and FTP hosting on a Windows 2000 computer. |
| interfaces | The devices that connect a computer to a network, interfaces include NICs, modems, and ISDN adapters. |
| IP addresses | An IP address is a 32-bit number used to identify each computer on a TCP/IP network. |
| IP data packets | With TCP/IP, data is sent in discrete packages, called IP data packets or IP packets. |
| IP packet header information | The information at the beginning of each IP packet defining the source and destination IP addresses. |
| ISDN | Integrated Services Digital Network transmits data over digital telephone lines. |
| ISP | An Internet Service Provider connects users to the Internet through remote access servers. |
| LAN | A Local Area Network is a collection of computers in a single location, connected by a cable. |
| MMC | The Microsoft Management Console provides a common interface for many Windows 2000 tools, including Proxy Server and IIS. |
| name resolution | The process of converting a computer name to an IP address. |

| Term | Description |
| --- | --- |
| NAT | Network Address Translation converts private IP addresses to a single public IP address that can be used on the Internet. |
| NIC | A Network Interface Card connects a computer to the network. |
| PPTP | The Point-to-Point Tunneling Protocol is a tunneling protocol used to create a VPN. |
| private IP address | A private IP address is one that cannot be used on the Internet. |
| Proxy Server | Generically, a computer that provides NAT services. Capitalized, the name of the Microsoft product that provides proxy services. |
| PSTN | The Public Switched Telephone Network is the collection of standard analog telephone lines. |
| public IP address | An address that is valid on the Internet. |
| RRAS | Routing and Remote Access is a Windows 2000 service that provides remote access, routing, and VPN support for a Windows 2000 network. |
| saturation | When a server receives more network requests than it can handle. |
| scope | A range of IP addresses. |
| SSL | Secure Sockets Layer provides a secure means of transmitting Web data. |
| TCP | Transmission Control Protocol is part of the TCP/IP protocol suite. |
| TCP port | A channel within the TCP/IP network through which specific data travels. |
| UDP | User Datagram Protocol is part of the TCP/IP protocol suite. |

| Term | Description |
|---|---|
| URL | The Universal Resource Locator is a means of finding a specific resource on the Internet. An example of a URL is http://www.lightpointlearning.net. |
| VPN | A Virtual Private Network creates a tunnel on the Internet through which data can travel securely. |
| Windows Clustering | A service that combines two or more servers into a single logical server. |
| WINS | The Windows Internet Naming Service resolves NetBIOS names to IP addresses. |

# In Brief

| If you want to... | Then do this... |
| --- | --- |
| Provide Internet connectivity for a small office environment | Establish an Internet connection on a Windows 2000 computer. Enable the dial-up connection with Shared Access (or Connection Sharing). |
| Provide a small office the ability to pass SNMP packets across a single VPN connection to another network | Install a Windows 2000 server with Proxy Server. |
| Keep a log of Internet accesses | Configure the Proxy Server to log accesses. |
| Monitor a ICS server for failures | Select the Log Errors Only option. |
| Prevent unauthorized access through a shared connection | Implement IP filtering, blocking all accesses except those that are absolutely necessary. |

# Lesson 10 Activities

Complete the following activities to better prepare you for the certification exam.

1.   Referring to Proposed Solution 1 and Proposed Solution 2, which of these choices most accurately meets all of the needs and expectations of WCA?

2.   Which solution will cost more to implement?

3.   How does Proposed Solution 1 increase network connectivity speeds?

4.   Which solution provides faster Internet connections?

5.   Does either proposal meet the requirements for server availability? How?

6.   Describe how both solutions provide for expected growth of the network.

7.   What are two unexpected benefits to be gained by using Proposed Solution 2?

8.   The CEO has decided to establish his one FTP server in his office, from which he can share personal files with friends and family. When he tries to set up his FTP server, he discovers that no one can access his files. Using each solution, what could be a possible reason for this?

9.   WCA still occasionally uses an old, proprietary software program called ChiroLink. ChiroLink uses RPCs to connect to a database. Will it continue to work under both solutions? If not, why not?

10.  The CEO wants a list every month of the most commonly accessed Web sites, so that he can keep an eye on employee productivity. Which solution best meets this need?

# Answers to Lesson 10 Activities

1.  Neither solution is complete. Proposed Solution 1 fails to address the desire to place the external Web server within the intranet. IP filtering in Proposed Solution 1 prevents Internet users from accessing the company's Web site.  Proposed Solution 2 fails to meet the expectations regarding security. ICS does not provide the level of security expected. Furthermore, issues about employee productivity are not met, since this plan does not allow for filtering or centralized access logging.

2.  Proposed Solution 1 will probably be more expensive, since it requires the purchase of two Windows 2000 servers and two copies of Proxy Server. Proposed Solution 2 does not require the purchase of additional computers or extra lines.

3.  Performance did not significantly increase with the installation of a much faster Internet connection. This suggests that the proxy server is the bottleneck. By replacing the single proxy server with two servers, you distribute the network demands. By creating an array, you increase caching abilities, as well.

4.  Proposed Solution 2 provides faster Internet connections. Although the connections are established through ISDN lines at each regional center, data from each of these regional centers needs to pass through ISDN to reach the proxy servers in Raleigh, anyway. Distributing the network demands and placing ICS servers at these remote locations result in much faster access.

5.  Only Proposed Solution 1 meets the requirements for availability. With either proposal, more than one server provides Internet connectivity. However, with Proposed Solution 2, connectivity between the regional centers and the national center depends upon the same server that provides Internet connectivity. If this server fails, users cannot access the Internet, and they cannot connect to the national office or other regional centers. Only the national center has a redundant connection.

6.  The servers in Proposed Solution1 will become saturated after much more growth. Proposed Solution 1 will be adequate for a little more than a year before additional servers (or more powerful servers) will be needed. Proposed Solution 2 does not currently provide enough connectivity for the full-time employees in Raleigh, and additional growth will only compound this.

7.  By using the ISDN lines to connect to the Internet and then creating VPN connections to Raleigh, you increase the security of data traveling between the regional offices. Furthermore, once connected to the Internet, each regional office can establish a VPN connection to other regional offices, enhancing communication and providing strong fault tolerance in the network.

8.  Using Proposed Solution 1, IP filters prevent access to all internal resources except the Web server. You need to enable access to the IP address of the CEO's computer, and to allow access over TCP port 21. Additionally, a reverse proxy needs to be configured on the proxy servers.

    Using Proposed Solution 2, you need to configure ICS to allow access to the CEO's IP address using TCP port 21.

9.  The software is likely to continue to work with Proposed Solution 1 for two reasons. First, intranet data does not pass through proxy servers, so the internal network structure is not changing. If ChiroLink works now, it will work after implementing the first proposal. Also, Proxy Server supports the forwarding of RPC data. ChiroLink will not work under the second proposal. With Proposed Solution 2, all data must pass through the ICS servers, and ICS does not support RPC data forwarding.

10. Proposed Solution 1 provides detailed logging of all Internet site accesses through Proxy Server. If this is an important requirement, you must implement Proposed Solution 1. Not only does Proxy Server provide logging, you are forcing all Internet connections through a centralized connection. With Proposed Solution 2, you would need to configure logging for every ICS server (which is not an option), and then combine the lists.

# Lesson 10 Quiz

These questions test your knowledge of features, vocabulary, procedures, and syntax.

1.  By default, for how long is a TCP mapping valid in Connection Sharing?
    A.    24 minutes
    B.    24 hours
    C.    24 days
    D.    1440 hours

2.  Which of the following is a valid way to implement filters? (Choose all that apply).
    A.    Ignore filters for administrators
    B.    Block all data that meets filter criteria
    C.    Accept only data that meets filter criteria
    D.    Filter only some IP traffic

3.  What does ICS provide that Shared Access does not?
    A.    A shared dial-up connection
    B.    An inexpensive internet connection method
    C.    NetBIOS name resolution
    D.    Automatic IP assignments

4.  Which of the following can be used as filtering criteria? (Choose all that apply).
    A.    Domain name
    B.    Destination IP address
    C.    Source IP address
    D.    IP packet type

5.  When you install Shared Access, what happens to the configuration of the NIC attached to the intranet?
    A.    It retains its IP address, but receives a new subnet mask.
    B.    The IP address changes to 168.192.0.1
    C.    The IP address changes to 192.168.0.1
    D.    Nothing. You must manually change the NIC configuration.

6.    What is the Windows 2000 service that provides Web hosting?
    A.    IIS
    B.    Connection Sharing
    C.    Proxy Server
    D.    TCP

7.    Which of the following increases Proxy Server performance? (Choose all that apply).
    A.    Adding additional proxy servers to the network
    B.    Increasing the cache
    C.    Creating a cluster
    D.    Creating an array

8.    Which of the following increases ICS performance? (Choose all that apply).
    A.    Adding additional ICS servers
    B.    Increasing the cache
    C.    Creating a cluster
    D.    Creating an array

9.    What is the protocol used by proxy arrays to distribute the cache?
    A.    CARP
    B.    TUNA
    C.    TROUT
    D.    BASS

10.    Which ICS logging option generates the largest log file?
    A.    Log Warnings
    B.    Log All Events
    C.    Log All Warnings, Errors, and Events
    D.    Log the Maximum Amount of Information

# Answers to Lesson 10 Quiz

1.     Answer B is correct. The default duration is 1440 minutes, or 24 hours.

       Therefore, answers A, C, and D are incorrect.

2.     Answers B and C are correct. You can set filters to block data that either meets the filter criteria or does not.

       Answers A and D are incorrect. All of the filter criteria (or none of it) must be met to pass IP data packets, and you cannot base filtering on user accounts.

3.     Answer C is correct. Shared Access does not provide NetBIOS name resolution.

       Answers A, B, and D are incorrect. These are all characteristics of both Shared Access and Connection Sharing.

4.     Answers A, B, C, and D are all correct. IP filtering criteria can also include the packet filter type (TCP or UDP).

5.     Answer C is correct. The NIC receives a new IP address, which is always 192.168.0.1.

       Answers A and D are incorrect. Unless the IP address changes, the other computers on the network will not be able to access the computer.

       Answer B is incorrect. The address is 192.168.0.1, not 168.192.0.1.

6.     Answer A is correct. Internet Information Services provides Web and FTP hosting services.

       Answers B and C are incorrect. ICS and Proxy Server provide Internet connectivity, but not Web site hosting.

       Answer D is incorrect. TCP is part of the TCP/IP protocol suite. It is not a service.

7.    Answers A, B, C, and D are all correct. These are all valid ways to increase the availability and performance of the proxy service on a network.

8.    Answer A is correct. Adding additional ICS servers will increase performance of Connection Sharing.

      Answers B, C, and D are incorrect. ICS does not support caching, arrays, or the Windows Cluster service.

9.    Answer A is correct. The Cache Array Routing Protocol distributes cached files to all members of a proxy array.

      Answers B, C, and D are incorrect. These are all fictitious terms.

10.   Answer D is correct. The Log the Maximum Amount of Information setting will generate the largest log file.

      Answers A, B, and C are incorrect. None of these are valid log settings for Connection Sharing.

# Glossary

| Term | Description |
|---|---|
| 3DES | Triple Data Encryption Standard uses three 128-bit keys for data encryption and is the highest level of encryption supported by Windows 2000. |
| 40-bit DES | A Data Encryption Standard that uses one 40-bit encryption key. |
| 56-bit DES | A Data Encryption standard that uses a single 56-bit key. |
| Active Directory | The directory database that provides the foundation of every Windows 2000 network. |
| Active Directory-integrated DNS | DNS zone information integrated with the Active Directory database for enhanced security and easier replication. |
| ADSL | Asymmetric Digital Subscriber Line is a technology that uses standard telephone lines to transmit digital data. |
| APIPA | Automatic Private Internet Protocol Addressing, supported by all Windows 2000 computers, allows computers to assign themselves an IP address if a DHCP server is unavailable. |
| area | One part of an AS, areas define small zones of a large routed network. |
| array | A collection of two or more proxy servers sharing Internet connectivity responsibilities. |
| AS | An Autonomous System is a management zone within a large routed network, and consists of one or more areas. |
| authentication protocol | A protocol used to authenticate users connecting through a VPN. |

| Term | Description |
| --- | --- |
| auto-static mode | A RIP setting that enables a router to receive manual updates to the routing information tables across demand-dial connections. |
| backbone area | Within each AS, the zone identified with the IP address 0.0.0.0. |
| bandwidth | The amount of data that can be transmitted across a network connection. |
| BGP | Border Gateway Protocol is a routing protocol used by routers on a TCP/IP network to transmit information between autonomous systems. |
| BOOTP | Routers use the Bootstrap Protocol to forward DHCP broadcast messages. |
| boundary routers | Routers that transfer information between ASs. |
| broadcast forwarding | The ability of routers to pass certain broadcast messages on to other network segments. |
| broadcast messages | Messages that are sent on the network with no specified destination IP address, so that all computers on the subnet will act upon the message. |
| broadcasts | TCP/IP data messages sent to every computer on the network without a destination IP address specified. |
| burst-mode name registration | When a WINS server becomes overloaded with registration requests, burst-mode name registration provides a short-term solution until the server can fully process the requests. |
| byte | 1 byte is equal to 8 bits. |
| CA | A Certificate Authority provides X.509 certificates for IPSec authorization. |
| cache hit | When a cached file fulfills a request for an internet resource. |

| Term | Description |
|---|---|
| caching | Storing recently accessed Web pages and files on the proxy server. |
| caching-only servers | DNS servers that do not contain any zone information. They only contain a list of recently resolved hostnames and IP addresses for quick retrieval. |
| CARP | The Cache Array Routing Protocol distributes cached files among all members of a proxy array. |
| CHAP | Challenge Handshake Authentication Protocol is one of the security protocols RRAS supports. |
| CIDR | Classless Inter-Domain Routing is a way of customizing IP addresses and subnet masks. |
| client | A computer requesting information from a server (like a DHCP or DNS server). |
| clustering | The combining of two or more servers into one logical server. |
| CMAK | You use the Connection Manager Administration Kit to configure Connection Manager and customize the software that clients receive. |
| Connection Manager | A service in Windows 2000 that provides connectivity and phone book services to clients. |
| Connection Sharing | A Windows 2000 service that acts as a basic proxy server and firewall. |
| cryptography | The method of encrypting data, rendering it unreadable to all but the intended recipient. |
| data encryption | Applying a mathematical formula to data, rendering it unreadable by anyone other than the intended recipient. |
| datagram | A single piece of network data on a TCP/IP network. |

| Term | Description |
| --- | --- |
| default gateway | A TCP/IP configuration setting that defines the IP address of the default router used on a segment. |
| default name server | The first DNS server a client queries when name resolution is needed. |
| demand-dial | A feature of Windows 2000 that allows routers to establish a connection to other routers only when the connection is needed. |
| demand-dial routing | Demand-dial routing is a Windows 2000 service that provides an inexpensive way to connect to networks and to provide a backup WAN connection. |
| DHCP | The Dynamic Host Configuration Protocol automatically assigns IP addresses and other TCP/IP configuration information to requesting clients. |
| DHCP relay agent | A computer that forwards DHCP broadcast messages directly to a DHCP server. |
| dial-up access | Connecting to a network using a modem and standard telephone lines. Dial-up access also includes using an Integrated Services Digital Network (ISDN) line or Asymmetric Digital Subscriber Line (ADSL). |
| dial-up connection | A connection between two computers that involves dialing the connection using a modem or ISDN adapter. |
| dial-up connections | A connection to a network established through telephone lines or ISDN lines that use a modem. |
| distance vector algorithm | The mathematical function used by RIP to determine the best route on which to send an IP packet. |
| distributed scope | A DHCP scope that has been divided into two or more parts and placed on several DHCP servers. |
| DNS | The Domain Name System resolves IP addresses to hostnames and FQDNs , and hostnames and FQDNs to IP addresses. |

| Term | Description |
|------|-------------|
| DNS integration | The Windows 2000 implementation of DNS and DHCP are designed to work together so that DHCP can update the DNS database when IP address changes occur. |
| DNS round-robin | A feature of DNS that allows multiple computers to share a single hostname. |
| domain | A logical grouping of computers, a domain is the basic unit of organization in a Windows 2000 network. |
| domain name | The name assigned to a logical collection of computers, the domain name can be used as an IP filter criterion. |
| domain namespace | A hierarchical structure of domains that groups computers in a logical fashion. |
| Dynamic DNS | The ability of the DNS database to be updated by DHCP and DHCP clients. |
| dynamic routing protocols | Windows 2000 supports two dynamic routing protocols—RIP and OSPF. Routers using these protocols automatically update their routing information. |
| dynamic updates | When the IP information changes on a DHCP client, the client or DHCP updates the DNS database. |
| EAP-TLS | Extensible Authentication Protocol-Transport Layer Security (EAP-TLS); one of the security protocols supported by Windows 2000 RRAS; uses public keys for mutual router authentication. |
| fault tolerance | The ability of a network or computer to recover from a single failure. |
| filter | A TCP/IP filter prevents data from transmitting unless it meets specific TCP/IP characteristics. |
| firewall | A firewall is a hardware or software filtering device that connects an intranet to the Internet, and provides security by preventing certain traffic from flowing in either direction. |

| Term | Description |
| --- | --- |
| FQDN | The Fully Qualified Domain Name is the hostname appended with the entire domain name. |
| FTP | The File Transfer Protocol, part of the TCP/IP protocol suite, is a protocol used to transfer files on the Internet. |
| GUI | The Graphic User Interface is the user-friendly interface that allows people to use a mouse to select choices. |
| hardware routers | Hardware devices that are specifically designed for routing data and typically serve no other function on the network. |
| hierarchical DNS structure | In a hierarchical domain structure, a DNS server will pass queries it cannot resolve to a higher-level name server. |
| host | Any object attached to a TCP/IP-based network. |
| host ID | The part of an IP address that specifies the host. |
| hostname | A user-friendly name assigned to each host on a TCP/IP network. |
| hostnames | A TCP/IP name given to each host on a network. DNS resolves hostnames to IP addresses. |
| HTTP | HyperText Transfer Protocol is part of the TCP/IP protocol suite, and is used to transfer Web pages from servers to clients. |
| IAS | Internet Authentication Service is the Windows 2000 service that provides RADIUS server capabilities. |
| ICS | Internet Connection Sharing is a Windows 2000 service that provides shared Internet connectivity. |
| ICS server | Any Windows 2000 computer with a shared Internet connection using ICS. |
| IEAK | Connection Manager is installed when you install the Internet Explorer Administration Kit. |

| Term | Description |
|------|-------------|
| IGMP | The Internet Group Management Protocol is part of the TCP/IP protocol suite and provides the foundation of Windows 2000 multicasting. |
| IIS | Internet Information Service provides Web and FTP hosting on a Windows 2000 computer, and is a necessary part of Connection Manager. |
| incremental zone transfers | The transfer of DNS zone information in which only changes are transferred, rather than the entire database. |
| interfaces | The devices that connect a computer to a network, interfaces include NICs, modems, and ISDN adapters. |
| intranet | An internal network of computers. |
| IP address | The 32-bit number assigned to each host on a TCP/IP network. For each host on a network, the TCP/IP number must be unique. |
| IP addresses | An IP address is a 32-bit number used to identify each computer on a TCP/IP network. |
| IP data packets | With TCP/IP, data is sent in discrete packages, called IP data packets or IP packets. |
| IP filtering | Filtering prevents information from traveling on the network, based on specific TCP/IP information (such as the originating computer's IP address). |
| IP packet header information | The information at the beginning of each IP packet defining the source and destination IP addresses. |
| IP packets | Data is segmented in packets before transmission on a TCP/IP network. |
| **IPCONFIG** | The **IPCONFIG** command displays information about the current TCP/IP configuration information on a computer. |

| Term | Description |
|---|---|
| IPSec | The Internet Protocol Security provides data encryption and computer authentication for VPNs, intranet and network security. |
| IPSec policies | IPSec policies define how a computer uses IPSec. There are three default IPSec policies in Windows 2000. |
| IPX | Internet Protocol Exchange is part of the Novell's proprietary IPX/SPX network protocol. |
| ISDN | Integrated Service Digital Network is a networking and communications standard for transmitting information across digital phone lines. |
| ISP | An Internet Service Provider connects users to the Internet through remote access servers. |
| Kerberos | An authentication method used by Windows 2000 Active Directory and IPSec. |
| L2TP | Layer 2 Tunneling Protocol is one of two tunneling protocols used by Windows 2000 to create a VPN. |
| LAN | A Local Area Network consists of computers within a single area, connected by a cable. |
| lease duration | The amount of time a DHCP-assigned IP address remains valid on a client. |
| local | A host that is on the same network segment as your computer is said to be local. |
| logon scripts | A small program that executes when a user logs on to a network, and is used to automate steps that occur at every logon. |
| MD5 | Message Digest 5 provides 128-bit data encryption. |

| Term | Description |
|---|---|
| MMC | The Microsoft Management Console provides a common interface for many Windows 2000 tools, including Proxy Server and IIS. |
| MPPE | Microsoft Point-to-Point Encryption is an RRAS data encryption protocol that works with PPTP and PPP. |
| MS-CHAP | Microsoft Challenge Handshake Authentication Protocol |
| MS-CHAP v1 | Microsoft Challenge Handshake Authentication Protocol version 1 is one of the router authentication protocols. |
| MS-CHAP v2 | Microsoft Challenge Handshake Authentication Protocol version 2 is one of the router authentication protocols, and the only CHAP-based protocol that supports mutual authentication. |
| multicast forwarding | The ability of a Windows 2000 computer to pass multicast information from one network to another. |
| multicast heartbeat | A method used by Windows 2000 routers to verify that multicasting is working properly. |
| multicast proxy | A Windows 2000 server that acts as a multicast server on a private network by receiving multicast information from the Internet and passing it to local multicast clients. |
| multicasting | Sending a single copy of data to multiple computers simultaneously. |
| multihomed | Any computer with two or more NICs and attached to two or more subnets. |
| mutual authentication | The ability of both routers in a connection to authenticate the other simultaneously. |
| name resolution | The process of converting a hostname or NetBIOS name to an IP address. |
| name server | A DNS server. |

| Term | Description |
| --- | --- |
| NAT | Net Address Translators, like proxy servers, allow multiple computers to share a single Internet connection. |
| NBT | NetBIOS over TCP/IP allows the functionality of NetBIOS to work with TCP/IP. |
| NetBEUI | NetBIOS Enhanced User Interface is an older, non-routable protocol designed to work with NetBIOS. |
| NetBIOS | The Network Basic Input/Output System is a Windows proprietary network protocol. |
| NetBIOS name | The name used on NetBIOS networks to identify each computer. |
| network ID | The part of the IP address that defines the subnet on which a host is connected. |
| NIC | The Network Interface Card connects a computer to the network medium (cable). NICs may also be called network cards and network adapters. |
| OSPF | Open Shortest Path First is one of two dynamic (automatic) routing protocols supported by Windows 2000. |
| PAP | Password Authentication Protocol is the least secure of the router authentication protocols, sending authentication information in an unencrypted state. |
| PBA | The Phone Book Administrator is a service included with Connection Manager that provides a means of updating the phone book database. |
| PBS | The Phone Book Service provides access to the phone book database. |
| PBS server | A Windows 2000 server running the PBS. |
| phone book file | A database file that contains a listing of the local dial-up access numbers clients use to connect to the network. |

| Term | Description |
|------|-------------|
| POP | The Point of Presence is a local dial-up access number entry in the phone book database. |
| PPP | The Point-to-Point Protocol is one of two dial-up protocols. |
| PPTP | The Point-to-Point Tunneling Protocol is a tunneling protocol used to create a VPN. |
| private IP addresses | IP addresses that cannot be used on the Internet, and so are suitable for use on intranets. |
| profile | Part of the information sent to Connection Manager clients, which defines the local access numbers. |
| protocol | A protocol defines the rules of communication on a network. |
| protocol suite | A collection of several protocols designed to work together, TCP/IP is an example of a protocol suite. |
| proxy server | A computer that allows many computers to share a single internet connection. |
| Proxy Server | Generically, a computer that provides NAT services. Capitalized, the name of the Microsoft product that provides proxy services. |
| PSTN | Public Switched Telephone Network consists of the standard telephone lines used to carry voice information and data when used with a modem. |
| public IP address | An address that is valid on the Internet. |
| public lines | Telephone lines and other cables that provide the backbone of data transmissions. Public lines are used to carry voice, data, video, and television signals. |
| pull replication | During pull replication, a WINS server requests changes from other servers. |

| Term | Description |
|---|---|
| push/pull replication | With push/pull replication, a WINS server will notify other servers when changes occur. |
| querier | The computer responsible for identifying the multicast hosts on a network segment. |
| query | A query is a request to a DNS or WINS server to provide name resolution. |
| query | A client computer queries (sends a request to) DHCP for TCP/IP configuration information. |
| RADIUS | Remote Authentication Dial-In User Service centralizes remote user authentication and removes this work from the RRAS server. |
| RADIUS client | A remote access server that passes user authentication requests to a RADIUS server. |
| RADIUS server | A server that handles remote access user authentication. |
| RAM | Random Access Memory is the memory in a computer that programs use to run. |
| recursive request | A request for name resolution, a recursive request expects a complete answer, not partial information. |
| redundancy | Providing one or more additional servers to a network to distribute network demands and to provide fault tolerance. |
| redundant DNS servers | Two or more servers that provide the same DNS zone information to the network and provide load balancing and fault tolerance. |
| redundant server | A server that provides the same service as another, and is primarily used in case the first server fails. |
| registration | WINS clients record their IP address and NetBIOS names with a WINS server. |

| Term | Description |
|---|---|
| release | WINS clients, when shutting down, notify the WINS server that their NetBIOS name and IP address are no longer being used on the network. |
| remote | A host attached to a different network segment from your own is said to be remote. When you send data to a remote host, it must pass through at least one router. |
| remote access | Access to a network from a location not connected by a permanent cable. |
| renewal | Before a WINS registration expires, a WINS client renews its registration with the WINS server. |
| replication | The process of copying information from one server to another. WINS and DNS servers copy information to other servers through replication. |
| resolution | When WINS clients request the conversion of a NetBIOS name to an IP address. |
| resolve | Convert a hostname or NetBIOS name to an IP address, or IP address to hostname or NetBIOS name. |
| RIP | Routing Information Protocol is one of two dynamic routing protocols supported by Windows 2000 that enables routers to automatically update the routing information tables. |
| RIP for IPv2 | Routing Information Protocol for IP version 2 is one of the routing protocols supported by Windows 2000 routers. |
| rogue server | A DHCP server that is not authorized to be on the network. |
| root-level domain | The highest domain level, the root domain is represented by a period (.). All domains on the Internet are members of the root domain. |
| round-robin DNS | A configuration of Windows 2000 DNS that allows multiple computers with different IP addresses to share a single common hostname. |

| Term | Description |
| --- | --- |
| routable | A protocol or network message that can be passed on by routers from one subnet to another. |
| route | The path an IP packet travels from its source to destination. |
| router | A hardware or software device that connects two or more network segments and passes information between them. |
| router authentication | The ability of one router to verify the router to which it is connected, before transmitting network data. |
| router saturation | When too many network packages need to be routed simultaneously, the router may become saturated. |
| routers | Software or hardware devices that connects network segments, and passes and filter the network traffic that passes through them. |
| routing table | The list of network segments a router uses to determine the best path on which to send an IP packet. |
| RRAS | Routing and Remote Access is a Windows 2000 service that provides remote access, routing, and VPN support for a Windows 2000 network. |
| SAP | The Service Advertising Protocol is a routing protocol used with IPX. |
| saturated | The state of a router or server that has received more requests for service than it can handle. |
| saturation | When a server receives more network requests than it can handle. |
| scope | A range of IP addresses from which DHCP will assign addresses to requesting clients. |
| second-level domain | Below top-level domains, second-level domains are usually organization-specific. |

| Term | Description |
|---|---|
| segment | Synonymous with subnet, a segment is one portion of a TCP/IP network and is connected to other segments with routers. |
| server cluster | Connecting several servers so that they act as a single logical server. |
| service | A program that runs on a server and provides functionality to the network. |
| SHA | The Secure Hash Algorithm provides 160-bit data encryption for IPSec. |
| SID | The Security Identifier is a number assigned to each object on an Active Directory network and is used to positively identify a computer. |
| SLIP | Serial Line Interface Protocol is one of two dial-up protocols. |
| SMS | Microsoft Systems Management Server provides overall network management solutions, including hardware inventories, computer monitoring, administrative alerts, and software distribution. |
| software routers | Computers that also serve as routers on a network, the computer must be multihomed and must run the Windows 2000 RRAS service. |
| SPAP | Shiva Password Authentication Protocol is a security protocol supported by RAS specifically for Shiva clients. |
| SSL | Secure Sockets Layer provides a secure means of transmitting Web data. |
| standard DNS | A DNS system that is not integrated with Active Directory but is compatible with other DNS servers. |
| static | Does not automatically change; must be configured manually. |
| static table | A routing table that only changes when manually updated. |

| Term | Description |
|------|-------------|
| subdomains | Domains below the second-level domain, subdomains are used for organization within a company. |
| subnet | Synonymous with segment, a subnet is one portion of a TCP/IP network, connected to other subnets with routers. |
| subnet mask | Part of the TCP/IP configuration information, the 32-bit number subnet mask defines the host and network identifications. |
| supernetting | Combining two or more IP address ranges into one range that can be used on a single network subnet. |
| TCP | Transmission Control Protocol is one of many protocols in the TCP/IP protocol suite. |
| TCP port | A channel within the TCP/IP network through which specific data travels. TCP directs information based on a port number. Some services have default ports, like port 80 for HTTP. |
| TCP/IP | The Transmission Control Protocol/Internet Protocol is the networking protocol used on the Internet and is the default protocol in Windows 2000. |
| top-level domain | One level below the root-level domain, top-level domains are two- or three-letter names that define the type of organization (com, net, gov, for example). |
| transport mode | One of two IPSec modes, transport mode is useful on intranets. |
| TTL | The Time To Live defines the lease duration for a NetBIOS name registration. |
| TTL | The Time To Live indicates the number of routers through which a message will pass before it is stopped by a router. |
| tunnel | A virtual path through which data travels securely in a VPN. |

| Term | Description |
|---|---|
| tunnel mode | One of two IPSec modes, tunnel mode uses L2TP to create a tunnel for VPNs. |
| UDP | The User Datagram Protocol is one protocol in the TCP/IP protocol suite. |
| unicast | The traditional way to send a message, unicast messages travel from a single source to a single destination. |
| URL | The Universal Resource Locator is a means of finding a specific resource on the Internet. An example of a URL is http://www.lightpointlearning.net. |
| user authentication | The process of verifying a username and password before granting the user access to network resources. |
| VPN | Virtual Private Networks use tunneling protocols to create a secure channel for data transmission across the Internet. |
| WAN | A Wide Area Network consists of two or more LANs connect by leased lines, Virtual Private Network, or other long-distance connectivity methods. |
| Windows Clustering | A Windows 2000 service that combines two or more servers into a single logical server. Windows Clustering provides the highest availability for services on a network. |
| WINS | The Windows Internet Naming Service provides name resolution for NetBIOS names by resolving NetBIOS names to IP addresses. |
| X.25 | One of many packet switching, high-speed WAN technologies. |
| zone of authority | The range of hostnames for which a single DNS server is responsible. |

# Index

3DES, 154, 265, 278, 281

access, 1, 6-8, 27-30, 36, 70, 74, 77, 82, 106, 113, 118, 130-131, 146-147, 149-161, 163, 165, 167, 169, 171, 173-176, 179-180, 182-183, 195, 198-201, 203-204, 210, 213, 229, 233, 235, 237, 240-241, 243, 248, 262, 264-269, 271-273, 277-281, 283, 296, 300-301, 303-306, 309, 318, 321, 323-325, 327, 330, 332

    Internet control, 8

accounting, 150

Active Directory, 2, 6, 24-26, 70, 74, 76, 80-81, 103-106, 109-110, 112, 114, 151, 156, 158, 195, 268, 273-274

    database, 1, 6, 46, 74, 76, 101, 105-109, 111, 113, 117, 119, 127-128, 130, 155-156, 160, 175, 178-182

    DHCP integration, 77, 109, 156

    domain, 1-4, 25-26, 31, 60, 65, 70, 74, 76, 79, 97, 99-103, 113, 156, 195, 202, 240, 268, 271, 274, 281-282, 299

    integrated DNS, 104-107, 112, 135, 144

    integration, 74-77, 81, 104, 109-110, 127, 129, 156, 182, 240-241, 327

    replication, 25, 106-112, 117-126, 128-129, 179, 195

Add/Remove Programs Control Panel, 62, 103, 121

addressing, 2-3, 25-27, 29-30, 32, 36, 45, 80, 85, 316, 329

    IP support, 36

administrative, 28, 42, 61-62, 75, 77, 79, 81, 85, 105, 109-112, 122, 128, 156-157, 180, 198,
203, 211, 229, 233, 235, 237, 243, 264, 279-280, 306, 309, 318

    task, 81, 104, 210, 213, 240, 265

ADSL, 197, 281

APIPA, 27, 32

AppleTalk, 18, 148, 167

area, 1, 5-6, 37-38, 45, 70, 106, 114, 146, 173, 179, 195-196, 238-239, 247, 262-263, 275, 304

array, 300, 325-326, 328-329, 332

AS, 1-9, 11, 24-26, 30-31, 33, 35-36, 44-46, 61, 69, 74, 77, 79-81, 85, 97, 100, 104-107, 109-113, 115-116, 118-119, 127-130, 146-147, 150, 154-159, 175, 178-182, 195-197, 209-213, 227, 233, 238-242, 245-248, 262-263, 265, 267-268, 271-275, 278-281, 283, 296, 299-300, 323-324, 326, 328-329, 332

Asymmetric Digital Subscriber Line, 197, 281

authentication, 6, 25, 106, 146-147, 149-150, 152-156, 158, 160, 197, 203, 208-210, 213, 248, 264-265, 270-275, 277-278, 281-282

    client, 3, 7, 10, 24, 31-32, 36, 61, 66, 68-69, 73-74, 76, 79, 100-102, 108, 113-116, 119-120, 127, 146, 149-152, 155-158, 161, 173-176, 178, 180, 272-275, 283, 327

    mutual, 197, 208-209, 213, 248

    protocol, 1-8, 24-25, 27, 31, 36-38, 42, 45-46, 60-63, 65, 67-69, 71, 73, 75, 77, 79, 81, 83, 85, 87, 89, 91, 93, 95, 97, 100, 106, 109, 126, 147, 153-154, 156, 178, 195, 197, 199, 208-210, 226-228, 230-232, 235-236, 238, 240-242, 246, 248, 262, 264, 270-271, 297, 299-300, 305, 307, 309, 313, 317, 323, 326, 329

    remote access protocol, 153

www.ingramcontent.com/pod-product-compliance
Lightning Source LLC
Chambersburg PA
CBHW080145060326

40689CB00018B/3854